The Visual Arts in Education:
Completing the Circle

The Falmer Press Library on Aesthetic Education

Series Editor: Dr Peter Abbs, University of Sussex, UK

Setting the Frame

LIVING POWERS:
The Arts in Education
Edited by Peter Abbs

A IS FOR AESTHETIC:
Essays on Creative and Aesthetic
Education
Peter Abbs

THE SYMBOLIC ORDER:
A Contemporary Reader on the
Arts Debate
Edited by Peter Abbs

THE RATIONALITY OF
FEELING:
Understanding the Arts in
Education
David Best

The Individual Studies

FILM AND TELEVISION IN
EDUCATION:
An Aesthetic Approach to the
Moving Image
Robert Watson

LITERATURE AND
EDUCATION:
Encounter and Experience
Edwin Webb

THE VISUAL ARTS IN
EDUCATION
Rod Taylor

DANCE AS EDUCATION:
Towards a National Dance Culture
Peter Brinson

MUSIC EDUCATION IN
THEORY AND PRACTICE
Charles Plummeridge

THE ARTS IN THE PRIMARY
SCHOOL
Glennis Andrews and Rod Taylor

EDUCATION IN DRAMA:
Casting the Dramatic Curriculum
David Hornbrook

Work of Reference

KEY CONCEPTS:
A Guide to Aesthetics, Criticism and the Arts in Education
Trevor Pateman

The Falmer Press Library on Aesthetic Education

The Visual Arts in Education:
Completing the Circle

Rod Taylor

 The Falmer Press

(A member of the Taylor & Francis Group)
London • Washington, D.C.

UK   The Falmer Press, 4 John St., London WC1N 2ET
USA   The Falmer Press, Taylor & Francis Inc., 1900 Frost Road, Suite 101,
            Bristol, PA 19007

First published 1992

**A Catalogue Record for this book is available from the
British Library**

ISBN 1 85000 769 1
ISBN 1 85000 770 5 pbk

**Library of Congress Cataloging-in-Publication Data are
available on request**

Typeset in 9.5/11pt Bembo
by Graphicraft Typesetters Ltd., Hong Kong

*Printed in Great Britain by Burgess Science Press, Basingstoke
on paper which has a specified pH value on final paper
manufacture of not less than 7·5 and is therefore 'acid free'.*

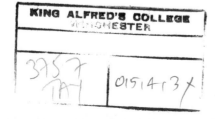

Contents

Acknowledgments

I am indebted to my wife Dot Taylor. An accomplished sixth form college teacher and head of department, she puts into daily practice the philosophy of art and design education that we both passionately believe in and share. The practical, written and spoken testimonies of her students illuminate these pages and ensure an effective wedding of theory with practice. It is testimony to her teaching that, for every case study example drawn upon, countless others could equally as effectively have been chosen. Thanks are also due to my colleagues at the Drumcroon Education Art Centre and in the Wigan Visual Arts Service for their support, as well as to all the Wigan classroom practitioners who have provided information and practical material essential to the writing of this book.

The warmth and friendship of Greg and Lorna Dick during the month I spent with them while undertaking a Fellowship at Curtin University in Perth, Western Australia, were also invaluable. They enabled me to pick up the thread of writing again after it had been severed by the poll tax 'capping' of Wigan and the considerable damage this inflicted on a carefully conceived and highly effective Visual Arts service which had been built up over many years.

Finally, I would like to acknowledge how much benefit in the writing of this book I have derived from the constant support, ideas, promptings and sympathy of Peter Abbs. It has been a real pleasure to collaborate so closely with one who believes passionately in the life-enhancing force of the arts in education, and in the notion of the enlightening potential of education in general, in these mechanistic times in which the arts so often suffer for reasons of expediency. I only hope that *The Visual Arts in Education* proves a worthy addition to the Library on Aesthetic Education which he has worked so hard and over such a time-span to realize.

Preface

It was the major contention of *Living Powers*, the first volume in this series on aesthetic education, that the teaching of the arts had been narrowed by the intellectual movements known as Progressivism and Late Modernism and that a new synthesis in our understanding of arts education was now urgently required. In this volume Rod Taylor demonstrates with a wealth of ideas and good practice what such a synthesis might look like for the teaching of the visual arts. That it is so close to the model proposed by the Art Working Group for the National Curriculum makes it both timely and realistic. Indeed, it provides certain grounds for hope that a comprehensive education in art and design for every child in this country is now possible.

'Comprehensive': that is the key word. Perhaps more than any other arts discipline, with the exception of drama, visual arts teaching has suffered from intensely partial conceptions ever since it began. A short history of art education was provided by Robin Morris in *Living Powers* and is again retold in an essential chapter of this book.[1] Yet a historical perspective remains vital to any proper understanding of the importance of the model proposed by Rod Taylor, for it is in the history of art education that we see, at their clearest, the limitations of Progressivism and Modernism.

We can see the negative features of Progressivism most clearly at work in some of the formulations of Herbert Read. In *Education through Art* (1943), for example, Herbert Read seemed particularly anxious to hold back the influences of culture in order to preserve the spontaneity of the child. 'The real problem', he wrote, 'is to preserve the original intensity of the child's reactions to the sensuous qualities of experience — to colours, surfaces, shapes and rhythms. These', he continued, 'are apt to be so infallibly "right" that the teacher can only stand over them in a kind of protective awe.' That protective awe, as it became a widespread disposition, began more and more to exclude the great artefacts of the culture or any informed appreciation of them. The children were largely left inside the real but enclosed bubble of their own indigenous creativity.

In fact, similar versions of child-centred Progressivism (not without an element of truth and also to be partly understood as a most necessary reaction against earlier overprescriptive teaching) can be found across the teaching of all the arts between 1940 and 1970. What the teachers of 'self-expression' valued was improvisation, originality and the process of making; what was largely excluded was the aesthetic field in which these creative acts need to be placed. In particular, there was little reference to achieved work, few conventions were explicitly introduced and there was a corresponding poverty of terms, critical, historical and practical. As Rod Taylor points out, the progressive movement concentrated only on 'making' and overlooked the complementary needs of 'presenting', 'responding' and 'evaluating'.

In this respect one of the distinctive achievements of Rod Taylor has been to insist on the place of Critical Studies (creatively conceived) and to provide coherent models for its realization in the classroom. What he has done is to expand the circumference of art activity until it has become a brilliant and articulate whole. He has revealed the interacting segments which together comprise the whole circle. This circle includes a living awareness of all kinds of achieved art, of nature and landscape, of the environment, design and technology. It includes also the reciprocal play of critical response and dynamic making within the context of a natural and symbolic order. His model makes that of the Progressive's look lean and insubstantial; yet, at the same time, it employs their main premise, namely that the student should be envisaged as a creative agent, a being with an innate disposition towards symbolic expression and transformation.

Yet, our brief historic overview is not complete. For in the 1960s there was a swing against Progressivism and a further orthodoxy (also described by Rod Taylor in these pages and by Robin Morris in his contribution to *Living Powers*) related to Modernism and especially as Late Modernism developed. It wanted no truck with either tradition or self-expression. It wanted to start the world as if from nothing and from nowhere. Through a mode of organized 'problem-solving' it was thought that students could best discover naturally 'a visual language' –– line, shape, tone, texture. Quite often this movement abrasively confronted the notions of high art, culture and aesthetic meaning. Typically, a tutor at Cardiff School of Art, for example, could claim: 'we should be establishing a non-art situation, not a process of self-conscious art-making, not endowing the artefact with the "mystique" of esoteric difference.'[2] A non-art situation *meant* what it so cumbersomely said. It meant that there need be no reference to works of art, to the history of art or to the criticism and understanding of it. Thus in the space where there had once been self-expression, there arose the habit of observing visual stimuli, of problem-solving and of employing what Peter Fuller called in his essay in *The Symbolic Order* the anaesthetic practices of the mega-visual tradition. From the artistic and symbolic point of view this was even more limited than what had gone before.

In responding to this functional reaction to the progressive spirit, Rod Taylor wants to retain, obviously, observation and the connection with design and technology, but, once again, he works to expand the range of possibilities so that it includes all the varieties of art-making inside the vast symbolic order of art, traditional and contemporary, Western European as well as non-European. In particular, he is anxious that art is seen as engaging through perceptual response with the problem of meaning or what he calls 'content' and that the area of Design and Technology is not left on the edge of any aesthetic programme but is grasped as a necessary part of it. Anyone with any doubts on this matter should turn at once to Louis Arnaud Reid's eloquent description of a spoon in the chapter significantly titled 'Art, Nature and Heightened Environmental Awareness'. Reid's articulate response to the spoon shows that there need be and should be no divide between beauty and function, between aesthetic response and utile object.

What is involved in Rod Taylor's critique of the Modernist movement towards design and visual objectivity is, then, not so much a rejection, as an extraordinary expansion which, in effect, transforms the earlier programme entirely. He works to place the concern for functional elements in an infinitely broader matrix, a matrix which includes subjectivity (as elaborated in the chapter on Surrealism and Adolescence), an awareness of the whole cultural continuum (from the cave paintings to the latest exhibition) as well as the means of personal and critical appreciation, made possible through the introduction of an informed language. The elements from both the Progressive and Modernist movements are picked up and duly placed in a wider order. This is why I said at the beginning that 'comprehensive' is the keyword. The outcome is an education of the individual sensibility of *all* children in relationship to the whole cosmos of art.

One further quality of Rod Taylor's approach to the teaching of the visual arts needs to be stressed. While it may strike some as an overorganized programme, the reader will quickly detect that what the author values most is the empowering of students to respond to the artistic and historic culture which is rightfully theirs. The eloquent and precise testimonies of individual students run like a single resonant thread through nearly all the chapters of the book. It is this free and developing response to chosen art works, painters, movements which is cherished most. (This is why the chronicle of the Illuminating Experience is given such prominence.) Yet, to be sure, the formal model for responding to art-works laid out in Chapter 4 *is* programmatic; it is there to guide the perception of the students by asking them to attend to *the form, the content, the process* and *the mood* of the work; but it is not there to procure a list of factual answers. It is an open-ended way of productively directing attention so that any student can stop by a work of art and have questions to put to it which will quickly sharpen and deepen aesthetic response. The schema is a vehicle to promote sensuous curiosity and reflective activity and to do so to some purpose. It is this creative engagement which lies at the heart of the model. Indeed, the whole book is about this one thing: pupils finding their own creativity within the collective creativity of our inherited culture.

This volume has been written by a person who both loves the visual arts and has enormous experience of teaching and working with art teachers. The theory illuminates the practice; and the practice, in return, confirms and extends the theory. The argument possesses, simultaneously, breadth of vision and good common-sense. At this critical moment in arts education the argument is much needed for it could play an important part in seeing that the structures and strictures of the National Curriculum are wisely used to deepen and enlarge aesthetic awareness. What is so hopeful is that there is sufficient common ground between the vision of the book and the formal demands of the Art and Design curriculum to make this a possibility worth fighting for.

Peter Abbs
Centre for Language, Literature and the Arts in Education
University of Sussex
April 1991

Notes

1 See Robin Morris (1987) 'Towards a Shared Symbolic Order', in *Living Powers*, ed. Peter Abbs, Basingstoke, Falmer Press.
2 *Ibid.*, p. 194.

Chapter 1

The Visual Arts, Critical Approaches and the Aesthetic Field

We want to see not only a programme for the arts, but also a body of arts teachers who actively feel they form a unified community with a common purpose and a common aesthetic ... we believe that the individual arts — literature, drama, dance, music, film and art — must be conceived as forming a single community in the curriculum. This does not necessarily mean that they should be integrated in their teaching, but that they should be understood as serving similar aesthetic processes and purposes. They all belong together under the category of the aesthetic. (Peter Abbs in *Living Powers*).[1]

A Library for Aesthetic Education

The Visual Arts in Education is but one volume in a series of twelve which, in total, comprise a unique Library on Aesthetic Education — a manifesto of the arts. *Living Powers*, the first of the series, lays the ground and is consistent in its arguments with those of the influential 1982 Gulbenkian Report, *The Arts in Schools*.[2] It maintains that the arts should be seen together as comprising an essential and substantial area of the curriculum to do with the aesthetic. It is the aesthetic which is the common bond which gives them their common purposes, though this need not mean integrated arts teaching. As such, *Living Powers* defines the philosophical framework of the library as a whole, acting as a kind of microcosm for it in layout and structure. Having made a strong case for the arts in education through the aesthetic, *Living Powers* then uses this as the focus through which to examine each art form as it manifests itself in education. *Living Powers* is followed by two further books of a theoretical nature, and then the central feature of this series are the individual volumes representing each major art form in turn: *The Visual Arts in Education* is one volume in this central section.

Living Powers was published in 1987 in close proximity to the National Curriculum consultation document. The last books to complete the series will be published with the National Curriculum firmly in place and all the resulting programmes of study and attainment targets in the ten designated core and foundation subjects known. The testing by law of 7-year-olds who have been taken through the Key Stage 1 phase of the National Curriculum will have become reality. The series has therefore been written and published against the dramatic and constantly shifting backdrop of sweeping educational reform through legislation. *Living Powers* highlighted the inadequacy of arts practice and provision in the majority of schools at the outset of this process. The most ardent advocate of the National Curriculum will readily concede that, whatever its virtues, it most certainly does not present any coherent view of the arts, or for aesthetic education to comprise an essential part of young people's entitlement.

Living Powers articulates the case for more arts time, the arts representing as they do one of the fundamental areas of human achievement, expression and understanding. If anything, time available for the study of the arts has noticeably diminished since 1987, with combined arts courses introduced not to promote aesthetic education but to conveniently place the arts into a predetermined timetable slot. An arts mish-mash characterized by superficial and generalized approaches at the expense of essential in-depth experiences necessary for engagements at an aesthetic level is all too frequently the result. The need for a library for aesthetic education is probably even more pronounced now than when *Living Powers* was published a relatively short time ago.

The Aesthetic Field

A central argument in *Living Powers* is that it is the aesthetic which the six major art forms of literature, music, drama, dance, film and the visual arts share in common. Because each of these disciplines has different and distinct histories, having come into the curriculum at different times and for different reasons, arts teachers themselves do not always necessarily recognize what it is they share in common, to the overall detriment of aesthetic education. Abbs, the editor of the series and author of the overriding philosophical argument with which *Living Powers* begins, argues that the aesthetic constitutes one of the fundamental ways of knowing, being to do with apprehension through the senses.[3] 'Aesthetic denotes a mode of sensuous knowing essential for the life and development of consciousness; aesthetic response is inevitably, through its sensory and physical operations, cognitive in nature.' The significance of the aesthetic to human insight and understanding can be perhaps best understood by focusing on its opposite, anaesthesia. Interestingly, this word was in use in 1721, decades before 'aesthetic' came into the language, and it of course denotes 'loss of feeling or sensation: insensibility'. An education which ignores the aesthetic is therefore one which risks impoverishment by failing to cultivate and develop feelings, sensations and sensibilities.

> The aesthetic, then, must be concerned with all that works through and on feeling, sensation and sensibility.... Touch, taste, feel, tact: these are the words, suggesting in their uses the intimate relationship between sensation and feeling, which best bring out the nature of the aesthetic mode.

The traditional problems of lack of continuity in arts teaching and inadequate time allocations are further compounded, Abbs asserts, in that 'much of what is done in these art periods is not deeply aesthetic in nature'. Many of the activities undertaken lie virtually outside what he defines as the aesthetic field. Taking all three factors into account, on the basis of one comprehensive school timetable, he calculates in *Living Powers* that their second year pupils experience, on average, 'no more than an hour or so of genuine aesthetic activity each week'. He argues that a major cause behind the neglect of aesthetic activity in arts education emanates from an intertwining of modernism in art with progressivism in education, with the most articulate and eloquent advocate of both being, of course, Herbert Read. It is now possible to see that just as art, in the latter phases of modernism, failed adequately to replenish itself by drawing upon the wider cultural tradition, so arts teaching likewise turned in on itself, with the resulting work becoming too narrow in its scope and hence predictable.

As opposed to a notion of art as constituting a series of discrete artefacts or art objects, Abbs uses the word 'field' metaphorically to suggest that the aesthetic field implies 'a highly complex web of energy linking the artist to the audience, and both artist and audience to all inherited culture as now an active, now a latent shaping force'. In order to chart this aesthetic field, he proposes the four-phase model of making, presenting, responding and evaluating.

Making, Presenting, Responding, Evaluating

The concept of a dynamic aesthetic field 'in which all art moves and has its being' is summarized diagrammatically in *Living Powers* (p. 56). The central significance of making, presenting, responding and evaluating is immediately apparent.

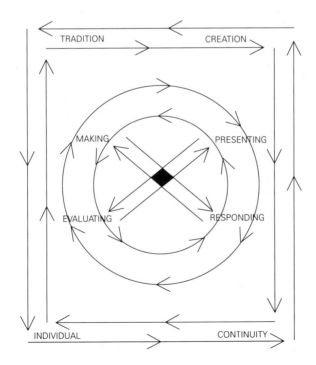

The arts teacher can break into the aesthetic field at any point and be led by an invisible pattern of relationships into the whole circuit — for the parts are not self-contained but gain their meaning through connection with all the other parts. All points, therefore, can be starting points and there can be no one way of sequencing the teaching of the arts. What is important for the teacher is to discern the whole complex interaction of the field and to use that knowledge in the organising and planning of work.

The art medium is the tangible material which makes the act of making possible. Its particular character invites certain movements, resists others. It is through technique that definite shape is given to 'an unknown entity already possessed but not yet intelligible'. Every artistic material has its own history, with which the artist also engages, at both conscious and unconscious levels, during the creative process; the artist might actively study other artists' work as an essential part of that process. 'Each work of art in its making manifests the whole field.' The artist can identify so passionately with the material that he or she can be 'lost' in it, but there comes a stage in the making process, most obviously as it nears resolution, when the work begins to assume its own independent existence.

John Dewey observed that 'the completed artefact is not in itself an aesthetic object but an object that invites aesthetic response from others'; the aesthetic meaning resides in the dynamic interaction between the work and those who engage with it: 'No audience — no aesthetic.' Presenting, then, is an essential act of communication without which the work remains incomplete — it is the viewer who completes the work, though in aesthetic education 'the students move constantly from one position to the other, now making, now responding, now performing, now evaluating.'

Response can be to the work as a whole but might be to some compelling part which, in turn, draws us deeper into the work as a whole. There may be the wish to submit oneself further to a work so that it might release more fully what was sensed to a degree but somehow withheld in the initial engagement. At this stage, expressions of response are likely to be along the lines of 'Terrific!', 'Fantastic!', 'Dreadful!' or 'Deeply moving!', for all these responses 'are not logical but intuitive apprehensions working through our senses and our feelings, through our sensibility.' The educational temptation must therefore be resisted to overlay this stage with too much theory, explanation and knowledge for, in isolation from aesthetic experience, this can block the sensuous, physical, dramatic and imaginative 'indwelling' aspects so crucial to artistic response at this essentially pre-verbal stage. 'The point and purpose of the art lies in the field of its action.'

Nevertheless, we do wish to make judgments and to understand the nature of the transformation of media brought about by the artist — and at many crucial moments in responding we require information to help us make sense of what we see. 'Evaluating is, then, in large part, an attempt to organise the complex elements of our aesthetic response — to state intellectually our relationship to the work of art, to formulate the aesthetic response ... conceptually.' Great pleasure can be derived from this process of seeing how something works and how it has been made to add up to a unified whole. 'Evaluation makes intelligible (and communicable) the aesthetic response'; 'It is post-event.' It is here that knowledge of traditions, awareness of history and culture, understanding of craft — and possession of an appropriate critical vocabulary — can develop and deepen aesthetic judgments and responses.

It is the major aim of the Library on Aesthetic Education as a whole to demonstrate that all the major art forms in the curriculum, irrespective of their different origins and developments to date, fit into this dynamic aesthetic field. In this respect, the visual arts have been at the forefront of noteworthy beneficial change and development over the last decade through what has become known as the critical studies movement. Some of the aspects of this work were taken up and developed in other art forms through the SCDC Arts in Schools Project, which began in 1985 and gave rise to *The Arts 5–16 Project Pack* (Oliver and Boyd, 1990). It is worth looking at some of the circumstances which gave rise to this movement in the visual arts field, however, and the nature of the developments which it brought about.

Critical Studies in Visual Arts Education

If the aesthetic field is to be genuinely dynamic, making is an essential element, for it not only denotes that of established artists but also the significance of pupil practice in relation to that of the established artist. A long-standing problem in visual arts education was that art history teaching and studio practice were out of tandem; art college students still frequently fail to make essential connections between the two because it is still commonplace for them to be taught in different ways at different times by different tutors — it is not uncommon for the art historian to have no practical skills or interests, for example. In turn, many art college students on becoming teachers have felt loathe to inflict on their pupils an aspect of the discipline which had been unpalatable to them in their training. In rejecting that particular art history lecture model, though, they would frequently be rejecting critical studies approaches in general, failing to devise an alternative systematic range of strategies.

By the beginning of the 1980s this had led to a growing concern that the vast majority of pupils were leaving school having had opportunities to make art of their own, but having acquired little or no knowledge, understanding, or sense of enjoyment concerning the wider world of the visual arts as a whole. The 1981–84 Critical Studies in Art Education (CSAE) Project was set up through the joint funding and support of the Arts, Crafts and Schools Councils with the aim of exploring this issue and finding constructive ways forward in how it might be addressed in the classroom and through closer collaboration between schools and art galleries. The recently opened Drumcroon Education Art Centre in Wigan became host centre to the project and proved ideal in that it ensured that in an environment where children of all ages were engaging with art works in a variety of ways, on a daily basis, the research would be practical and action-based as well as theoretical. As such, it proved relevant to teachers from the outset. Enjoying, as it does, particularly close ties with teachers while clearly functioning as an art gallery within a locality, Drumcroon breaks down some of the traditional barriers which separate the two. Its work has continued at a local authority level beyond the life of CSAE, and some of the implications raised by this work are explored further in this book.

'Free expression' were two commonly used words in 1981 when the CSAE Project began. They indicated the considerable influence which the Child Art movement still exerted. Yet there were contradictions. It was widely accepted that, with the onset of adolescence, the natural spontaneity, which was seen as essential to child creativity, began to dissipate. At this stage, therefore, there was frequently a return to a diet of skill-based exercises which, after about three years, gave way — at the upper secondary phase — to demands that pupils once again be imaginative and expressive. This all too often led to a predictable form of art derived from secondhand sources. These stop-go approaches made it extremely difficult to invest visual arts education with any balance, coherence or continuity. The CSAE Project demonstrated that it was possible for children of all ages to be educated in such a manner that they could both study and enjoy the art of others and engage in studio practice to the benefit and enrichment of each aspect. In the process, continuity and coherence can become realizable concepts, as opposed to being abstract notions inviting only theoretical discussion. Instead of the engagement with adults' art stultifying children's imaginations, as had been argued for so long, there was ample evidence of the opposite: these contacts opened up a wide range of possibilities which enable pupils to move outside and beyond the clichés of classroom art — the crumpled coke can, the half pepper, the sci-fi magazine copy, etc.

Hand in hand with the emphasis on free expression was the deeply held belief that art galleries were boring to children anyway. Why give up valuable practical time to something that was more than likely to prove a negative experience? The CSAE Project made extensive use of pupil interviews and case studies, and these certainly indicated that the gallery was initially perceived as such: 'I'd always thought that it would be boring'; 'At first on both occasions I wasn't keen to go'; 'I was bored out of my mind!' What their testimonies vividly revealed, however, was the dramatic way in which this assumption could so easily be turned around into something positive. Even where young people had some prior knowledge, their reactions consistently highlighted the special qualities inherent in experiencing works in the original:

> ... I was thrilled to bits. I thought, 'It's great, this!' We went to the National and even the Turners and the Constables, I got really excited about them, because I thought that they were the first steps towards going in different directions, like Constable with his snowflaking and Turner with his sort of command over the elements ... they were really exciting to look at.[4]

As Project Director, I coined the term 'Illuminating Experience' to describe both the initiating moment which takes the pupil from the outside to the inside of an art form, and all subsequent ones of a similar nature to which one can be subjected throughout life.

The Nature of the Illuminating Experience

Using adult informants who had a love of a particular art form, David Hargreaves collected their aesthetic autobiographies by encouraging them to reflect over their key formative experiences. The CSAE Project effectively built upon this research,[5] following a brief collaboration with Hargreaves in September

1981. It was the art gallery, theatre, opera house and concert hall which proved the natural arenas for the illuminating experience — these informants rarely, if ever, mentioned the classroom in this regard. Much of school learning is of an incremental nature, whereas the art gallery has an important potential for surprises — even shock — which can open up new dimensions and aspects of the art form. This 'is of singular importance to aesthetic learning in matters which relate to appreciation as opposed to skill acquisition.'

The pupils and students I interviewed substantiated Hargreaves' research through testimonies which provided further evidence of key characteristics and outcomes of the illuminating experience. In the most marked examples there was reference to what Hargreaves calls concentration of attention. One can literally lose sense of time and place as one is drawn into the orbit of the art work: 'It just flew past ... it didn't seem like an hour and a half — more like ten minutes'; 'It almost seemed to be in the whole of your view ... your attention was drawn to it.' The second element is sense of revelation: 'It seemed a totally different form of Art'; 'It was a complete eye-opener.' It is not just the art form, or a new and unexpected dimension of it, which is being opened up, but it is 'as if some already existing core of the self is suddenly being touched and brought to life for the first time, and yet inevitably so.' The third element is inarticulateness. I have described this as the art educator's nightmare for, whereas pupils often have no inhibitions about informing the teacher that 'it was boring', those positively affected do not necessarily formulate the experience into words for their own sake, let alone to communicate with others. Some people will keep the experience to themselves for years. How can the teacher constructively harness what he or she is not even aware of? There can be important signs, though. A key one is memory retention; the actual experience is remembered because it was disturbing, but many youngsters' testimonies make it clear that they remember with extreme clarity and detail the associated works themselves. This poses the seeming contradiction that inarticulateness is complemented by another element which provides the young person with the basis to talk (or write) about the work or works in question with more precision, clarity and feeling than was hitherto the case. Another key element is arousal of appetite. 'One simply wants the experience to continue or to be repeated, and this can be felt with considerable urgency.' Even in weaker versions of the experience 'there is still a lingering fascination which leads people to say that they felt "hooked" on the art object in some way.' Arousal of appetite can be highly motivating, meaning that commitment and the desire for further exploration are two important outcomes of the illuminating experience. In contrast to that earlier perception of the art gallery being boring, the young person is now likely to want to revisit in order to get a similar 'buzz' again. A sense of discrimination begins to develop as the person gauges the impact, nature and relevance of one experience against others. These outcomes do not necessarily come about in any discrete order, but, a fourth, the search for background knowledge, is the most likely to follow in the wake of the others. In some cases the person will only begin to read about artist, period or movement some years later. This is interesting, as it highlights that what often comes last in these situations is that which usually comes first in the school context: Abbs warns of the dangers of killing aesthetic responses with too much theory, explanation and knowledge divorced from them, and Hargreaves emphasizes that this can in itself be aversive and turn the pupil off at a crucial stage. Nevertheless, through adequate provision of book, slide, reproduction and video resources, the teacher can constructively satisfy the need for background knowledge, and short-circuit something that might take a long time otherwise, harnessing it in the process.

The traditional problem of the split between art history and appreciation teaching and studio practice has already been highlighted. In this respect, one further outcome, that of heightened environmental awareness, can be of crucial importance. Under the influence of the art work(s), the individual can become unusually receptive to aspects of his or her immediate surroundings, or of the inner imaginative world. Young people of all ages can be affected in this way, as the responses to the same stimulus, one by a 10-year-old and the other by an A-level student, vividly illustrate. The stimulus is that of Gerd Winner's 1981 Drumcroon exhibition, with his many treatments of London's East One dock-land area and of New York tenements with their fire escapes:

> Buildings at the side of busy roads that seem to hug the clouds and block out my upward view. Blind alleys with buildings looming over them. Alleys small, dark and desolate. Alleys where buildings have been made higgledy piggledy, all shapes and sizes. Ancient stone buildings with towers, brick semis with boards over windows or bricked up.[6]

> ... a brick wall would now be a Winner wall if you looked at it right, and a lamp post stood out rather than just being something at the side of a road. You came to look as a camera might, you'd walk round and see with Winner's eyes, just walking. Especially when you went to the canals and warehouses, the fire escapes seemed to be more prominent. You seemed to get a totally different viewpoint.[7]

Heightened environmenal awareness is therefore of special significance in that it can act as a potentially important bridging link between the study of art and its practice by virtue of making aspects of the visible world suddenly of un-expected relevance: 'Before, you'd just see something outside like the buildings, and you'd just draw that. You look at things differently now. Things that you wouldn't have found interesting before, now you do. It's changed the way that I look at things.' Rather than experience of adult art impair pupil practice, the evidence was that it actually made them aware of a wider range of practical possibilities which were directly related to their responses and concerns.

The main characteristics of the illuminating experience can be set out in diagram form for added clarity as follows:

ILLUMINATING EXPERIENCE =
CONCENTRATION OF ATTENTION + SENSE OF REVELATION
+ INARTICULATENESS + MEMORY RETENTION
and of particular educational significance
AROUSAL OF APPETITE
These lead to, but not necessarily in discrete order,
COMMITMENT — EXPLORATION — DISCRIMINATION —
SEARCH FOR BACKGROUND KNOWLEDGE
+ HEIGHTENED ENVIRONMENTAL AWARENESS,
an important bridging link between the study
and practice of art.

Though the illuminating experience, with its surprise element, is far more likely to take place in the art gallery and involve art works encountered in the original, this does not negate the importance of books, reproductions, video and slide material — far from it. It became abundantly clear in 1981 that the majority of schools were lacking in these resources, and yet many young people felt the need of appropriate preparation for the gallery visit, epitomized by the student who met a friend in a London gallery who was on another course, had had no adequate preparation, and was not enjoying herself: 'The only reason she wasn't enjoying it as much as me was because they hadn't looked at the paintings before and they hadn't had it explained, and that was the only reason.' This student further emphasizes that when 'I go to the galleries I — at the moment — go up to the ones I've read about.' If the wrong types of explanation can be aversive, preparation which whets the appetite is nevertheless desirable, and secondhand stimulus is also invaluable as a means of substantiating gallery experiences after the event.

Home Art[8]

Many children spend varying amounts of time and varying degrees of commitment in the production of art at home. One of the important findings of the CSAE Project was that it was often through the practice of home art that children were working out the connections they made with particular art works to which they had been personally responsive. This was in large measure because the prescribed practical syllabus of the school invariably allowed insufficient scope for these connections to manifest themselves there: 'We couldn't use what we had seen unless we broke the rules.... He was telling us what had been and then he wouldn't let us try it out!' 'It had to be standardized. It had to be in the vein of what O-level Art is.' School art could all too easily become a distinct genre of art in its own right, divorced from all other types and areas of art. In such instances the phases of making, presenting, responding and evaluating become separated, with aspects uncovered to the detriment of aesthetic learning as a whole.

In 1981 many art teachers vigorously maintained that the prime aim of the art lesson was to enable children to be expressive and that the art room was one of the few places within the school where this could happen. The pupils were of the opinion that they were carrying out instructions here as elsewhere in the school, though — particularly in the early years of secondary schooling: 'You knew what it was going to be like from the beginning'; 'Everybody's was exactly the same'; 'I sort of felt though that everybody should have got the chance to do different things.' Though sometimes dismissive of the quality of their home art products, they nevertheless saw these as providing the means whereby they gave expression to their particular interests and concerns. As such, home art often remains private, the teacher unaware of its very existence. Equally, when known about, it is frequently dismissed as being of poor quality because the materials used are often the only ones to hand within the home context.

An important and intriguing feature of home art, however, was that it was abundantly clear from the pupil testimonies that it was sometimes produced as an alternative, and in opposition to, school art. It was invariably content-led, whereas much of school art — particularly that done in the first two or three years at the secondary level — was often exclusively focused on formal and technical concerns. The more extreme this focus, the more likelihood of the pupil

9

Resulting in No links between home/school

resorting to a purely content-based art at home. A not uncommon consequence was that what was done at school failed to inform what was done at home, and vice versa. Home art could all too easily degenerate into repetition, wither and die. School art was seen as set tasks to be dutifully carried out, but without necessary levels of motivation. It was sometimes suggested that the child should be entitled to some privacy, and therefore home art should remain separate. This could be the case, if the child so chose, but the underlying impulse — obviously related to content and hence pupil interests — could nevertheless be harnessed to give extra significance and meaning to school practice. The teachers' desires to develop formal understanding and technical proficiency in their pupils could be better realized if the pupils saw added meaning in what they were doing through it being imbued with more relevant content. Similarly, courses could benefit from the added impetus which they would gain from pupils being able to make explicit the connections with art gallery works to which they had been responsive, rather than these be worked out privately or not at all.

A Model for Engaging with Art Works

The young informants would often choose to talk about the gallery works they had latched onto between the guide finishing and the coach drawing up outside to return them to school. This in no way reflects badly on the gallery guide; it may well be that the more formal sessions provided necessary criteria to enable the pupils to operate more effectively on their own. It does emphasize, however, the importance of personal choice within the gallery context and the need for informal, as well as formal, approaches to be adopted. Though pupils might initially seek out those works about which they knew something, no teacher can anticipate all the works to which pupils will have been drawn by the conclusion of the visit. In 1981 it was extremely rare to see other than pupil work displayed in art rooms, the art teacher often being seen as the only arbiter of taste, values and judgments. In the interplay between gallery response and pupil practice, highlighted by the CSAE Project and some of the home art practice, the need is made clear for a wide variety of art works to be made accessible through visual arts courses, and not only those which reflect the teachers' own tastes — important though the teachers' enthusiasms obviously are!

Equally important, no teacher is an expert about everything to do with the vast world of the visual arts as practised through time and across places. Temporary exhibitions, particularly by certain contemporary or unfamiliar artists, or those from other cultures, can pose problems about prior preparation as well as actual gallery usage. Likewise, loan collection works brought into schools without supporting information risk being used as teaching aids at only a minimal level. Gallery visits risk becoming aimless where there is no clear focus for engaging with the exhibited works themselves. It was in attempting to address these kinds of issues that I wrote in the book arising out of the CSAE Project, *Educating for Art*:

> Four fundamental areas all have teaching potential.... They are relevant to all art and craft objects, though the emphasis on particular aspects will inevitably vary from work to work. The four areas are:

1   The techniques, processes and methods involved in the making of the work.
2   The formal qualities of the work; its arrangement into shapes, its form, the colour scheme employed, etc.
3   Its content in terms of subject matter; its significance, how the artist has accumulated the information, etc.
4   The mood, atmosphere or feeling evoked by the work.

The CSAE Project emphasized that critical studies was integral to visual arts education and as such had potential to invest it with added and fresh meaning and impetus. Particularly with critical studies establishing a foothold in GCSE examinations, there has been a subsequent need to help teachers find positive ways in — especially as many confess to feeling constrained because of the inadequacies of their own art college training in this respect. The nature of art in the National Curriculum is likely to intensify this need at both primary and secondary levels. Many BEd and PGCE college lecturers are now keen to ensure that their students acquire an enhanced range of teaching strategies, appropriate to the purpose. The four areas identified in *Educating for Art* have therefore been developed into what is now widely recognized as an invaluable Content, Form, Process, Mood model.[10] It is well tested at both the initial and in-service levels in workshop contexts, and there is evidence of its relevance to primary and secondary pupils in the gallery and the classroom.

Its significance in relation to acquisition and use of a critical vocabulary and to practical needs is further highlighted in *Approaching Art and Design: A Guide for Students*.[11] I wrote this book with Dot Taylor, utilizing her extensive experience in the sixth form college sector and the work and testimonies of her students. Content, form, process and mood are explored fully in *The Visual Arts in Education*, and provide an important cornerstone of the text, amplified by further student usage as well as that of teachers.

Personal Appraisal: A Critical Studies Approach to Recording Achievement

An intriguing feature of *Approaching Art and Design* is the evidence it provides of a demanding and rigorous course which is flexible enough for students to identify and pursue their own specific interests and concerns, with encouragement to develop these in highly individual ways according to their particular dictates. Negotiated learning is central to this balance and is facilitated by the personal appraisal (or assessment review) approach adopted. This arises out of a perceived critical studies need, and is therefore integral to visual arts education, as opposed to being the grafted-on chore which so often makes students and teachers alike resentful of recording of achievement. By contrast, many of the students involved approach their personal appraisals with enthusiasm and seriousness, recognizing them as a potent vehicle through which to evaluate their practice, give expression to their concerns, and as a mode of communication. Much of what they write is not only reflective but throws light on their aspirations and intentions about possible future work and its directions.

To encourage such insightful speculation, students are provided at the outset of the course with all relevant information about the course principles and

PLATE 1.   Critical studies approaches facilitate individual learning and one-to-one teaching: Helen painting at Winstanley Sixth Form College during her A-level course

content, the examinations on offer, and what is required of them in terms of such extra demands as, for example, the use of sketchbooks outside the college. This knowledge enables students to take responsibility for their own learning and is obviously crucial to meaningful negotiation; young people are frequently disempowered through ignorance of what is to come next. In contrast, hints as to future, possible directions and the importance of negotiated learning to the ethos of the art room are reflected in appraisal statements from the outset. It is only five weeks into the course that one student feels able to record:

> The atmosphere in the art class and the relaxed, equal relationship between teacher and pupil is very different from the 'teach and learn' approach I experienced in my feeder school.... My interest in the work of mature artists encouraged me to go on a school trip to Glasgow ... now I am eager to study Art History but my main goal, after seeing Degas' Ballerinas, is to master the art of figure drawing.

What invaluable information for the teacher to be able to act upon in negotiation with the student!

Approaching Art and Design was written when A-level modifications in the light of GCSE were envisaged but not yet implemented. Some of the changes are dramatic. JMB candidates now mount exhibitions of coursework as an important element of the examination. Besides choosing their topic for the written assignment arising out of their art history and appreciation course, they are also responsible for identifying the nature of the practical assignment for external moderation. This means that this assignment can grow directly out of their course concerns and provide their culmination, while relating equally directly to their studies of art and artists. The examination therefore encourages students to

PLATE 2.   Jane's interests in personal adornment can be traced back to her work with an artist-in-residence when she was eleven: as an A-level student she is encouraged fully to explore these interests

enter into the aesthetic field at a point of their own choosing and fully to explore it through all the phases of making, presenting, responding and evaluating. Examples of this fresh scope, provided by the first generation of students to sit the modified examination, are incorporated into the text of *The Visual Arts in Education*. The significance of their personal appraisal statements to negotiated learning with a view to constantly entering the aesthetic field is made richly and abundantly clear.

Notes

1   Peter Abbs (1987) in *Living Powers*, Basingstoke, Falmer Press, pp. 2, 3.
2   *The Arts in Schools: Principles, Practice and Provision* (1982), London, Calouste Gulbenkian Foundation.
3   Abbs, *op. cit.* The following section on the aesthetic field and the phases of making, presenting, responding and evaluating is based on pp. 52–63.
4   Rod Taylor (1986) *Educating for Art: Critical Response and Development*, Harlow, Essex. Longman, p. 49.
5   See, in particular, Rod Taylor, *ibid.*, pp. 18–28. For elaboration of argument, see also David Hargreaves (1983) 'The Teaching of Art and the Art of Teaching: Towards an Alternative View of Aesthetic Learning', in *Curriculum Practice: Some Sociological Case Studies*, Ed. Martin Hammersley and Andy Hargreaves, Lewes, Falmer Press.
6   Taylor, *op. cit.*, p. 112.
7   *Ibid.*, p. 68.
8   See Taylor, *ibid.*, pp. 70–82 on the issue of home art.
9   *Ibid.*, p. 181.
10   This model was first set out in detail in *Wigan Schools, Critical Studies and GCSE Art and Design* (1988), a Drumcroon Education Art Centre, Wigan, occasional publication.
11   Rod Taylor and Dot Taylor (1990) *Approaching Art and Design: A Guide for Students*, Harlow, Essex. Longman. See, in particular, pp. 103–11.

Chapter 2

Working within the Aesthetic Field: A Short Recent History of the Teaching of the Visual Arts

Field, then, in our context, implies an intricate web of energy where the parts are seen in relationship, in a state of reciprocal flow between tradition and innovation, between form and impulse, between the society and the individual, between the four phases of making, presenting, responding and evaluating which mark the four essential elements of the aesthetic field.... The arts teacher can break into the aesthetic field at any point and be led by an invisible pattern of relationships into the whole circuit — for the arts are not self-contained but gain their meaning through connection with all the other parts. All points, therefore, can be starting points.... (Peter Abbs)[1]

Introduction

During a recent trip to Australia I visited an artist and his wife who had just returned to their home having spent several months on an island north of Arnhem Land.[2] It was a restricted access area to white people, but they had been invited to work there, and through art, to do something for the Aboriginal people of the island who were in a demoralized and depressed state. Once inside their home, one was surrounded by a rich abundance of Aboriginal art. It covered every wall and even all available floor surfaces. There were paintings both on bark and in acrylic on canvas — virtually all executed in the four basic colours of black, red and yellow ochre, and white. Woven mats were piled on top of each other and there were baskets, bags, beads and carvings in abundance. When they first arrived on the island, there were just five of the Aboriginals painting, but this number steadily rose to well over seventy. There was also extraordinary evidence of rapid progress in skills and treatment from their first attempts to what they were achieving only a few months later. After about two months, the artist and his wife received a visit from the hospital's nurses. What were they doing? What was going on? There must be something happening: the local hospital was empty!

One could not have a more powerful example of the power of the visual arts, or one that points up some of their significance within education. What happened was not by chance, of course, nor does it mean that all artistic activity is, by definition, therapeutic. What it does illustrate is the sensitivity which the artist brought to his task, and which makes the project a model of its kind. When appropriate, he introduced them to new materials, in their terms, such as acrylic paint and canvas, but equally he encouraged them to work within, and draw upon, their own well established artistic traditions and to make use of their own well-tried methods and materials. In the process, they were put back in touch with their own rich history as embodied within their Dreamtime. This combination of factors enabled them to endow their work with unusual vitality and to marry innovation with tradition. Their new-found confidence and feelings of self-esteem were not too dissimilar from the motivations arising out of being able to give expression to personal ideas and concepts which characterize the work of the students, practising within a flexible critical studies context, which I record in the next chapter. Their course, too, was sufficiently full and rounded to enable them to draw upon artistic traditions and conventions yet be innovative within their terms of reference, with obvious implications for course construction.

Of all the major art forms, none is currently better placed than the visual arts to provide a rich, broad and fully rounded education relevant to the needs of young people, irrespective of age, intelligence and background. Large numbers opt to study art and design to GCSE level, while recent curriculum initiatives provide both theoretical underpinning and practical evidence demonstrating the worth of courses in which the four phases of making, presenting, responding and evaluating are all present, and in interactive ways which benefit and enrich each other. Yet an historical emphasis on making alone goes very deep; in its wake there is an inevitable reluctance on the part of some to broaden what is on offer.

The Emphasis on Making

Making will always occupy a pre-eminent place in visual arts education; learning through practical involvement is a crucial dimension of the subject. But should it be the sole preoccupation? Might this not actually limit activities and be counter-productive? When I began teaching in 1961, I rapidly became aware that the prevailing art education wisdom of the day was adamant that children's art making was separate from the wider world of the visual arts as practised by mature artists and crafts people, whether past or present. There had been earlier warning signs to alert me. On the first day of the teacher training year we were told that we had been self-indulgent art students for years. This was now at an end and was quite separate from and unrelated to the issues of children and education we now had to address. Whatever skills, knowledge and understanding all those years of specialist training had given us were now apparently seen as irrelevant to the requirements of teaching art to children. Could this really be the case? Might not such a view actually restrict our teaching approaches?

I had been taken on gallery visits as a child and these were affirmed by virtue of my art student experiences when the joys and pleasures of gallery visiting intensified. I soon began to acquire my own art books, avidly studying their plates and enjoying finding out more about art and artists. Gallery visits would conclude with the purchase of postcards and new works, and sometimes new artists were discovered in the postcard sections of book and art material shops.

I recall spreading these postcards on the lounge carpet, sometimes grouped thematically, formally or according to artists. A moderate student grant ensured that most of the books acquired were secondhand, but a small plate of a Vuillard vase of flowers instilled the ambition one day to compose in a similarly delectable range of warm greys and purples. Daumier rapidly became a firm favourite, along with Degas. A hitch-hiked journey to Swansea to see a relatively large grouping of Daumier's art was followed by a visit to the galleries of Paris, and a lifelong desire to travel in pursuit of art was born. Under Daumier's influence, street workers and washerwomen pushing old prams assumed a powerfully moving grandeur and nobility, opening up a whole new world of compositional possibilities and subject matter found in the ordinary and everyday. Hours were spent discussing matters to do with art with student friends, and the links relating artists to music and literature stimulated concert-going and the reading of a wide variety of literature. Were all these key formative experiences alright for an art student but irrelevant — indeed harmful, as some argued — to the young urban comprehensive pupils in my first school?

Abbs' four-phase model would have stood little chance of achieving any recognition in the art education climate of 1961. Likewise, that formulated by the GCSE Grade Criteria Working Party in Art and Design could never have been conceived of then, with its suggestions of three domains relating to the conceptual, productive and the contextual and critical.[3] Both emphasize that visual art and indeed all other artistic experiences can and should be of a multifaceted nature, challenging the ingrained notion that pupils should engage exclusively in making activities. In these circumstances making inevitably becomes a limited and restricted activity and one-dimensional as compared with Abbs' generous view of what it entails.

> The appetite — the impulse to expression — animates the specific medium of the art-maker ... and in the encounter between appetite and medium the art-work begins to take shape.... The material also carries with it a history, a repertoire of previous uses, of working conventions, of established connections and meanings, both covert and hidden. In engaging with the material the art-maker thus engages both consciously and unconsciously with tradition, with the forms already used and the modes and the techniques those forms have employed and passed on. Indeed, sometimes, the art-maker in the process of composition will actively study other artists' work. And so, art does not come solely out of appetite but also out of other art.[4]

This is a process understood by virtually all artists. As Constable once expressed it, 'A self-taught artist is one taught by a very ignorant person', while Lucian Freud now accepts that he hindered his development for a time because he attempted to rely on appetite alone,

> I always felt that my work hadn't much to do with art; my admirations for other art had very little room to show themselves in my work because I hoped that if I concentrated enough the intensity of scrutiny alone would force life into the pictures. I ignored the fact that art, after all, derives from art. Now I realise that this is the case.[5]

Abbs' broader view of making, consistent with recent critical studies' developments in art and design education, accepts the interactions between study and practice, seeing the reflective and contemplative as being of an active, rather than passive, nature. To see the possibilities which this opens up for the future, it is worth first reflecting upon some of the broad trends which have characterized the visual arts in education over the last thirty years or so.

As a pupil, my art lessons took place in the single room of a boys' grammar school. It was typical of its time and type of school, the trestle tables and above-average classroom size being the only features to distinguish it from any other room in the school. It was otherwise devoid of any equipment and tools or stimulus appropriate to the requirements of the subject. The course was even then outmoded, comprising an unalleviated diet throughout the five years of making still-life drawings but always from arrangements of a set of white wooden cubes, spheres and pyramid forms. Then there was manuscript writing copied from a poem written on the blackboard, and the writing down and learning for testing purposes of architectural words and their definitions read out to us in alphabetical order by the teacher. The subject was held in low esteem and, unfortunately, the attitudes of many who hold posts which determine educational decisions today were irrevocably shaped by the low status and undemanding nature of art as practised in the schools where they were educated. It has always seemed ironical and somewhat amusing to me that I had to move down into the science stream in order to continue 'studying' art! My first teaching practice was in a tough boys secondary modern, similar to my old grammar school in size but with the benefit of two art rooms, one equipped with a kiln. Though the practice in one was at not too far a remove from my schooldays, pupils were encouraged to make large, ambitious pots in the other — an aspect of craft was allied to art.

My first teaching post was in an early comprehensive school with a purpose-built three art room suite, a concept which characterized the establishment of comprehensive schools. When properly designed, furnished and equipped — and staffed — these opened up a dramatic range of new possibilities, with opportunities provided for painting and drawing, printmaking and graphics, photography, fashion and textiles, ceramics and three-dimensional studies with, of course, the addition of computer design and graphics in more recent times. Just as features of primary open-plan practice permeated schools of traditional design, so those stimulated by comprehensive provision likewise took root in secondary schools of other types, in both the public and private sectors. The subject rapidly changed beyo⸱d recognition; few other curriculum areas have changed as dramatically and significantly in the range and breadth of what is on offer as art and design did during the 1960s and 1970s, compared with what it was.

Expansion took place so rapidly that there were often problems recruiting teachers with specialisms relating to those of the provision, and a prime concern rapidly became that of constructing courses around the many disciplines now made possible. It was not uncommon for the overriding aim of departments to be that of 'providing opportunities for pupils to experience as wide a range of media, processes, and techniques as possible'. Over a relatively short time-span the range and scope of the subject were transformed, at least in the range and scope of the practical activities on offer. The subject now had the potential to relate more closely to the art and design courses available at the higher education level, and the numbers opting to study art and design to 16+ level began to increase to the

PLATE 3.   Comprehensive art and design suites expanded the range of activities on offer: the textiles area at Golborne High School, Wigan

point where it becomes a foundation subject in the National Curriculum with around half the school population already choosing to study it to GCSE level.

On the debit side, though, the emphasis on an ever-increasing range of processes and activities could become an end in itself, with the absence of any coherent critical studies basis causing a risk of fragmentary and unrelated practical experiences, each of relatively short duration, following one from the other. This lack of continuity is graphically conveyed by one 14-year-old; she had completed one exercise, but,

> As soon as we had done that we went onto something else, and I did not really know what the point of the previous lesson was. We went onto something different, and it just didn't relate to anything else that we did before or after — as soon as we had finished it, that was it.[6]

There was little evidence of any genuine appraisal. This meant that the assumed logic of the syllabus was rarely actually put to the test, with pupils often unable to make the connections between activities which were presumed to be being made.

Attractively designed free-flow suites often went ahead of the fresh thinking and departmental philosophies appropriate to their adequate exploitation. What constituted a fully rounded art and design education? How might pupils develop an individual say in how they might gain access to what was now on offer? How might staff skills and roles complement and affirm each other in order to add up to an appropriate coherent whole? What kind of syllabus was necessary to maximize what was now possible? How might the timetable facilitate more constructive usage in terms of, for example, blocking of a whole year of pupils at the same time? As these issues were beginning to be addressed, the problems were compounded by the advent of design education.

Design Education and Faculty Structures

Beginning in the late 1960s, design education was particularly influential throughout the 1970s when the setting up of large faculties incorporating art and design, home economics, and craft, design and technology became widespread. Problem-solving was seen as the main means whereby major links could be established across disciplines, with courses again constructed around materials. Clay and fabrics, photography and printmaking were likely to be areas identified as art and design responsibilities, with the 2-D teacher often taking responsibility for a range of colour, line, tone, texture exercises, for the acquisition of an 'art vocabulary' acquired through the practice of a range of basic skills was deemed necessary. Following on from the essentially child-centred primary approaches in which spontaneity and use of the imagination were still dominant, art college foundation-level basic course attitudes involving 'wiping the slate clean' began to find favour at the secondary school level — only now could 'real' learning commence!

Complementing the clay, fabrics, photography and print art and design could offer, food, metals, plastics, wood and so on were on offer elsewhere in the faculty. Block timetabling was introduced to facilitate movement from one materials area to another; it still exerts its influence today. In an eight FE school, 240 pupils might be divided among twelve teachers, ideally four from each of the three departments, providing groups of twenty. By moving pupils round on a 'rotation' or 'carousel' system, each set of materials could be sampled in turn. Over a three-year cycle pupils would move every nine weeks — on a two-year one, every six weeks! Teachers could not learn the names of most pupils and, though experimentation was very much in vogue, the pressures of devising six week courses frequently led to an overemphasis on completed products at the end of the period, sometimes obviously contrived ones. In attempts to provide a semblance of unity, themes and topics were often devised to run concurrently across all faculty activities, but there was a persistent unease that these invariably emphasized overlap between departmental concerns at the expense of what was seen as the central core of each.

One design education proposal which found little favour was that of the 'lead' or 'key' lesson. Besides slabs of practical time, pupils could also come together for shorter periods of a more theoretical nature for the introduction of faculty-wide projects with opportunities to illustrate possibilities and to discuss problems. Common concerns, maybe relating to formal considerations, the nature and properties of particular materials, or correct usage of tools and equipment, could be addressed. An expert or enthusiast on a particular topic might take the lead, and there might even be opportunity to see and hear a resident craftsperson talking about his or her work. The rejection of the whole notion of this key lesson can be seen, with hindsight, as a lost opportunity to introduce a dimension of critical studies a full decade prior to its eventual recognition. Not only that, but essential developments might then have taken place in critical studies at the design level, as opposed to those of a more fine art nature which have so illuminated that area of practice. The rejection of the key lesson is but one more illustration of the stranglehold exerted by making alone.

Visual Studies

Though many visual arts teachers remained sceptical about design education, they were remorselessly sucked into it, for it was wholeheartedly embraced by curriculum planners and schools administrators alike. Ernest Goodman warned against 'the education of the consumer' being elevated into a major aim leading to 'promotion of Habitat or House and Garden cliches — a sort of middle-class "dolce-vita".'[7] Many art educators felt more sympathy towards visual studies, which ran almost parallel and shared some of the same characteristics. It, too, put a great emphasis on colour, line, tone, texture exercises, and it, too, was in large part a reaction to an overreliance on the imagination as children's sole means of producing art. In marked contrast, Alan Simpson highlights that with visual studies,

> The emphasis has been on direct observation and recording — object drawing — the 'object' being the 'environment'. In primary and secondary school respectively we have been through the dragons of egg cartons and other junk, the drawings of twigs, shells, sections of any fruit or vegetable you care to name, skulls, bones, bits of bikes, lamps and those tedious pencil studies of crushed coke cans and toothpaste tubes; all now definitely passé.[8]

Perhaps so — except that a Canadian art educator recently came to see me, three years after Simpson's article was written, disillusioned at the number of British schools she had visited where 'predictable' objective drawing lessons were still the order of the day and with that crumpled coke can still very much in evidence. Visual studies, in spite of laudable attributes, often degenerated all too easily into spades always being spades and no more. Simpson observes, 'However, it has been taken for granted that what art is wholly about is observing, recording and responding to visual and tactile stimuli from which either freely personal interpretation (fine art) or design work is developed.'[9] Drawings would be translated directly into paint or print, or a detail be selected by use of a rectangular viewer being moved across the surface, the chosen area then being blown up into a large, seemingly abstract set of shapes. The same initial drawing might, on occasions, be variously reworked, emphasizing first its colour qualities, followed by those emphasizing line, tone and then texture. In ceramics, making pots was replaced by fungus and seed pod forms, and so on. Simpson notes that words like 'creativity' and 'self-expression' gave way to talk about the 'artistic process' and the 'design process'. For the most part, though, 'there has been little, if any, reference to works of art or art history, while criticism, although covertly implied throughout, has overtly been disclaimed completely.'

Indeed, writing in 1976 and reflecting the attitudes of the time, Ernest Goodman was forcibly arguing that all connections with art and art history should be irrevocably severed once and for all. Essays of 'numbing detail and derivative banality on Michelangelo, would be passed with approbation' around staffrooms while the 'creative leap of a less academic child, embodied in his personal response in a painting or drawing to an aspect of his environment goes unheeded and unheralded.' To remedy this state of affairs,

> ... the whole subject of art as generally understood in schools needs to be undone. The subject carries with it a false notion of the cultural heritage. Such a heritage renders us all modest — not modest in action, but modest in passivity. ART as presently understood means reception. What is needed is questioning. The space that ART now usurps must be filled with experience instead of with handed-down and spurious cultural values. Probably the field should be given another name in order to start clearly — instead of art the subject might be called Visual Studies.[10]

This statement is particularly interesting as a potent reminder of the dominant attitudes which were influencing art and design practice at the time when it is remembered that Goodman played an influential role in the setting up of the 1981–84 Critical Studies in Art Education (CSAE) Project, which was initially jointly funded by the Arts and Schools Councils and subsequently by the Crafts Council also. I was Director of that Project and well remember his important contribution to the Society for Education through Art 1981 Conference at a key stage in the early life of CSAE. His contrary views of the mid-1970s were typical of those of the art education establishment then, however, when it was commonplace to hear contemptuous talk of adult art being 'out there', irrelevant to pupil needs, and to be assiduously avoided as being potentially harmful to the children's own artistic expression.

The Child Art Movement

Design education and visual studies were both, therefore, unified in the sense that each was, at least in part, a reaction to the child-centred approaches which had held sway for some considerable time. There were irreconcilable differences between child art and both the former, yet it was values that had come to be seen as implicit in child art which permeated attitudes in the others, particularly with regard to cultural tradition and adult art values. The history of child art goes back considerably further, its most influential initial advocate in this country being Marion Richardson through her teaching at the Dudley High School for Girls, and through her inspectoral work and writing.

> She contended that all children are gifted with the power to create and should therefore be given equal opportunity to express themselves.... In the year 1930 she was appointed District Inspector of Art by the London County Council, and it was in this capacity that her influence on the art teaching of children became most active and effective.[11]

Roger Fry exhibited her children's work, establishing a tangible connection between the Modernism in art which he championed and Progressivism in art education, an intertwining which has subsequently been seen as of great importance. This link was further affirmed with the publication of *Education through Art* in 1943, written by Herbert Read, another ardent champion of Modernism. In its implications and influence it was to become one of the most far-reaching books ever to be published on art education. Through the child art movement, the vision and individuality of each child as artist came to be highly prized. With it, though, came the unfortunate by-product of the teacher all too often being side-lined, on occasions becoming little more than the provider of materials and encouragement and creator of a warm ambience. A widely accepted assumption gained currency that it must also be necessary to take steps to protect children from adult values and influences, particularly as epitomized in the works of 'great artists' and 'high art'. By taking pupils on gallery visits, teachers were subjecting them to influences which would inevitably impair their originality, spontaneity, natural creativity and imagination, the argument went. One presenter some months before the advent of the CSAE Project, speaking at a secondary schools' heads of department DES Conference, sought to illustrate this notion anec-dotally. He had visited the Picasso Museum in Barcelona that summer. It was now Easter, eight months later, and olive greens and purples were still dominating his colour schemes. If this was the effect on him, an experienced adult, what on earth will be the effect on the impressionable child!

So entrenched had these attitudes become that it can come as quite a shock to realize that the major influential pioneers and practitioners of child art adopted diametrically opposed stances and ones quite compatible with current critical studies thinking. Marion Richardson, for example, surrounded her children,

> ... as far as possible, with reproductions of great pictures of all sorts. In this good company taste will have had the opportunity of developing unconsciously, and can prove an armour of defence. The children may not yet understand or even care for what is fine, but, as a pupil once said to me, 'It has an expression on its face'. She recognised it. This ex-pression is the look of sincerity. In its own infinitely humble way, the children's work has it too, and they can dimly feel it as a broad and common denominator, the thing that makes their own efforts more worthwhile than anything borrowed or secondhand.[12]

Herbert Read was also arguing — as long ago as 1937 — that:

> If the number of those who are trained as painters, sculptors and 'creative' artists generally should be restricted, on the other hand the numbers of those to be trained in the appreciation of the arts should be vastly increased; indeed, no person would be exempt from such training except those hopelessly disqualified by stupidity or mental atrophy. For common sense as well as psychology tells us that the aesthetic impulses ... are the normal possessions of children....[13]

In *Education through Art* he expresses his preference for schools being decorated with the children's own pictures 'properly mounted and decently framed', and continues:

> Children should, of course, be shown the work of mature artists, both of the past and of the present (and preferably not through reproductions),

but these again should be treated with respect, and shown in an appropriate setting. But it should always be remembered that the school is a workshop and not a museum, a centre of creative activity and not an academy of learning. Appreciation ... is not acquired by passive contemplation; we only appreciate beauty on the basis of our own creative aspirations, abortive though these be.[14]

Recent critical studies initiatives affirm the relevance of such active participation as opposed to appreciation lessons being taught in a manner which is distinct and divorced from the pupils' practical involvements. However, Read's emphasis elsewhere in *Education through Art* on preserving 'the original intensity of the child's reactions to the sensuous qualities of experience — to colours, surfaces, shapes and rhythms' prior to adolescence, became a central platform for the child art movement and justification for denying younger pupils access to art and artists and to leaving everything to the imagination and nature.

R.R. Tomlinson entitled his book *Children as Artists*, but in it he also stresses the importance of the works of mature artists to the children's lives. Writing in the aftermath of the Second World War, he is in no doubt that 'Environment can and does have a profound effect ... upon the form which conceptions take. It is, therefore, of great importance that children should be made acquainted with the world's great art and craft in addition to well designed things of modern manufacture, and that they should live and work in as suitable and beautiful surroundings as possible.'[15] Sybil Marshall regarded the lifelong implications that can develop out of this kind of contact with mature art as being of paramount importance.

To believe in their own potentiality for creativity was for children the first half of their journey towards being educated beings. The other half could be completed only when they could see their own lives surrounded, sustained and indeed explained by the general experience of all humanity. This part of the journey will take them all the rest of their lives, but to know this is the greatest wisdom they can learn at school. To be able to approach the classic works of art without fear, and with pleasure, interest, understanding and love is to be able to tap the inexhaustible well of past human experience.[16]

Teaching in days prior to the existence of schools loan collections of original art works, Marion Richardson naturally turns to reproductions as the means through which to surround her pupils 'with great pictures of all sorts', whereas Read stresses the importance of the original work. Such variations notwithstanding, the unanimity of the views expressed by these important child art advocates and pioneers makes it all the more intriguing that the need to 'protect' children from exposure to mature art and artists gained the widespread acceptance that it did, and for so long. The positive desire to help children 'tap the inexhaustible well of past human experience' seems a far more laudable aim than the negative one of applying rigid forms of censorship to restrict pupil access and knowledge out of a fear that the resulting experiences might not be properly harnessed in relation to the pupil's own practice.

The positive aspects of these interactions, which can enable young people better to locate themselves within their culture in active ways, are highlighted by Seonaid Robertson through her belief that it is:

> Only through a sincere study of the masters (both old and contemporary) as people doing the same sort of thing as himself, only far better, who show the variety, the flexibility, the potency of the language of painting to fix an image, and convey an experience — only through this will he grow from childhood to manhood in art, with expression and appreciation interweaving. So can a child and an adolescent grow into his own culture and root his present in its past. This much about creative work I understood ... but I did not know hòw far back the roots might reach or how rich was that compost of ages which may fertilise his growth.[17]

The last sentence reveals Robertson's ever-deepening awareness of the significance of this basic truth she has always recognized, and with her we see the perfect fusion of the children's art making and their engagements with the works of others. It was the neglect — even conscious denial — of this fundamental relationship which caused child art to turn in on itself and become predictable and diluted, without adequate potential for growth and further development. It also contributed to that 'wiping the slate clean' mentality, already noted, at the secondary level. It was frequently argued that the natural spontaneity and creativity of the primary school child were not available for the secondary teacher to draw upon; by the age of transfer, these qualities had already begun to dissipate and peter out. Nevertheless, the majority of secondary teachers did not adhere rigidly to any one of the trends noted, most syllabuses containing amalgams of aspects of each, and with 'imaginative' and 'expressive' lessons taught amongst those emphasizing objective approaches or the acquisition of basic skills. However, diverse the elements within the course, though, the one powerful unifying factor bringing them all together was the overriding concern with making alone.

Critical Studies: The Missing Element

One important dissenting voice was that of Brian Allison. Throughout the 1970s he was arguing that making art was but one facet of any properly balanced art and design education. There were the analytical, critical, historical and cultural domains as well as the 'presently pervasive expressive practical domain'; all had their rightful place within the subject.

> To be 'educated in art' means considerably more than being able to manipulate some art materials, however skilful and expressive that manipulation might be. It also means to be perceptually developed and visually discriminative, to be able to realise the relationships of materials to the form and function of art expression and communication, to be able to critically analyse and appraise art forms and phenomena, to be able to appreciate the contributions to, and functions within, different cultures and societies that art makes.[18]

It was the preparedness of art educators like Allison to swim against the hostile tides of the 1970s in order to present a more rounded picture of what being 'educated in art' might mean that helped pave the way for the critical studies initiatives and developments which were to become a very real characteristic of the next decade.

Overlapping these two decades was the Art and the Built Environment (ABE) Project, set up in 1976 and eventually giving rise to the book of the same name, published in 1982.[19] ABE explored the means whereby pupils might become more conscious and critically aware of their immediate built environments, and with reference to vernacular architecture rather than just 'famous' buildings. Simpson stresses that criticism, while covertly implied, was actually overtly disclaimed completely by the visual studies protagonists. In contrast, ABE set considerable store by the development of language skills as an essential aid to critical appraisal and evaluation;

> Jerome Bruner says that 'the child sees the world differently through the use of language which reorders his experience' and concludes, 'the limits of my language are the limits of my world'. The Project revealed that most people's schooling leaves them with an inadequate vocabulary, verbal or visual, for understanding the reality of aesthetic experience.[20]

The Project sought to address this task of taking 'deliberate action to counterbalance this lack of language. At the most basic level it was even important to introduce visual and verbal vocabularies', and lists of words are detailed which were 'used effectively to widen students' vocabularies'. Such attention and concern were in marked contrast to the then prevalent assertion that the visual arts were a form of non-verbal communication and that it followed, by definition, that ideas and concepts to do with them could not be expressed through words to any worthwhile degree. However, ABE brought forward tangible evidence to support Allison's assertion that:

> The acquisition of an art vocabulary is fundamental to learning in art. Even a most limited art vocabulary is necessary before one can begin to adequately, or even minimally, describe, discuss or communicate feelings about art objects. From the infant school onwards, a child's art vocabulary should grow at levels of range and complexity commensurate with his developing intellect. It is important in the acquisition of any art vocabulary that the child is given as much opportunity as possible to actively use it.[21]

Reference has already been made in the previous chapter to the Critical Studies (CSAE) Project which, running from 1981 to 1984, overlapped ABE. Its concerns inevitably meant that it too placed considerable emphasis on the use of language as an integral aspect of visual arts education, one of the main aims being: 'To explore methods and approaches which will enable pupils to develop a critical vocabulary, to enable them to adequately express the ideas and insights which reflect a developing awareness of their own work and that of established artists and designers.'[22] Its case study approaches emphasized the extent to which the young people themselves, once they had become acquainted with art and artists, had few of the inhibitions which had been causing art educators to argue that such access should be denied to pupils. One 15-year-old emphasized that:

> Everybody is influenced by somebody else and if you could just start to formulate your own ideas, just follow the guidelines of somebody else's work and not exactly copy, just understand how they have done it, what they were thinking of and how they put it all together, instead of just doing one simple print of just a figure or something like that — and really going to town on things like that. Just to have the chance to tax your brain —![23].

The CSAE Project demonstrated that this close relationship between the study of artists' work and pupils' own practice can open up a wide range of possibilities, rather than cause young people to produce predictable art because it was done in imitation. On the contrary, pupils' art frequently took unexpected imaginative leaps which took it outside the usual conventions of school art — '... painting pomegranates, and a half cabbage, and your reflection in a kettle and things like that',[24] as one pupil expressed it. To make the connections fully, young people could be stimulated to express their responses to the art works to which they were drawn in a precise language born of their desire to give expression to a strong fusion of thoughts and feelings. Witness the evidence of Martin's exacting scrutiny of Manet's Bar at the Folies-Bergère in the Courtauld Institute.

> The champagne bottles on the left are superbly painted, especially their golden foiled tops, for they seem to shine and portray an extreme element of realism. From a distance they do actually look real, and as you approach the painting to inspect it further it is then that you can appreciate and absorb Manet's fantastic painting process. Thick dark colours consisting of dark evergreens mixed in wetly with dark browns and strong bold blacks mixed with deep ocean blues are applied to the neck and base of the bottle.... Strong lightning whites are enhanced with the addition of delicate blues and flesh pinks to make strong reflections on the bottle and a smooth hard table. The foil on the bottles is a masterly maze of brushstrokes.[25]

This awareness of the nuances of painting cannot but help the person so affected to look at the real world in a more heightened way, discovering unexpected new sources of subject matter and ways of approaching them in the process.

Following hard on the heels of CSAE was The Arts in Schools Project, one of the first to be set up by the Schools Curriculum Development Council, formed as part replacement for the Schools Council. It began in 1985 and culminated in the publication of the 1990 *The Arts 5–16 Project Pack*. It identified that the relative absence of critical studies approaches which had given rise to the CSAE Project in the visual arts was a problem across the arts. In stating that 'the arts teaching in all disciplines is often on promoting pupils' own creative work', it noted that, '... the best practice in primary as well as secondary schools gives equal weight to developing young people's critical understanding of other people's work and their knowledge of different cultural practices and traditions. This calls for a shift in the balance of work in many classrooms'.[26]

CSAE had taken account of race, gender and special needs issues, and The Arts in Schools emphasized that these should have ongoing consideration. An effective multicultural education involves pupils in 'analysing and comparing their own cultures in relation to others'. 'In the practice of the arts young people can be enabled to clarify and communicate their own ideas and values. Through critical engagement with existing works they can be brought into vivid contact with the ideas, values and sensibilities of other people in their own and in other cultural communities.' Arts education should therefore, of necessity, 'extend pupils' cultural experiences by drawing on forms and styles of work from beyond Western/European cultures.'[27]

Through engagement in the phases of making, presenting, responding and evaluating, all pupils can therefore effectively begin to locate themselves within such a broad view of the cultural tradition. Given adequate resourcing in schools — neglected for far too long — pupils can envisage the tradition as complex and three-dimensional, ranging across time, place and cultures, and not as a purely linear one extending back in time. Whatever the pupil's particular concerns, others can be identified as having travelled a similar road, helping the pupil — in turn — to envisage a wider range of possibilities. The Arts in Schools helped many practitioners open up these possibilities to countless pupils by being practically based in authorities and through constant attention to the issues of race, gender and special needs.

Two-Directional Pulls: To the Arts and to Design and Technology

The Arts in Schools undoubtedly gave added momentum to the impetus towards arts faculties. These invariably involved only the performing and visual arts, however, the verbal arts remaining firmly within English. Often disillusioned with their years spent in design faculties, many visual arts teachers felt more natural affinities towards other arts practitioners, and readily embraced the trend. In practice, once within combined arts faculties they often found themselves working within reduced amounts of time. Rather than the place of the arts being strengthened, they could be weakened by being marginalized, and the in-depth experience essential to true aesthetic engagement be replaced solely by more generalized approaches with all the emphasis on breadth. The democratic principle of dividing whatever the time available equally among the component art forms was particularly damaging to the visual arts, as they invariably entered the faculty from a position of relative strength yet found essential discussion and practical time eroded without adequate debate having taken place.

How could visual arts teachers construct courses within such constraints which effectively embraced the spectrum of art, craft and design activities, and of 2-D, textiles and 3-D experiences? How could courses be adequately imbued with and informed by the critical studies developments pioneered in the visual arts and crucial to aesthetic learning? How could essential time be found to enable pupils to experience the rigours of drawing, to experiment, research and investigate in order to bring true meaning to the activities of making? Did the broader view of the arts in general afforded through faculty involvement compensate for some or all of these subject concerns being lost or only superficially addressed? By eschewing faculty involvements, was there not a risk of all the important developments through The Arts in Schools being lost through fragmentation? Might not other natural liaisons with subjects allow the arts to permeate the wider curriculum, particularly as links with the verbal arts already had to be fostered outside timetable groupings?

These dilemmas were exacerbated in that all this was happening while core and foundation National Curriculum subjects were being introduced into the curriculum. As the National Curriculum either subsumed art forms into other disciplines — drama, dance, the verbal arts — or dealt with them last — art and music (and dance within PE) — the arts inevitably suffered badly in a period of hybrid timetables during which previously accepted needs had to be reconciled with the new requirements of each National Curriculum subject being introduced with its new status and added clout. In this complex scenario it was essential to hang on to Abbs' arguments as set out in *Living Powers*: arts teachers should recognize that they form a unified community through concern for the aesthetic; but this did not necessarily mean integration. These concerns could be subverted where the real reason for the creation of a faculty was expedience and not to facilitate the realization of a higher set of aims.

While this debate was still taking place, Art was named as one of the five major subject contributors to technology as a foundation area of study. The subject's widely accepted title of 'Art and Design' underlined its importance to the design aspects which became increasingly important to the Technology Working Party to the point where they would have actually preferred the title 'Design and Technology'. A decade ago, it was commonplace to hear visual arts teachers emphasize the importance of 'free expression'. However, many of the leading designers in society come through the visual arts route, and the capacity to design by visualizing in the mind's eye something which does not yet exist, and then to work out the necessary steps to bring it into being, is a special human capacity of which education should obviously take account.

> Design is the way in which we try to shape our environment, both in its whole and in its parts. Anybody setting out to design anything — an object, a room, a garden, a process or an event — will be trying to mould the materials, space, time and other resources which are available to meet a need which she or he has identified.[28]

Though not the prerogative of any one curriculum area, the role of the visual arts is vital to this area through its engagement in fashion and textiles design, ceramics and three-dimensional studies, graphics, etc. Equally, the recording from the real world, the research and investigative processes fundamental to all good visual arts practice, and the critical studies developments pioneered in the subject, are all vital contributors to technology. The visual arts are ideally situated to imbue technology with the aesthetic, essential for the future of our beleaguered environment.

Inevitably, this development before an Art Working Party had even been formed, posed an obvious dilemma: should the visual arts be in arts or design and technology faculties? Perhaps, in the final analysis, the National Curriculum has underlined their importance to each and their central position between the two.

This means that whatever school structure is expedient, the visual arts must be able to extend outwards to make their contribution to the other aspect. They must therefore be allowed to retain their own identity and integrity in order that they can operate from strength in their own right and in the interests of the arts and design and technology in general.

Examinations

Most of this book has been written in the period prior to the setting up of the Art Working Party and, once it had been formed, in anticipation of the Art Interim Report. Some of its findings could be reasonably anticipated because of the developments which had taken place through the replacement of O-level and 16+ examinations with GCSE, pupils embarking on the new courses in September 1986. O-level epitomized the examination model of producing work under supervised conditions in a rigidly prescribed time. Coursework therefore tended to be a preparation for it, with some candidates practising the same type and scale of drawing over and over again, for example. The Certificate of Secondary Education (CSE) had been introduced in the mid-1960s and it placed the main emphasis on assessment of coursework. It was designed to meet the needs of an additional stratum of the school population, however, and therefore existed alongside O-level. A decade later, though, a successful 16+ pilot scheme led to some O-level boards likewise accepting a combination of coursework and a set-piece for assessment purposes. This led to a varying picture across the country, with some areas predominantly coursework in approach, but others still dominated by external assessment of the rigid O-level type.

GCSE gave an added impetus to the visual arts on a number of fronts. Greater importance was placed on coursework at all levels, with the emphasis on what pupils know, understand and can do an incentive to encouraging individual approaches and development of ideas, as opposed to the conformity epitomizing so much of what was done to O-level. An added emphasis on process in relation to product likewise encouraged more investigative approaches and the development of ideas through, for example, the use of sketching from firsthand stimulus; one of the things which had debased both 16+ and CSE was the amount of mindless copying that had arisen because of the undue significance given to the product alone. With GCSE the prospect also opened up of examiner, teacher and pupil all being in possession of the same criteria for assessment, with obvious implications for negotiated and independent learning. If examination boards did have clear criteria in the past, they had remained a well-guarded secret!

Finally, albeit unevenly from board to board, GCSE acknowledged the place of critical studies. Under O-level requirements, it was non-existent with regard to practical papers, and separate art history and appreciation papers attracted very few candidates and were widely seen as representing a distinct and separate area of concern. Most GCSE syllabuses emphasized the importance of critical studies to any balanced course, 'both for the student personally and for the consequent stimulus it can provide for other work', for example. Some actually added assessment objectives in critical studies, and each year its importance is increasingly stressed in chief examiners' reports; one for 1989, for example, observes that,

PLATE 4. GCSE, with its emphasis on process and critical studies, can facilitate broader approaches than were possible under previous examination systems: an Abraham Guest High School studio showing large-scale irregular-shaped abstract canvases

> ... an ever increasing number of centres are beginning to develop crit-
> ical and contextual work as an integral part of each unit of coursework.
> Some centres were highly commended because within the coursework
> they lay emphasis to show that candidates had explored methods and
> approaches which had enabled them to acquire a critical vocabulary....
> As a consequence, candidates were able to express ideas and insights
> which reflected a developing awareness of the place of their own work in
> relation to that of other artists and designers past and present.[29]

Nevertheless, though considerable advances have undoubtedly been made, there is still GCSE work — and, indeed, sometimes whole exhibitions awarded the higher grades — which are still lacking in evidence of any worthwhile critical studies engagement!

One major reason for this was that the in-service preparation for GCSE, particularly with it following in the immediate wake of a prolonged teachers' dispute, was often inadequate. Another was that what should have been the first GCSE building blocks actually came last. Teaching patterns were largely determined, sometimes simply perpetuating existing practice, by the time draft grade criteria were published in 1988, by which time they were in danger of being submerged under the weight of National Curriculum legislation and reforms. Grade criteria proposals suggested that account should be taken of three domains for assessment purposes: the conceptual, productive, and critical and contextual. Though proposed for assessment purposes, this three-domain model had obvious implications for course construction and content and could be regarded as fundamental to any balanced visual arts course.

Art in the National Curriculum

In June 1990, in conjecturing about the possible nature of art as a foundation subject at a point where the National Curriculum Art Working Party was being set up, I wrote that it would doubtless take account of these three domains, for:

'Each can be addressed in its own right, but they are interconnected and inter-active. This framework, or a near equivalent, could provide the basis for a fully-rounded, coherent and rich visual arts education appropriate to all ages'.[30] *The Interim Report*, published in late January 1991, is encouraging in this respect. The Chairperson, in his accompanying letter to the Secretary of State, emphasizes that while a substantial part of the proposed curriculum 'involves the practical activ-ities of actually making art, we have stressed also the central role played by train-ing in art and design in the promotion of visual literacy and in equipping pupils with the ability to "read" and evaluate images.' While welcoming that design is linked with technology, he also stresses that 'we feel that the design component in a broadly-based art cannot be overlooked.' The terms 'art' and 'art and design' have therefore been used almost interchangeably in the report.[31] It emphasizes that art and design cannot be made in a vacuum.

> We consider the processes of art and design to be integrated and holistic.... In teasing out the various strands of the processes, our purpose was not to separate them from each other, but rather to under-stand better the way they each interact within an indivisible whole. We propose the use of the following three attainment targets for art in the National Curriculum:
> AT1: Understanding and evaluating art.
> AT2: Making.
> AT3: Observation, research and developing ideas.
> These are objectives for an art course, separated only for ease of com-munication and understanding. They are presented in an order which is deliberately non-sequential, to avoid any suggestion of a fixed proce-dural sequence.[32]

These can be seen to relate reasonably closely to those GCSE draft criteria, with AT1 relating to the critical and contextual, AT2 to the productive and AT3 to the conceptual.

In his response to the Interim Report, the Secretary of State suggested 'simpler, even one word, titles', and that the working party consider whether two attainment targets covering 'making' and 'understanding' or 'knowing' might not suffice. Is there not a degree of overlap between the first and third attainment targets? He also suggested that they 'make clear the importance and centrality of "making" in Art, especially for the early primary age-groups, while still reflecting the importance of appreciation and evaluation.' There are certainly areas of overlap as the Interim Report unfolds but nothing which cannot be satisfactorily resolved.[33]

Each attainment target has been 'divided into three strands or components, grouped under broad headings', and used consistently throughout the four key stages. These are then used as the basis for the formulation of end of key stage statements, providing the following format:[34]

Attainment Target 1	Attainment Target 2	Attainment Target 3
Understanding and Evaluating Art	Making	Observation, Research and Developing Ideas

A. Describing and evaluating own work	Materials, tools and techniques	Recording from firsthand experience
B. Relating own work to that of other artists and designers	Formal elements	Collecting and using information from secondary sources
C. Art and design in a wider context	Understanding of making processes	Describing perceptions and research

The Secretary of State requests one-word attainment target titles, if possible, and these could help identify more precisely the function of each within a holistic view of the subject. Understanding for AT1, Making for AT2 and Investigating for AT3 might suffice, though the necessity to be constantly inventing new ways to describe the activities of the discipline can in itself confuse. For example, understanding would become the area which best exemplifies what has been developed through critical studies, and teachers should be able to recognize that what is to be required of them in the future has relationships with what they have already been incorporating into their teaching, to whatever degree. The Working Group should point up these connections in the Final Report.

The most widespread criticism of the Interim Report is its neglect of the imaginative and expressive dimensions of the subject. Whether or not these are the most problematic in assessment terms is no reason to distort the visual arts by shaping them according to only that which is most easy to assess. Indeed, the recurrent absence of these aspects from a school's or pupil's work is in itself an essential criterion for assessment, as the printmaker, Michael Rothenstein, recently illustrated to me anecdotally. He and David Hockney were on a print biennale selection panel. Example after example of technically accomplished, but empty, studio editioned prints had passed by. Eventually one with genuine content appeared. Hockney turned to Rothenstein and said, 'I do like my art to be about something, don't you?'

Any Making attainment target must therefore allow scope for the imaginative and expressive, and not preclude them. As the descriptions of what each strand represents are initially described in AT1 in terms of activity, it would be helpful to retain this format throughout. AT2,A could then become 'Using materials, tools and techniques' rather than simply 'Materials, tools and techniques' — though I will seek to demonstrate later that 'Processes' implies more than the combination of these words. AT2,B could become 'Applying formal elements', but these two strands alone add up to no more than basic art courses designed to teach an art vocabulary as a prerequisite for any *future* activity in the field. AT2,C actually uses the word 'understanding', for which there is already an attainment target, and this already contains a strand — AT1,A — specifically concerned with pupils' understanding and evaluation of their own work. AT2,C should therefore be subsumed within AT1,A, releasing an important Making strand for something specific and crucial to this activity, and the vital missing element is Content.

Art educators have been attempting to absorb the Interim Report against the backdrop of the Gulf War. Major issues about life and death have been brought

PLATE 5.   The 'Price of Victory' *Observer* photograph; an image that highlights the need for content to be fundamental to making activities in the National Curriculum

sharply into focus, as have matters to do with power and authority, privilege and disadvantage, order and chaos, oppression and control, strife and conflict. There have been concerns expressed about colossal ecological damage. Throughout time, the visual arts have provided one of the most potent means whereby humankind has confronted and addressed these and life's other major issues and concerns. Any visual arts education which does not naturally accommodate these must be deficient. There must be a Making strand devoted to content, therefore, and AT2,C should therefore be worded along the lines of 'Addressing issues through content' or 'Realizing ideas in relation to content'.

This concern was brought forcibly home to me as I first drafted my response to the Report on the day *The Observer* newspaper published its photograph, 'Price of Victory', depicting the charred head of an Iraqi soldier leaning through the windscreen of his vehicle, burnt-out during the retreat from Kuwait.[35] It will probably become one of the most memorable of all war images. Nobody could believe that the photographer who took it was only thinking about, or concerned with, technical and formal matters: its content is its message. A week later, there were inevitably letters of protest that such a shocking image should be shown, but a sixth-former acknowledged that he had been affected by the 'buzz of excitement' about the war and, until seeing that photograph, 'hadn't woken up to the fact that there are real people dying in a real war.' He adds, 'In the beginning I had no forgiveness for the Iraqis, but now I don't see Iraqis dying but human beings.... I pray that I will never see pictures like that again.'[36] One could not have a more powerful reinforcement of the importance of Content and therefore its place within any art National Curriculum structure; the student has glimpsed the universal through the content of the specific image.

Unless there is scope for content, pupils will only make limited reference to the qualities inherent in the works of others under the AT1 strand B, 'Relating own work to that of other artists and designers'. Is it acceptable only to study Picasso's 'Guernica' from the standpoints of technical accomplishment and formal arrangement? Equally, as a holistic part of an integrated visual arts education, the door is opened by content for the full range and scope of the art of others, as practised across time, place and cultures, to be introduced through AT1,C, 'Art and design in a wider context'. The wording of this strand could nevertheless be beneficially modified to ensure that pupils actually study and learn to enjoy art works themselves, rather than just learning about facts, dates and surrounding data to do with contexts, with the art works never becoming more than a generalized backdrop. To this end, a wording like 'Engaging with art and design works and their contexts' would be an important improvement.

Content in itself does not, of course, guarantee that the imaginative and expressive elements will assert themselves, but by removing the overlaps in AT3 as has now been proposed to AT2, there is increased scope to accommodate them in the third attainment target. By proposing 'Investigating' as its one-word title, observation has been removed. Given its crucial importance to visual arts education, it can be reintroduced by terming AT3,A 'Observing and recording from firsthand experience'. The Interim Report is flawed, though, by according equal status to secondary sources in AT3,B. By changing this to 'Researching to develop and clarify concepts', appropriate use of secondary sources where necessary would be accommodated, but that strand implies far more in what it encourages in terms of essential investigating to make both the making and understanding processes more clear and informed.

'Describing perceptions and research', the AT3,C strand in the Interim Report, ought also to be subsumed within AT1,A, as has already been proposed for AT2,C. This, likewise, releases a crucial strand essential to Investigating, and it is surely here that the imaginative and expressive can finally be afforded their rightful due. A wording such as 'Responding to stimuli in imaginative and expressive ways' would provide scope for school pupils to investigate in ways which have countless precedents in art history, with responses to the observed providing an essential springboard for the imaginative leap. Gauguin advised that young painters dream before nature, Leonardo recommended that they study walls splashed with stains, the ashes of fires, clouds or mud as the basis for stimulation of marvellous ideas, providing essential means of invention.[37] Vasari, likewise, described how Piero di Cosimo sat 'plunged in contemplation of a wall upon which certain sick persons had formed the habit of spitting. Out of these stains he formed equestrian battles, fantastic towns and the most magnificent landscapes.'[38]

During a childhood illness Max Ernst gazed at a panel opposite his bed and the wooden grooves began successively to assume 'the aspect of an eye, a nose, a bird's head, a menacing nightingale, a spinning top and so on.' Many years later this memory was recalled as he gazed at 'floorboards upon which a thousand scrubbings had deepened the grooves.' To aid his 'meditative and hallucinatory faculties', he made a series of rubbings of them and was 'surprised by the sudden intensification of my visionary capacities and by the hallucinatory succession of contradictory images superimposed, one upon the other, with the persistence and rapidity characteristic of amorous memories.' Ernst went on to experiment with other materials — 'leaves and their veins, the ragged edges of a bit of linen, the brushstrokes of a "modern" painting, the unwound thread of a spool.' On the one hand, then, objective study is about more than a spade being a spade, and on the other some of Ernst's experiments are not too dissimilar to some of those of the art room.[39]

In the school context, though, such experiments all too often remain as exercises to do with texture but without allowing for essential imaginative leaps. In the process, exploration of the visual and tactile worlds and the use of the imagination can come to be seen as distinct and separate activities, to the detriment of each. The 'imaginative' has become discredited in many eyes because of this polarization, being associated with predictable cliché art made without any recourse to essential stimulus or by pupils forced to resort to copying from comics, sci-fi magazines and the like. A broad-based approach to observation and research is therefore crucial not only with regard to giving pupils control over their use of the world at an objective level, but as a means of feeding and nurturing the imagination; hopefully the final report will reflect this more clearly. These modifications produce a revised matrix as follows:

Attainment Target 1	**Attainment Target 2**	**Attainment Target 3**
Understanding	Making	Investigating
A. Describing and evaluating own work	Using materials, tools and techniques	Observing and recording from firsthand experiences
B. Relating own work to that of other artists and designers	Applying formal elements	Researching to develop and clarify concepts
C. Engaging with art and design works and their contexts	Realizing ideas in relation to content (or: Addressing issues through content)	Responding to stimuli in imaginative and expressive ways

This matrix facilitates a wide range and variety of visual arts activities, whereas the Interim Report is restrictive because of its omissions. It also makes clear why three attainment targets are necessary, for the strands are all essential to their attainment targets, each of which identifies a clear area of activity. Each end of key statement, programme of study and supporting examples can now be constructed without fear of overlap, for every strand is quite specific in what it addresses. The matrix provides a firm structure through which such major issues as those of race, gender and special needs can be approached and accommodated in a coherent way.

It also throws into relief the inadequacy of the arguments regarding art in relation to the expressive arts in paragraph 3.20. This recognizes 'the past and present achievements of fruitful collaboration between the arts, especially at professional and adult levels', but proceeds to deny the possibility of any in education on the grounds that the basic teaching of art 'has its own autonomy and is not something which can be combined.' Similarities in the arts obscure deep differences: 'It is tempting to suppose that a common vocabulary exists in art and music because they both use words such as tone, texture, form, scale, colour and rhythm, but the precise meanings used in each subject highlight how different they are.' The ability to compose a picture does not enhance the ability to compose a piece of music or choreograph a dance, the Report continues.

I have already warned against the dangers of combined arts courses formed for the sake of expedience without time allowed for in-depth learning. It is, however, surely wrong to follow this argument to the point where it denies the important commonalities which the arts might share at the educational, as well as professional and adult, levels. Colin Renfrew, who chairs the Working Group, emphasizes 'the central role played by training in art and design in the promotion of visual literacy and in equipping pupils with the ability to "read" and evaluate images.' The great themes of life which find expression through the visual arts are likewise dealt with through all the other art forms. Is it really true to say that pupils' abilities to read and evaluate images cannot be enhanced through the parallel study of Britten's 'War Requiem' or the poems of Owen and Sassoon in relation to that charred Iraqi soldier, Goya's 'Disasters of War', Nash's paintings of blasted trenches or Breugel's 'Triumph of Death'?

Equally, is it not important that pupils understand that the great sweeps of civilization can, and usually do, manifest themselves across the arts — the Renaissance, Baroque and Rococo, Romanticism, Impressionism and Surrealism? Seen within the larger contexts of the arts, those words associated with formal elements likewise assume added significance? Why should musicians choose to 'borrow' words like tone, colour and texture, and artists harmony, rhythm and improvisation? What do these words share across art forms and how do they change in the process from literal to metaphorical usage? These larger connections should not be denied because combined arts are sometimes introduced for cynical reasons. Similarly, much excellent primary school arts practice within whole-school policies should not be denied because of specific problems of secondary school timetabling.

It might therefore be seen as contradictory to advocate that art and music are set against each other at Key Stage 4 level, but the eleventh-hour decision to make both art and music optional at this stage is disastrous.[40] It makes mockery of the claim that the National Curriculum would provide a broad and balanced education for all pupils. Concern is not allayed by the Secretary of State expecting that all schools will 'provide appropriate opportunities to 16 for all who wish to take advantage of them.' Without him taking further steps to ensure this, it is totally predictable that the too-long history of certain schools devising option patterns which, on the surface, provide access but, in reality, deny it to whole categories of pupils — those doing a second modern language, for example — will be maintained. In these circumstances all pupils having to study either art or music at this level would ensure that an aesthetic subject remained a part of their educational entitlement throughout every key stage — art and music being the only named ones at foundation level which could therefore focus on the aesthetic other than on a spasmodic basis.

Art being now optional at Key Stage 4, programme of study proposals become non-statutory at this level. The Working Group will still offer advice, though, because of the need 'for new GCSEs and equivalent qualifications to build on National Curriculum requirements at Key Stages 1–3.' The numbers studying art and design to GCSE should increase whether art and music remain optional or are set against each other. The Working Group has gone a long way towards identifying what might constitute a broad and properly rounded visual arts education. The kinds of modifications I have proposed would ensure that the holistic view of the subject which they seek could become a desirable and much-needed reality. GCSE examinations marked an advance when introduced; pupils at every level of education might begin to engage in an education in which the four phases of making, presenting, responding and evaluating provide them with constant access to the aesthetic field.

Postscript

That most influential art educator, advocate for the crafts, and another closely associated with child art, Robin Tanner, also produced a considerable body of his own work. In emphasizing the significance of artistic experiences by reflecting on his own childhood experiences, he too emphasizes that holistic view which might at last become a reality for the majority of young people.

> When I was six years old, one of my greatest pleasures was to be left alone with a few sections of a Bible, issued in parts on very large paper with enormous margins, and illustrated with steel engravings of an intimidating, melodramatic kind by Gustave Doré.

> I was most blissfully at home in this world of Black and White. The infinite range of tones, from brightest shining white, through countless silvery and darker greys of many textures, to richest, deepest and most velvety black, positively enthralled me.

> Etchings and engravings became my chief obsession, and they still are today.

He did not have to go far to find the appropriate content for his own etchings; it was all around him in the immediate environment.

> All that I wanted to say on copper — indeed, all that I still want to say — is contained in a few square miles of N.W. Wiltshire — a land of Cotswold stone, but a countryside that is Cotswold with a Wiltshire difference: warmer and more lush than Gloucestershire: pastoral dairy country with small meadows and high hedges. And there is an ancient church every three miles or so in any direction.

He is conscious that he transposes this immediate world into an etched world which is also an ideal one, '... a world of pastoral beauty that could be ours. So I make my escape, but it is an escape into what Blake called the "real and eternal world"; my "corn is orient and immortal wheat"; in my world ... "everything is at rest, free and immortal".'[41] Tanner charts the aesthetic field in relationship to his personal responses first as a 6-year-old and then to the practice of making etchings as a mature adult. In turn, the intensity with which he scrutinizes a particular corner of England, and his imaginative interpretation of it, can enable us to respond to aspects of the world around in a heightened way — a process not unique to the visual arts, but very important and significant to them. Tanner reflects upon formative childhood experiences and their relevance to his mature achievements; a group of sixth-form college students equally amply demonstrate the significance of the aesthetic field to their adolescent artistic insights and achievements.

Notes

1 Peter Abbs, *op. cit.*, pp. 55, 56.
2 Des Brennan, the artist in question, lives and works in Darlington, Western Australia, where I visited him in October 1990.
3 The Art and Design Working Party was set up in January 1986 by the Secondary Examinations Council (SEC, now SEAC). The Draft Grade Criteria Report was published in 1988.
4 Abbs, *op. cit.*, p. 57.
5 Robert Hughes (1988) On Lucian Freud in the Lucian Freud paintings catalogue, Hayward Gallery Retrospective, The British Council.
6 Taylor, *op. cit.*, p. 183.
7 Ernest Goodman (1976) 'The Place of Art in the Curriculum', *Athene* 64, Autumn 1976, p. 12.
8 Alan Simpson (1987) 'What Is Education Doing?', *Journal of Art and Design Education* (JADE), 6, 3, 1987, p. 255.
9 *Ibid.*, p. 255.
10 Goodman, *op. cit.*, p. 12.
11 R.R. Tomlinson (1944) *Children as Artists*, London and New York, Penguin Books, p. 21.
12 Marion Richardson (1948) *Art and the Child*, London University Press, p. 23.
13 Herbert Read (1937) *Art and Society*, London, Heinemann, p. 223.
14 Herbert Read (1943) *Education through Art*, London, Faber and Faber, p. 298.
15 Tomlinson, *op. cit.*, p. 27.
16 Sybil Marshall (1963) *An Experiment in Education*, Cambridge University Press, p. 171.
17 Seonaid Robertson (1963) *Rosegarden and Labyrinth*, Lewes, East Sussex, Gryphon Press, p. xxix.
18 Brian Allison (1978) *Journal of the National Society for Art Education* of a lecture given at Rolle College, Devon.
19 Eileen Adams and Colin Ward (1982) *Art and the Built Environment*, Harlow, Essex, Longman.
20 *Ibid.*, p. 54.
21 Brian Allison (1972) *Art Education*, VCOAD (Voluntary Committee on Overseas Aid and Development).
22 Taylor, *op. cit.*, xii. The fourth of the project's six main aims, they appear in all the project material. See, for example, Rod Taylor (1982) *The Illuminating Experience*, CSAE, Occasional Publication No. 2, Arts, Crafts and Schools Council.
23 *Ibid.*, p. 45.
24 *Ibid.*, p. 48.
25 From A-level Personal Study, 1989.
26 *The Arts 5–16: A Curriculum Framework* (1990) Harlow, Essex, Oliver and Boyd, p. 3.
27 *Ibid.*, p. 33.
28 *Design and Primary Education* (1987) London, The Design Council (pages unnumbered).
29 Chief Examiners' Reports, Section 2, *Creative Arts and CDT* (Summer 1989) GCSE, Southern Examining Group.
30 Rod Taylor (1990) 'Shapes of the Future', *The Times Educational Supplement*, 1 June 1990.
31 Letter to Secretary of State, Colin Renfrew (1991) Reproduced at front of National Curriculum Art Working Group Interim Report.

32   Art Interim Report, *ibid.*, p. 15.
33   Letter to Chairperson of Art Working Group, Kenneth Clark, Secretary of State, Interim Report.
34   Art Interim Report, *ibid.*, p. 17.
35   'The Real Face of War', *The Observer*, 3 March 1991.
36   Luke Waddington, Letter to *The Observer*, 10 March 1991.
37   Irma A. Richter (Ed.) (1977) *Notebooks of Leonardo da Vinci*, Oxford University Press, see p. 182.
38   David Larkin (Ed.) (1975) *Max Ernst*, New York, Ballantine Books (pages unnumbered).
39   *Ibid.*
40   First intimations that art and music would be made optional were in July 1990. The Secretary of State made the official announcement in his address to the North of England Education Conference, 4 January 1991.
41   *What I Believe: Lectures and other Writings by Robin Tanner* (1989) Holborne Museum and Crafts Study Centre, Bath, p. 5. The extracts are taken from *The Etcher's Craft*, published by Friends of Bristol Art Gallery (1980).

Additional Note: In June 1991 the Art Working Group's Final Report was submitted to the Secretaries of State for Education and Science and for Wales and was published as their proposals in August 1991, entitled *Art for ages 5 to 14*. The Working Group received nearly 500 comments on the *Interim Report*. 'Respondents made it clear that they agreed with our proposals for three attainment targets, closely linked to the programmes of study.' One-word headings as proposed in this chapter have now been used as follows:

Attainment target 1: Understanding
Attainment target 2: Making
Attainment target 3: Investigating

Each AT has been condensed to contain two, instead of three strands, providing the following basis for the formulation of end of key stage statements.

Attainment Target 1	**Attainment Target 2**	**Attainment Target 3**
Understanding	Making	Investigating
Respond practically and imaginatively to the work of artists, craftsworkers and designers.	develop skills and express ideas, feelings and meanings by working with materials, tools and techniques and the visual language of art, craft and design.	Observe and record, make connections and form ideas by working from direct experience, memory and the imagination to develop visual perception.
Explore art, craft and design in a wide historical and cultural context.	Review and modify own work in relation to intentions.	Visualize ideas by collecting and using a wide range of reference materials.

The Working Group has done an efficient and conscientious job. Overall, however, the report still lacks that essential broad sweep necessary to convey the essential place art and design occupies as one of the major forms humankind has always used to comment upon, and gain insight into, the great issues of life. Perhaps this is because Content is still not adequately accommodated. **4.12** of the report, for example, provides a rather pedestrian description of what Understanding might signify:

Through **attainment target 1 (Understanding)** pupils will begin to appreciate the methods and approaches of artists, craftworkers and designers and use them to inform and enrich their own work. They will recognize that there are different kinds of art made for different purposes. They will compare and contrast work undertaken in different cultures and contexts and evaluate how these influence meaning and interpretation. This definition, read in conjunction with the Report's end of key stage statements, presents — if anything — a vaguer picture as to exactly what it is that children should 'understand' than was conveyed in the Interim Report, compounded by all references to talk, describing, use of 'a developed art vocabulary' and reading having now disappeared from AT1 end of key stage statements. AT3 also looks insubstantial, relating only to making activities. Its equal relevance to understanding is not developed but would have substantially strengthened it — essential investigative skills are required to elicit relevant information from books, locate appropriate works in gallery or exhibition or in the use of reproductions, etc., and in identifying crucial intrinsic elements when studying works. Had these aspects been developed, the chances of three essential attainment targets being retained *might* have been strengthened. Views on the proposals are invited by 1 November 1991 with a view to the introduction of 'the attainment targets and programmes of study for all pupils in England and Wales in the first year of each of the key stages 1, 2 and 3 in autumn 1992.'

At the same time, a DES questionnaire was circulated to all secondary schools. Entitled *Art and music at key stage 4* it seeks to elicit views on the Secretary of State's decision to make art and music optional at that key stage and how schools are seeking to meet the Secretaries of State's view 'that schools should offer some form of aesthetic experience for all 14–16 year olds and that the great majority of schools should offer art and music to pupils who wish to continue their study of these subjects after 14.' Views on this issue likewise have to be received by 1 November 1991.

Chapter 3

Art as Felt Experience:
Surrealism and Adolescence

When we dream that we are dreaming we are close to waking.... What is outside me is right inside me, is mine and vice versa. (Novalis, 1772–1801)[1]

Magritte saw a painting by de Chirico and began to become Magritte, Patrick Hughes admired Magritte and began to become Patrick Hughes. (George Melly)[2]

We dream of journeys through the universe, but is the universe not within us? ... Inward is the direction of the mystic path. Within us or nowhere is eternity with its worlds of past and future. (Novalis)[3]

The Axes of Creativity

In this chapter five case studies of sixth-form students working on and with Surrealism are presented. They demonstrate the model of arts teaching I have just outlined; they also show how student art work at its best draws on both the inner and illogical as well as the historic and cultural dimensions of our lives, what Peter Abbs in *A Is for Aesthetic* named as the vertical and horizontal axes of true creativity.[4]

In that book, in order to understand the former, he suggests that we turn to the phenomenon of the dream which 'creates the imaginative powers that are then extended to other conscious activities in the course of evolutionary development.' In the dream state 'what was consciously hunted for rises spontaneously with the kinaesthetic sensation of water flowing.' Central to creativity in general, the dream obviously assumed particular significance to the Surrealists with their link to Sigmund Freud and concern for the unconscious. Magritte, for example, describes how,

When I open my eyes, thoughts crowd in on me. They are the things I saw the day before. I also recall things I dreamed about during the night. I always remember them with a sense of great happiness and it is like a victory for me when I succeed in reconquering the world of my dreams.

It had already occurred to me how strange my morning thoughts were; it seemed it was a matter of remembering the greatest possible number of things and however much I recall I never go back more than twenty-four hours into the past. I take account of it as soon as it occurs to me to check.[5]

In a letter dated 9 May 1967, in the last days of his life, the phrase 'an unpredictable image appeared to me last night' appears, followed by a sketch of a plant with three different types of flower. Forty years earlier he had written, 'If the dream is a translation of waking life, waking life is also a translation of the dream.' In distinguishing between hallucination and the recollection of an actual recent experience, he noted, 'In recalling these things, I discovered all at once that they did not belong to a dream. That woman on a bicycle — her I had seen on the previous evening as I came out of a cinema.' He made specific reference to what he called self-willed 'dreams', 'in which nothing is as vague as those feelings one has when escaping in dreams ... "Dreams" which are not intended to make you sleep but to wake you up.' He described how he once woke up in a room where there was a birdcage with a bird dozing in it. Through 'a magnificent error', instead of seeing the bird in the cage, he saw an egg in its place. One writer refers to this as a rare 'poetic shock' stimulated by the 'mental system' and the 'sensory system'. Magritte does not say that he awakened out of a dream, but he does say that waking caused him to see 'what was not there'. Max Ernst suggested that 'Magritte neither sleeps nor remains awake. He violates methodically, without laughing.'

To many minds this is the very stuff of Surrealism. By comparison it can come as a surprise to discover that a movement which epitomizes originality and the sudden flash of inspiration to many people is equally founded upon the principle of art growing out of art which the horizontal axis of creativity represents. Salvador Dali in particular seems to fulfil the view of the eccentric artist questing after novelty almost to the point of being an outrageous freak, completely out on a limb. This is contradicted by a rapid and fairly superficial skim through just one Dali monograph; it reveals how steeped in art and artists he actually was:

> The influence of Impressionism is clearly seen in the work of the young Catalonian artist up to 1919.... The influence of the Fauves and Bonnard is evident.... Influenced by Juan Gris, Seurat, and the Italian Metaphysical School, he then painted his first Cubist works ... techniques stemming from the precision of Vermeer to the blurred shapes of Carrière.... The influence of the masters of the Renaissance, seen in the museums of Florence and Rome, is recognisable in the groups of figures used at the time by the artist.[6]

Three trips to Italy gave rise to qualities derived from Palladio, Bernini, Raphael, Leonardo and Magnasco. He worked from a plaster model of a Phidias sculpture, originally situated on the west pediment of the Parthenon, and also found direct stimulus in the Venus de Milo.

He acknowledged a debt to Max Ernst, whilst emphasizing that 'instead of seeing an analogy with Max Ernst one should see what is absolutely the contrary ... because of my Mediterranean heritage and my almost scientific side.'

This scientific side was fed through his study of the mathematical works of an Italian monk, Fra Luca Pacioli, a Roumanian prince, Matila Ghyka, and the treatise on cubic form by Guan de Herrera, architect to Philip II of Spain, influenced his use of structure and proportions. His work contains reference to Houdon, Le Nain, Velazquez and Böcklin and draws upon the architectural forms of Gaudi and writings of Nietzsche, amongst others. In particular, 'The Angelus of Millet "suddenly" became for me the pictorial work which was the most troubling, the most enigmatic, the most dense and the richest in unconscious thoughts that I have ever seen.' His extremely long working life spanned most of this century's 'isms'. 'Tuna-Fishing' of 1966–67 is dedicated to a nineteenth century artist, Meissonier, but in it, 'The artist has brought together ... all his tendencies: Surrealism, 'quintessential pompierism', pointillism, action painting, tachisme, geometric abstraction, Pop, Op, and psychedelic art.'

At the age of 67 he was still making influential discoveries through such studies, for,

> In 1971 he came upon the work of the Dutch painter, Gerard Dou, and he noticed that several paintings by this pupil of Rembrandt, done in two versions, exhibited undeniable stereoscopic characteristics. He then decided to return to the experiments of Dou....

These interests and influences are extremely wide-ranging, varied and span many centuries. Surrealism can be appealing to adolescents, as five A-level case studies illustrate, but these students are fortunate and relatively unusual; they have been able to combine both the horizontal and vertical axes of creativity in their studies.

Each of them, with one exception, became deeply involved in Surrealism — or a facet of it, and the exception relates, though, through a direct link with Sigmund Freud, whose influence upon the whole Surrealist movement was profound. The examples could just as easily have been chosen to relate to Impressionism, Cubism, or an aspect of Post-Impressionism, but a significant distinguishing feature of Surrealism is that it is frequently 'prescribed' for the 13 to 18-year-old category on the grounds that it naturally appeals to that particular age group while also allowing them the necessary licence to distort and take liberties with natural appearances — all those things that it is assumed the adolescent cannot yet cope with but which have become important to the realization of the adult values and concerns of which he or she is now aware. Of the true essence of Surrealism there is often very little.

The Appeal of Dali

Some of the reasons for young people becoming involved with particular artists or groups can be quite surprising; Stuart certainly did not become involved with Salvador Dali and his work, and Surrealism, by a conventional route:

> I went on a trip with my parents to Florida to stay with my grandad, and it was in St. Petersburg and the Salvador Dali Museum was next door. At the time I was quite a bit younger and I hadn't heard of Salvador Dali. Because I wasn't into art history at that time I didn't go and I missed

out. My mum and dad came back and told me what I'd missed, so after that I decided to find out about this artist. I picked up a general book on art and there were some paintings of Salvador's in it; I just had a look and I liked them when I saw them. From then on it was just love of Salvador Dali, really.[7]

Stuart's parents successfully fulfilled an important aspect of any art educator's role — that of naturally transmitting enthusiasm. They effectively aroused in Stuart a fascination for what it was that had so obviously fascinated them. Many art educators have become involved in what they do because they have passionate interests in the subject, frequently pursuing these in their own leisure time. On occasions, though, these interests remain private, and the opportunity is missed of arousing similar fascinations in at least some of those they teach!

Stuart realized that he had 'missed out on a big opportunity', but he has tried to remedy this ever since. As an A-level student, he owned four books on Salvador Dali and had seen in the original those works of the artist owned by the Tate, both in London and in Liverpool. His attitudes to the artist are influenced by the impact of the works seen in the original and the knowledge gleaned from reading about him and by studying book plates and reproductions.

> I like the way it's very powerful. There are certain pictures that are, for me, the culmination of his work. I just don't see how any paintings could be better — such as 'Soft construction with Boiled Beans'. It's the power of the face, the way he's got each bit gripping itself, and the way the head is just thrust back with dramatic lighting on the face — just that against the really blue sky. For me, that sets it off and it just creates such a power in that figure. It just represents his hate of civil war, for me that is just an amazingly powerful figure!

This interest in Dali's paintings has, in turn, led to an inevitable interest in Surrealism in general — 'he's led me to look at the whole basis of Surrealism' — and of Yves Tanguy in particular, stylistic qualities being the main motivations.

> ... I'm interested in the whole group now, and especially Yves Tanguy. The original reason why I went there was because Dali specialises in slick painting, really, and I saw then Yves Tanguy, which is also a very slick type of style of painting, so it was like a very direct follow-on from Dali. And then I got more into what Yves Tanguy was about and what he was trying to create.

He would like to find out more about Tanguy, but he is not well represented in libraries and the only book Stuart has seen to buy 'was about 30 pounds and I can't afford that', so he has not been able fully to substantiate the interest through research 'which I would like to do'.

The special relationships which exist between Dali and his own art practice, though, are not lost on Stuart, though he has consciously avoided the whole idea of producing obvious 'cheap' imitations of the artist's works.

> When I've been painting, I've not directly started a painting and said, 'right, I'm going to do this in the style of Salvador Dali'. I mean, if

anything I've tried, perhaps, to get away from it and use my own view of what I see. But I'm sure it's affected my work subconsciously without me thinking about it.

More than that, Dali has brought him to a much more rigorous and demanding study of his own immediate world — and of his own foot!

> I know when I did my drawing of the foot, the big foot, the original starting point for that was in the Salvador Dali Museum.... There are two gigantic feet on the ceiling he has painted, and when I first saw that I started to have a good look at the foot, and I thought, 'well, what an interesting thing the foot is'. I decided I'd like to explore the foot, so I did a big drawing to show every curve of the foot.

Those by Dali were gigantic, and Stuart drew his on a large scale, joining a number of A1 cartridge sheets together to produce a foot the size of a person.

When it came to his A-level examination, Dali and Surrealism again played a significant part in the conception of his studies and resulting painting on the theme of the progression of time, not obviously in outward appearance, but in the sense that he has got to quite complex ideas of a psychological nature. He chose to address the theme by depicting his grandmother in a seated position and to the right of the composition. She is holding an almost empty hourglass.

> With the hourglass I was trying to represent the sands of time running out for the old lady. Behind was a mirror, and a drawing of myself reflected drawing my gran. And I had in my hand, as well, another hourglass which was almost full, symbolising the youth of life. The mirror was representing a record of the past — like a photograph — as I'm recording what I am seeing *now*, and that is something that will stay there for ever as a record of that present time. And around myself, as well, I tried to create a halo effect. It was light all around me gradually getting darker as it got towards the edges of the mirror. The colour of the top I was wearing was green to suggest youth and vitality. I painted my gran in a kind of sickly colour, a very yellowy ochre colour, like an illness of age — as they are getting old they are dying. And then I had the walking stick as well, to represent old age, and cracked and peeling wallpaper.... I was trying to show the effects of time — of getting old.

On seeing Stuart's preliminary studies, his grandmother 'wasn't too happy about the deepening of the lines across her face', but 'she didn't really understand all the symbolism too well.' Though he consciously tried to avoid 'apeing' Dali in any obvious sense, the influence is potently there. However, it has manifested itself through a sequence of transformation processes leading to the expression of something powerfully expressive of adolescence, and of feelings and thoughts which Stuart has made strikingly real as a consequence.

Stuart has certainly not just responded to Dali at a superficial level, either, for the effects are of a lasting and developing nature.

> It's not just like a passing thing. As I've grown older, I've grown more into finding out about the paintings. Before it was, 'that's a nice picture'

type of thing, whereas now it's also reading up about the painting, what the painting is about, that's interested me a lot. I like the fact that he does this slick type of painting. It interests me and fascinates me how technical it is. Many critics shun this, because lots of other artists can do this as well. They shun it and say that it is his 'sickly style'. I don't agree with them on that — but, of course, that's their own view!

Fundamental to artistic appraisal is the ability to relate one's own responses to those of others, and Stuart shows evidence of this process which is far more healthy than that of passively accepting the opinions of the assumed 'experts' as being the only ones possible or acceptable. He has read and understood what they have to say, but is equally convinced of the validity of his own viewpoint.

I just like the way he paints with the dark shadows and the range of colours. Although many critics say he uses the same colour palette all the time, I feel that is one of his themes that goes on and on through all his paintings — and it's meant to be like that. It's not just something that keeps happening accidentally, it's meant to be like that; it's a continuation.

A Crucifixion with Impact

The special experience of encountering a work in the original is of a different order than that of only knowing it through reproductions, and it is an ambition of Stuart's to visit *the* Dali Museum, that in Spain, and also to see the Glasgow City Art Gallery's painting of the crucified Christ, for reproductions can whet the appetite: '... because I don't think anyone has ever shown — well, to my knowledge — a view of Christ on the cross from above or such a different view. And the way he shows all the muscles in the back of the neck! And in the shoulders just as his head is leaning down ... that is really amazing!' But however powerful it appears in reproductions, Dali's 'Christ of St John of the Cross' is one of those paintings which has a remarkable capacity to affect dramatically many teenage students; Christian graphically conveys the nature of this impact writing in his unusually titled personal study, 'Light, Camera, Action', which in keeping with his chosen works is equally unusually subtitled, 'The Role of Chiaroscuro, Photographic Reality, and Drama'.

A visit to the Glasgow Art Gallery to see the magic of Dali takes you down long corridors, parallel to grand, echoing steps. You turn, hungry for the crucifix you have anticipated, when suddenly you rotate and find at the bottom of the labyrinth the illuminated, beautiful Christ seeming to expand as you walk towards it. There is just you accompanied by the echoing steps that you create as the Christ comes to greet you.

He contrasts it with Caravaggio's work in order to highlight an aspect of Dali's painting which sets it apart from many of the interpretations of the theme, past and present.

The purpose of a religious depiction of a crucifix originally was to draw the ordinary, illiterate person towards God through the sheer horror of what happened to Christ's martyrs. This can be traced easily with reference to Caravaggio's work during the Counter Reformation when he painted horrific pictures on the subject of death. Dali's work however seems to have none of this....

Because, he continues, Dali's 'aesthetic ambition' was the opposite of that of most modern painters who, Dali asserted, obtained 'emotion through ugliness' whereas 'My Christ would be beautiful.' Christian sees this as having been achieved through both the content and the form of the painting.

Indeed it is a beautiful picture (and so is the Christ). With regard to content, the dominating figure of Jesus attached to the cross is seen from a totally new angle — we the sinners looking down on him. Beneath this we have the tranquil clouds of a beautiful sunset evening which is in turn hanging over the rugged, yet calm scene of Port Lligat.

The form of the painting is also quite interesting. We see the shape of a triangle, created by the linear forms of the clouds, and also the oval shapes of the cliffs; a truly magnificent painting, worthy of the title 'masterpiece'.

He finds Caravaggio's use of an equally dominant triangular structure in 'The Supper at Emmaus' equally satisfying, and discovers that the two works share other similarities. In going back and forth between these two paintings making comparisons, he is spanning four centuries; he notes similarities in the treatment of drapery folds, foreshortened limbs and use of colour, as well as in their overall design. But in particular,

It is the foreshortening and the use of chiaroscuro in each work that ties these pictures together. When I looked closely at the figure of Jesus in Dali's work it is an amazing piece of painting; we see from the shoulders to the feet how foreshortening has been applied to the figure, helped with the shadow on his right leg and foot. The use of yellow ochre and murky greens mixed with flesh tint, give a truly convincing image and feeling of chiaroscuro modelling. Note the vein in the left foot and the rounded graduation of colour on both legs that convince the observer of the true extent of the image. Compare this with the raised hand of Jesus in Caravaggio's work. Closer scrutiny shows that the lower fingers are simply indicated by long lines of crimson and flesh tint, highlighted by a contrasting pink/red colour. These indicate the creases in the hand just like the Dali, although Dali chooses more muted colours than warm ones.

The first impact of seeing the Dali — and the Caravaggio — has subsequently led to detailed, intense and close scrutiny; to unravel what it was that made a work affect us so powerfully in the first place, this process of examination both of the whole and of the constituent parts can be involving over many years.

PLATE 6.   Dali's 'Christ of St John of the Cross', Glasgow City Art Gallery

PLATE 7.   Detail of Ann's A-level exhibition demonstrating her interest in foreshortening

PLATE 8.   A drypoint etching of a foreshortened figure by Ann

PLATE 9.   As preparation for her A-level assignment, Ann drew her boyfriend who had to pose in street hockey gear from 10.00 a.m. to 9.00 p.m. one hot Sunday

Like Christian, Ann was powerfully affected by her first sight of the Glasgow Dali, even though her 'preconception of Salvador Dali was that he was something of a freak'.

> Upon my approach to this huge and dominating art work the pulsation of admiration pounded from within me. Dali's melodramatic nature is typically demonstrated by the way he chooses to portray the dominant figure of Christ and by the foreshortened supporting cross. The importance of the figure is intensified by the suspension of the crucifix, the illuminated cloudscape and the tranquil setting.... It is ... the ultimate representation of what I consider to be art.

Ann is aware of Dali's 'cosmic dream' in which he visualized the 'nucleus of the atom' leading him to consider the 'very unity of the universe, Christ', worked out geometrically in the form of a triangle and circle.

> The geometrical construction of the pose enabled Dali to dramatically foreshorten the figure in a precise condensed manner, by using the space limitations within the triangle as a guideline of the composition. The positioning of the circle, to the lower region of the triangle enhances the image of depth, as this represents the figure's head. The face is looking downward and when thought of as a flat image the head is closer to the feet than to the hands. Yet, in reality, if it were possible to see such an unusual pose, the head would be progressing forward towards the viewer, so nearer to the hands rather than the feet. Again this is reinforced by the large outstretched hands. Dali has placed the hands towards the upper corners of the canvas which seem to lead the viewer's eye down the figure to the small fragile feet. This introduces the idea of the feet acting as a perspective point. The whole of the body is angled, so progressing to this point and the outstretched arms emphasise this idea.

Unusual Viewpoints

This incisive piece of analysis is particularly interesting when it is considered that Ann had never drawn the figure herself prior to the age of 16. At the commencement of her A-level course she therefore attempted to rectify this omission. Using her sketchbook at home, she 'decided to do a self portrait in order to prepare myself for this type of work at college.' It was 'very simply positioned', and her simple ambition was to 'just try and make it look like a person.' Though quite pleased with the outcome, she is nevertheless conscious that 'no doubt in the future I will consider it quite inadequate as a figure drawing as I think I shall improve with practice.'

As the weeks pass, she comments on the improvement she is making; she finds interest in lighting effects, tones and shades, and the texture of clothes. She becomes conscious of the problems of compositional placement on the sheet, and sequences of quick ink and brush sketches helped her to 'become more free and expressive'. She learned how to simplify the 'poses of the figure in order to capture the structure of the figure', relating 'all areas of the figure to the bone structure'. Ten months into the course, however, she records:

> After having to think of a project for my art exam, it seems that everything has suddenly become clear. Whereas before I was unsure of how my interests could be expressed in my art work, I now feel that I can visualise my exhibition; its content will consist of mainly drawings of the figure from unusual viewpoints. I want to create the illusion of depth.... I like to draw challenging poses and so I feel that if I can overcome the difficulties of the figure's position I will then be able to concentrate on the type of material (media) used.

She was soon putting her ambitions into practice, not only in college sessions but also, out of interest, at home, inevitably finding the work challenging!

> ... I wanted to continue with my theme of figure from the unusual angle, so I sat at the end of the bed therefore the pose was very foreshortened. I had extreme difficulty in connecting the legs with the rest of the body as not only were they much larger but the upper half of the body was also twisted. I also found the feet difficult to draw as the shoe was forward-facing and somehow didn't look quite right. I think if I will have time to study some feet I will be able to overcome the problem ... On the whole, in my opinion, it was a good attempt at creating an illusion of foreshortening and of the figure.

Four months later she is able to record that 'my interest in the figure has made me more confident in my art work overall', and that 'generally my drawing abilities have improved and I am much more confident in my approach.' Throughout, of course, her practice was progressing hand-in-hand with her wider studies of art and artists.

> I have liked researching for my project as it has influenced my own work and two of Lucian Freud's works have actually inspired me to start pieces of my own based on his ideas. The main problem I now face is not content but how to portray my ideas to their best advantage.

All the while she is continuing the exploration of her theme, deliberately setting herself new problems and challenges.

> I would like to continue with this piece because it was a challenge as I had to draw the head upside down (as she had her head hanging over a pillow). This was interesting as it totally distorted all sense of measurement. I therefore enjoyed this piece as I found it extremely difficult. However, I was extremely pleased to discover that when the drawing was turned upside down all the features were correctly placed. This drawing therefore was successful in helping my observation and measurement but alack I feel is not satisfactorily completed....

As the momentum gathers, she is not only concerned with the immediate piece of work in hand, but she is also envisaging her final exhibition and how all the works will relate to each other.

> *Exhibition* This will consist of many drawings of the figure from the unusual angle. Presently most are lead pencil but I would like to include colour pencil, pastel, charcoal??, Vinyl paintings and my etching. I want my exhibition to be striking and dominant not only in scale of work but the subject matter and the materials used. Although I prefer lead-pencil I think a colourful exhibition would be more eye-catching and attractive. I want to be able to have demonstrated that I not only *can* draw but I can develop my ideas and use other materials as well.

She concludes this piece with a really important statement pinpointing the dilemma of the young person of this age, studying art and design as just one of a number of subjects, but who is pushing herself hard and conscientiously monitoring her progress. 'However, my problem is finishing pieces of work, as I am continually developing and progressing my ideas to new and more challenging things, therefore leaving most work unfinished'.

Having toyed with the idea of including Freud in her written personal study at one stage, she eventually focused on works by Uccello and Degas as well as, of course, Dali. She found her study of these artists to be of crucial importance in the development of her own work.

> My selected paintings have influenced my own practical work and observational skills. I have begun to view everyday objects with new insight and I try to challenge them by scrutinising them from unusual angles. Although my accomplishments are not as significant as the above artists I have been fascinated by the experimentation and perseverance needed to record these phenomena and I now appreciate and accept techniques which are often acknowledged without consideration by the unconcerned viewer.

In Uccello's 'Rout of San Romano' she was fascinated by the 'miscalculations and mistakes' unintentionally made as, for example, in the scale of the lying down figure compared with the others but, she believes, 'present day artists concerned with this phenomena illustrate the perfection of illusionistic techniques, trading on past experiences of others.'

> Much experimentation has gone into the achievements brought about by my artists but what is peculiar to them all is amazing skills in drawing which have enabled them to demonstrate the scientific feature of perspective to their artistic ends. All of them love the figure but they present us with challenging unconventional views of it. They catch the figure lying down, hanging from the cross or even by their teeth in mid-air. Only a draughtsperson of great skill can produce these poses which are often transitory in nature.

Of the three paintings she studied, she had no doubts about which had the most impact, however.

Yet the most outstanding painting, in my opinion, is the magnificent portrayal of the sacrifice of Christ by Salvador Dali. The reason being that the picture captured my interest because it awakened previously unfelt respect for the Surrealist master.

She really penetrates beneath the surface of this painting. Like Christian, she picks up on Dali's assertion that he wanted his Christ to be beautiful, in contrast to all the modern painters who have obtained emotion through ugliness.

This preconception is evident in the radiance of the form, which is enhanced by the unusual golden light and the daring use of the thick black-painted background. The interpenetrable black shroud of death imprisons Christ in his own empty and dream-like dimension. The definition of the muscular structure of the figure is achieved by the bright illuminating light source, which casts deep shadows clinging to the clearly defined form. The intensity of light bleaches some areas of the body, such as the thigh and shoulder, thus defining the contrasting use of light and dark areas. The upper region of the cross is also illuminated by this pure and unnatural warmth, promoting the illusion of depth, as the apex of the crucifix is progressing upward whilst the base recedes down the surface or back into space.

His Surrealist nature, she suggests, is illustrated through his contrasting use of different eye levels used on Christ and on the harbour scene, and she concludes:

The tranquil harbour represents the beauty of the world which is so often taken for granted. It is a symbolic representation of a Dawn of a New Era, one which was created by Christ sacrificing his life for our souls. The tragedy of his death is depicted through this passionate portrayal of his sacrifice. These emotions have been dramatically and successfully recorded by the foreshortened figure, who seems to be suspended in space itself on a cross which looks as if it could fly off into infinity.

Aspects of Portraiture

Ann began her course by making a self-portrait study at home, but then found the whole figure viewed from unusual angles to be her most effective mode of enquiry. For Charlie, the portrait provided an abiding source of inspiration throughout his course. He commences his personal study with a definition of the portrait and an observation with regard to that definition.

'Portrait: A picture or drawing or photograph of a person or animal.'

In the Oxford dictionary, the portrait constitutes just two lines of text and yet portraits form one of the most important genres in art. They can be found on exhibition in almost every art gallery in the Western World. In my investigation I suspect that I will find that there are many dimensions to the portrait and ways in which it has been interpreted, thus making the dictionary definition seem inadequate.

His final A-level exhibition brought together his investigations into the portrait over two years, being composed mainly of self-portraits. The teacher's written assessment included the following statements:

> Previous experience was copying essentially — on his A-level course he has responded entirely to the demands of direct observation with amazing success.... The exhibition features portraits and figure work — some pieces are almost frightening in their intensity.... The bold black and white chiaroscuro figures are dramatic and 'eye-catching' — colour work has progressed especially since he moved into pastel.... A superb draughtsman — expressive and structural.

In his appraisal statements, Charlie documents his development through the course; two examples communicate something of the flavour. The first relates to a pencil-drawn self-portrait.

> Because it was of myself it didn't matter how the features looked and I therefore concentrated on the general feel of the piece. The pose is of my head cupped in my hands and symbolises depression, fed-upness along with a little frustration, and yet I feel that there's a comical aspect to it, a hidden humour. I look at it as a reverse of my real character, a mirror image, the reverse of me in all aspects but the physical.
>
> I also feel I was more bold with the use of the pencil. There is a depth and realism to the work which I feel I sometimes lack.

A later piece was to occupy an eye-catching central place in his final exhibition, being developed from a small sketchbook study.

> It shows just a portion of my head, mainly the eyes, with only a sliver of light illuminating the face. Apart from this flick of light the rest of the face is drawn in deep shadow. I then took this idea a step further. Taking a single light source I decided to pick out the lit areas and plunge the rest of the features into complete darkness. Charcoal was perfect for this as it enabled me to create smooth, very dark areas and also a great contrast from the white paper.

However, this particular area of investigation did not stop at that one work.

> Using this technique I have drawn three pieces which make a triptych. The works are to do with emotion and symbolise, for me, pain, despair and defiance. They are three figures from which I have tried to take away as much of their personality and character as I can. For example, I have placed the eyes into deep shadow. I have done this so that the viewer is not concerned about how well I have portrayed the individual, but is concerned with the image of emotion I have tried to create.

PLATE 10.   Charcoal provided Charlie with the ideal medium to express 'pain, despair and defiance' in his triptych, here seen displayed in his A-level exhibition

PLATE 11.   Detail showing the left-hand figure of the triptych

He had studied Francis Bacon's work closely, but he found strong affinities with the work of Lucian Freud. He concludes his written study by focusing on Freud's 'Interior in Paddington', in the Liverpool Walker Gallery, having previously written about Titian, Holbein and Ingres portraits. He discerns how Freud is pursuing concerns which relate to his own interests.

> He has by no means tried to flatter the subject, painting the skin tones in dirty brown/greens, pale earthy yellows and white. The effect is almost repulsive with few reds to give the subject any life. The sitter looks ill and the absence of warm pigments makes him look cold, almost like a corpse.... The feel of his work is often very enigmatic. The painting shows a number of puzzling elements which make you pause and try to fathom. For instance, the portrait is undoubtedly a portrait, yet why does the plant take up so much of the canvas? The figure is standing with his hand clenched as if in anger or frustration, yet his face holds no expression whatsoever. We are not even told who the sitter is. In fact, very few of Freud's portraits have been identified. In my view, this may be so that you are not bogged down thinking about whether the work is a good likeness of some named individual. We therefore are left to appreciate what the painting tells us 'about' the individual. Also, perhaps ... forcing us to consider something of humanity as a whole.

He acknowledges, though, that to Freud the identity of his sitters was 'probably the single most important aspect of his work'. Though reclusive by nature, Freud being a major, living artist — has inevitably been filmed, and Charlie found his manner as revealing as what he said.

> Having seen Freud on camera and the way he reacts to things, I am not too surprised that he has adopted such a unique and unusual approach. He appears to be wary all the time, always on his guard. His intense observation doesn't stop at painting. He seems to be constantly studying, poised as if at any moment he will dart out, pouncing on some unseen prey.

To Charlie, there seems to be something of this manner in his paintings — the man and his work are as one.

> Most of Freud's unusual characteristics have evidently transferred to his paintings. This is most noticeable when looking at pieces such as 'Naked Girl with Egg' and 'Small Naked Portrait'. Both these works are nudes, however, the way they have been tackled makes 'naked' a much more appropriate word. Freud takes a very high viewpoint and then almost attacks the figure, scrutinising each detail, making no compromises. He chooses poses which look uncomfortable, cold and vulnerable. The effect is dramatic, if a little disturbing.

Aware that Freud's family moved from Berlin to Britain in 1933, and that he was the grandson of 'the great Sigmund Freud', Charlie finds himself often wondering whether 'something of Lucian's interest in feelings and the psychological aspects of painting wasn't inherited from his predecessor', for:

PLATE 12. For his A-level assignment, Charlie featured the moist, transparency of the eyes as the main means of communicating his psychological concerns

... he is searching for something deeper with the people he paints.... His use of pigments and the swirling rich impasto persuades us that the paint is 'an actor', struggling over the difficult role of portraying a character's innermost feelings. I believe Freud is trying to communicate not only the presence of his sitters, but also his own presence at the event and his surroundings. He is struggling with the obvious task of translating his world, with his friends and feelings, into the medium of oil painting.

At the conclusion to his research, he returns to that two-line dictionary definition of portraits with which he began, now quite clear that it is inadequate and 'obviously unjust'. He suggests that 'perhaps it should read':

'Portrait: a picture or drawing or photograph of a person or animal. Is a record of an individual's appearance or that of the image that the individual projects. Can offer a great deal of information about the sitter, including his or her feelings and personality. Can sometimes suggest the state of mind of the artist in the action of painting the piece. Can offer more understanding about others in society and broaden our thinking when judging by appearance.'

These students, still in full-time education and subject to a whole range of course and examination pressures, nevertheless reveal evidence of an unusual involvement and commitment in what they are doing — not always by any means matched by students also engaged in full-time art studies at the art college stage. They are clearly capable of making informed aesthetic judgments about the works of Surrealist and other artists which are not limited to the learnable facts and dates. They are also willing to submit themselves to grappling with complex but essential drawing problems in order to realize more effectively their artistic ideas and concepts. The interconnections between these two important aspects of their course studies are apparent and they clearly inform each other.

PLATE 13.   Fiona's interest in Surrealism surfaced through the concerns which came to invest her own work with similar qualities

Hidden Meanings of an Intimate Nature

Not only that, of course, but the achievements and insights of the above students are also of obvious benefit to their well-being as individuals, involving them in fulfilling and personally relevant ways. The current emphasis on personal and social education sometimes leads to it being timetabled as a subject (PSE) in its own right. In the already overcrowded school week its time has inevitably to be 'stolen' from elsewhere: it is an unfortunate irony that the time is often taken from the arts, a curriculum area where personal and social issues are constantly being addressed in deep and natural ways. It rarely comes from, say, mathematics, where such issues rarely, if ever, surface to any marked or worthwhile degree.

The case study examples already used reveal important discoveries and insights obviously pertinent to these personal and social needs of the students, but Fiona's investigations into Surrealism are so redolent with implications of this nature that they provide a fitting conclusion to this section.

What drew her to an interest in the Surrealists in the first place?

The art works of Surrealist painters filled me with curiosity, and a need to explore the literal nature of their content. Because of my own interest in literature I felt a delight when I discovered that the Surrealist artists had been deeply influenced by contemporary literature and its COVERT or hidden language. This hidden language was to become so much the hallmark of their own practical expression and is today what holds the viewer in deep contemplation.

She had been aware of Surrealism for some time, but had perceived it negatively.

> Many Surrealist works had baffled me in the past and I dismissed these paintings as unfathomable. Now, through a connection with my own work I felt a need to understand.... My initial interest in Surrealism surfaced during a time when my own practical work was based on windows, doorways, rooms and the ambiguity and incongruity which could arise through the placement and juxtaposition of objects, the alteration of scale and time.

These concerns provided a natural link with, and interest in, Magritte.

> I could see obvious links between his paintings, 'The Human Condition' and 'The Door to Freedom' with the scenes in my own work. I like his style of painting, but I also wanted to know what was the meaning behind the Surreal images in his work. Once I began to look into Surrealism more deeply my interest intensified. I wanted to know why these forms and objects were put together and what was constituting their meaning.... As I expanded my knowledge of the movement, I realised that artists such as Max Ernst and Joan Miro were just as intriguing and complex in their approach. Each had developed his own individual style and language in response to their Surreal ideals.

She found herself 'intrigued by their philosophy and interests and their obsession with the psychological. It both disturbed and fascinated me.' She studied six specific paintings in the original, two each by Magritte, Ernst and Miro, writing, for example, the following about Ernst's 'Men Shall Know Nothing of This' (1923).

> At the top of the painting is a mysterious sun. We see a burnt orange circle, half black and half dirty blue. From it straight lines seem to represent rays that descend to a circle which represents the earth. The earth is a smaller version of the sun and this is partly hidden by a disembodied hand. The other circles represent other planets in the solar system. The circle above the earth is smaller than the earth. It has a pale blue border and is half burnt orange with royal blue in the middle. There is another planet which is also half royal blue and half pale blue and there is a small white moon that seems to be circling the earth. Between the sun and the earth the lower halves of a man and woman copulate in space. An upside down crescent/parachute supports a small whistle. From an arid desert of viscera/stones rise two strange objects.

So far, Fiona has provided a precise and concise description of the objects in the painting, but in puzzling for an explanation she begins to pose questions.

> On first seeing this painting I was confused yet fascinated by it. I could see the sun and astrology were represented in this painting, but what did the two half bodies mean? What were the large grey objects that towered into the sky? What was the significance of the viscera? And what did

the little whistle mean? These disturbing images have obvious sexual implications and yet I could not sensibly comprehend what the images meant. All I could see was that it was disturbingly sexual and this seemed to be controlled by the phases of the planet.

She obviously had to undertake wider research to progress further. This led her to the discovery that 'the stimulus for this painting stemmed from an interest in Daniel Paul Schreber who suffered from paranoid schizophrenia brought about by doubts as to whether he was male or female.' Artist and patient became friends, with Ernst studying Schreber's condition with interest. Fiona inserts the quotation, 'Ernst sets a mysterious sun, with strange emanating rays at the top of the picture', and continues:

Schreber had an extraordinary obsession with rays, which were asso-ciated with the sun and with God. They were also in his fantasies attached to the stars and his own body which was, he thought, being changed and dismembered under the impact of their activity. He imagined himself 'floating in voluptuousness' and he wrote.... 'I have to imagine myself as a man and a woman having intercourse with myself'. Hence, surely the ambi-sexual 'phalli' in the painting and the floating male and female forms.

The viscera at the bottom of the painting I discovered was inspired by Schreber's fantasies that his intestines were being removed by the 'rays' while the stones ... to him symbolised children.

She makes further important discoveries in relation to Schreber's father's obsession with 'one-sidedness' in children and the orthopaedic apparatus he designed to inhibit and control the various parts of the body, and concludes: 'Though we are viewing a product of Ernst's imaginings the forms and objects within the painting come together with the appearance of being real. We are convinced by them as objects, but disturbed by their relationships to one another.' Having become involved in the works of the Surrealists initially through seeing a connection between her own practice and qualities in Magritte, Fiona inevitably, in turn, is led into unforeseen and distinctly unusual territory in her own practice: 'I have been influenced by their work and I feel I have portrayed this in my own work but in my own style.'

In her last written 'Personal Appraisal', towards the conclusion of her course, under the heading 'Surrealism in my Work', she writes:

Once I had established the image of the woman I had many ideas about its connection with Surrealism and instead of the way the Surrealists harshly portrayed the female body I could use the design as a triptych to be more sensitive to the woman's body.

The pose is similar to that of Max Ernst's 'Men Shall Know Nothing of This'. In his painting the image is harsh and exposed. The pose in my design is also extremely exposed. The heart that appeared through the overlap of the mirror images covers the area between her legs (female

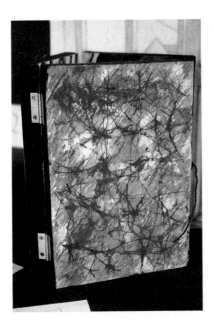

PLATE 14. Seen from the outside, closed, Fiona's triptych seems quite innocuous, with no hint of the treasures inside

PLATE 15. Once opened, however, the powerful impact of Surrealism on the work of Fiona is made abundantly clear

genitalia). The heart is the symbol of love and therefore appropriate with the image's obvious connection with sex.

There is also in the painting what could be the genitals of a man, but there is also the thought that the woman is in a child bearing position and maybe this is what is happening?

> I wanted the figure not to be exposed but to feel 'safe' within the painting. I do not want to shock the viewer by making them see the exposed nude. That is why I have decided to hinge the three pieces of wood together into a triangle.

She elaborates on how she organized the design across the various surfaces and how many different images appeared as it was turned round.

> Some were easily recognisable — the main image was that of a naked female figure sat with her legs apart.... The 'box' will be tied so if the woman is to be seen the viewer will have to open back the two hinged panels.

> The human, naked body is a personal thing and I feel that it should not be *exposed* in sexual poses.

> The outer design acts as a cover for what is inside the triptych just as we as human beings prefer to keep SECRET our 'bodies' <------- naked.

> Sex is also personal and should not be exploited. It should be 'secret' within a relationship — love → symbol of heart.

Fiona's final Surreal act is to write this statement in her 'Personal Appraisal', essentially a negotiated document agreed between her and her teacher. On untying the box she has made, one is confronted not by a female naked figure, sitting legs apart, but by a boldly painted floral design. However, the flowers depicted are distinctly erotic in their overtones and clearly suggestive of the actual content to which Fiona alludes — they are also powerfully reminiscent of, though quite distinct from, those painted by Georgia O'Keefe. Only rarely can the prescribed PSE lesson facilitate such complex multilayered responses of this deep and highly personal and private nature. By comparison, the visual arts, when effectively taught, constantly open up all manner of opportunities for young people to give expression to their innermost thoughts and feelings, sharing them with others in the process. Though the Surrealists are sometimes used as a sop to assumed interests, leading to cliché art, they nevertheless have the potential to engage adolescents in fascinating ways at many levels.

The five students provide abundant evidence of their capacities fully to chart the aesthetic field through having worked within a context which encourages and aids them to see the vertical and horizontal axes of creativity in relationship to each other. By coming together and intertwining, a spiral pattern of learning is established with each axis motivating the student to penetrate ever more deeply into the other. This only occasionally happens by chance: for sufficient numbers to benefit, appropriate course strategies must be in place. These students' involvement with Surrealism are intriguing in this respect, for they provide evidence of assimilated use of an invaluable model. Through awareness and use of four categories essential to engaging fully with art — content, form, process and mood — they have been able to envisage an intricate web of interconnections between their practical concerns and interests and Surrealism. It is now time to explore more fully these four fundamental categories of arts education.

Notes

1 David Larkin, *op. cit.* (pages unnumbered).
2 Brian Smith (1983) *Behind the Rainbow, Patrick Hughes: Prints 1964–83,* London, Paradox Publishing, p. 7.
3 David Larkin, *op. cit.* (pages unnumbered).
4 Peter Abbs (1989) in *A Is for Aesthetic: Essays on Creative and Aesthetic Education,* Basingstoke, Falmer Press; see in particular pp. 10–22.
5 A.M. Hammacher (1986) in *Magritte,* London, Thames and Hudson, p. 15; see also pp. 14–16.
6 Robert Descharnes (1976) in *Dali,* New York, Abrams, pp. 14, 15, 30, 39, 90, 162 and 168.
7 From a recorded interview with the student, June 1988. NOTE: All statements provided by Stuart come from this source. The student quotations throughout the rest of this chapter are drawn from either their A-level 'Personal Studies' on a topic of their choice, or from their 'Personal Appraisal' written as an essential part of their course. Stuart sat his A-level in 1988, the other students in 1989.

Four Necessary Categories
for the Teaching of Art:
Content, Form, Process and Mood

Works of art are among the most complex, demanding, and puzzling things created by human genius, and it would be odd indeed if learning to understand and appreciate them did not involve a prodigious amount of tuition and study, of plain hard work. Naive or unskilled voyagers into the art world might find much to admire and enjoy, but without proper preparation and a sufficiently long stay they would miss much that could enhance their enjoyment and increase their understanding. (Ralph Smith.)[1]

To like a work of art can be as dismissive as to dislike it, for either can be determined in the moment by an undiscerning cursory glance. How, then, might young people be educated so that they will want to linger and willingly submit themselves to 'a sufficiently long stay?' Numerous models and strategies have been formulated in an attempt to aid this process, with Feldman's Description, Analysis, Interpretation and Judgment being probably the most widely used.[2] In practice, though, many art educators confess that they find it useful but rather rigid and unnatural to apply to many situations. Equally, it is not lost on pupils that it carries with it an in-built assumption of them being expected to move from a stage of assumed lower artistic significance — that of describing — to the higher one of making judgments in a sequential manner; in other words, the model itself carries overtones of being a judgmental one with pressures on the pupils to move to the making of judgments. This suggests a need for an additional gallery model for engagement in which each of the elements is equal and can be addressed by pupils of all ages and levels of experience in this field. Feldman's model is ideal for use in conjunction with this, but as a tool for subsequent analysis and evaluation of what was done in the gallery.

Feldman does, nevertheless, point out that some individuals make judgments without going through the first three stages, and this has led others to suggesting a 'Pre-judgment' category at the beginning,[3] so that pupils can gauge their considered judgments against their initial ones. This carries with it the notion that initial reactions are invariably in need of modification through education — they are those of 'naive or unskilled voyagers'. It is all too easy, for the best of intentions, to alienate pupils at this formative stage by inadvertently indicating that their views are worthless. It will be remembered that Stuart's love of Dali, recorded in Chapter 3, was initially triggered by his parents' transmitting their enthusiasms to him. Similarly the natural transmission of teacher enthusiasms can provide a most effective way in at this early stage. This is especially so if they are conveyed in a manner which invites the pupils to share in them, but without feelings of censure towards the hesitant or reluctant pupil. When all is said and done, young people come with assumptions communicated by society at large that art galleries are boring places meant for a select group of people, but certainly not for their likes!

Account must also be taken of the fact that the illuminating experience *can* make its impact within the instant, and that this is a special peculiarity of the visual arts. All other art forms exist in time to which we have consciously to submit ourselves. We *know* the experience is incomplete if we see only half the film, play or dance performance, hear only half the song or concerto, read only half the poem or story. An intriguing aspect of the visual arts, though, is that a work can capture our attention, conveying complex, powerful and profound meanings — inseparable from what we choose to call the aesthetic experience — within the instant. In their wake, these experiences invite further study and can lead to a lifetime's investigation born of the desire to understand and unravel what it was that so powerfully affected us, and why.

Julie, for example, emphasizes that she 'will always relate to that Rothko as **THAT EMOTION** that it evoked the first time', whatever she might learn about him in particular or about colour field abstraction in general.[4] That will remain her thought, her idea, about those paintings. She also makes the important observation that, through such experiences, we become aware of something latent within ourselves being revealed for the first time. 'It was like a seed that was there — but it has to be triggered off.' It is all too easy to label a student who confronts Rothko for the first time, and without much prior knowledge, as a naive or unskilled voyager in art. However, what she points up is her need of an education which helps her unravel what has *already* occurred as opposed to one designed to educate her *out of* what it was she experienced. At these key formative stages, therefore, sensitivity is required on two counts: in leading the uninitiated, as yet unaffected by art, into this world in a manner free from censure so that they might more willingly and effectively enter, on the one hand. On the other, distinguishing between those who are, as yet, unaffected and those who need to understand more fully how and why they have already been so powerfully affected. In this respect, 'initial responses' is probably a more effective term to deal with than 'pre-judgments'.

The active participation, as opposed to passive acceptance, of the pupils should therefore be sought from the outset. Pupils should be encouraged to engage with works of art in an environment in which their attitudes and responses are elicited. This is consistent with that notion of Dewey's that the viewer completes the painting. Murray McDonald, writing about Patrick Hughes' recent paintings, highlights the relevance of Dewey's argument.

> Another meaning that attaches itself to this work is the importance of the viewer. Duchamp gave him a half share in the production of a work of art. The pictures are as much about you as about Hughes, There are no people in these paintings, the people in them are you. As you look at

them and move past them the pictures mix your perceiving, acting and thinking. You suspend your disbelief, and then pick it up again. The oscillation between what you see and what you know is the art. This can be joyous or uncomfortable. These are floors we cannot cross or roads we cannot walk. It is a closed world that seems to reject us until we give in to it, when it accepts us into its space.[5]

The oscillation between what each person sees and knows is, by definition, distinct, and young person as well as knowledgeable adult should be encouraged to participate in art on this basis; in front of Monet's waterlily canvasses, Rosemary found that they 'gave off a mysterious atmosphere; the stillness is almost disturbing.'[6]

We are aware of the feeling of light behind us, just as when we look into a pond.... A smooth, reflective surface can suggest space; in this case it is the space behind the viewer. I didn't feel claustrophobic when looking at the painting, as the sky suggests infinity. The spectator is surrounded by nature....

In relating what she knows to what she sees, Rosemary powerfully conveys the physicality, and the viewer's occupation of real space, which can be involved in the study of art, and which the young person can fully participate in.

To encourage this kind of direct engagement and participation, it is necessary to provide young people with analytical means appropriate to their needs. This book is liberally interspersed with numerous examples of writings by students who are conversant with Content, Form, Process and Mood as a model which facilitates 'in the round' study and interpretation of their chosen works. It is a neutral model in the sense that each of the four areas is equally as worthy of attention but without them carrying any inherent judgmental weighting. It constitutes an invaluable analytical tool which both encourages objective study and analysis on the one hand, and the possibility of eliciting a whole range of personalized responses of a more subjective nature on the other. Its relevance in enabling young people to approach unfamiliar, as well as known, works with confidence, of providing criteria for appraisal of their own practice, and in the relating of their studies of the art of others to their own practical needs, is highlighted by Nina in an A-level course 'Personal Appraisal' statement:

The idea used in the Art History Course of using Form, Content, Mood and Process to analyse paintings is very good. This helps me to understand paintings better, even ones I have not seen before. Learning about art feeds my imagination for my practical work; it informs me about colour combinations, structures of pictures, techniques, and subject matter.... Showing painters' Art Work also gives me insight to problems that may occur in my art work (i.e. design fault) and by showing how the painter gets around the problems he or she has encountered helps me too.[7]

In other words, Content, Form, Process, Mood provides an invaluable means of empowering young people so as to enable them to enter effectively into the aesthetic field of Making, Presenting, Responding and Evaluating.

PLATE 16. Content, Form, Process and Mood provide a basis for contextualizing exhibitions; a display at the Turnpike Gallery Leigh

It has the potential to encourage and stimulate pupils to conjecture before works of art in relevant and imaginative ways. It can aid them in the process of valuing and clarifying their own responses, opinions and judgments arrived at through the posing of a whole range of basic questions prompted by each of the four areas in turn. Questions such as, what is the work about? How has it been ordered and arranged? How has it been produced and with what? What mood, feeling or atmosphere does it encapsulate and convey? How does it affect me? The clarity of focus afforded through use of this model also offers potential for both the precise and vivid use of language, with each of the four areas likely to stimulate use of distinct types of vocabulary.

In *The Symbolic Order*, the third volume in the Library on Aesthetic Education, Maxine Greene's responses to a Cézanne Monte Sainte-Victoire canvas embrace each of the four areas.

> The situation is created by the transaction, by the grasping of a consciousness — drawn to a Cézanne painting, say, by a stir, a quiver of feelings, held rapt for a time as it intuits its presence — vaguely, at first, as landscape, as line, colour, shape. There is a taut awareness at work, and then a gradual focussing on images like mountain, tree, overarching sky. The more the beholder knows about picturing, about paint and canvas, the more he/she sees, the more details, the more appearances emerge. Apprehending it as a depiction rather than a representation of an actual mountain, noticing what there is to be noticed, the beholder may be able to see *into* the images revealed, see meaning condensed in symbolic forms. Taking time, he/she may single out the strokes of violet paint that model and give shape and contour to the transfigured mountain, watch the form of it jut forth against the pictorial plane, grasp the shifting perspectives that make its many profiles somehow visible, feel the touch of the textured sky, the play of light. When this occurs, it may be possible for the beholder to take his/her own journey through a world that dissolves what he/she may never have suspected, much less seen.[8]

This is not a description of a Cézanne, but *of the act of looking at* a Cézanne, and this is not the sole prerogative of the mature adult; young people, too, are perfectly capable of similarly engaging with art works, and content, form, process, mood offers an invaluable model to facilitate the process, as the student writings throughout these pages on Dali, Hepworth — and, in Chapter 6, on the student case studies on Millais, Goldsworthy — and so forth, abundantly reveal. It is both possible and desirable for all young people, commensurate with their age and stage of development, to be so educated that their abilities are likewise cultivated and developed.

Similar attempts have been made elsewhere, notably in the United States. In the days before the advent of what is now called Discipline Based Art Education (DBAE), Al Hurwitz described the 'exemplar approach' adopted by Ralph Smith, through which,

> ... a single work of recognised merit was examined for an extended period of time. In one series of discussion the children on Saturday morning classes were eleven and twelve years old. Discussions never ran less than an hour and at the conclusion of seven sessions, the class was discussing paintings by Rubens, Piero della Francesca, and Daumier in terms of mood, subject, content and compositional relationships. One can only imagine the levels such children could attain if such instruction were provided during the course of a year, or during the six years of elementary school.[9]

Smith defines interpretation as the 'apprehension of overall meaning' and argues that it emerges out of the 'interanimation of materials, subject matter and form'.

Though 'materials' is too restricted in meaning to stand for all that process implies, the main distinction between Smith's and the content, form, process, mood approach is the obvious reliance here on reproductions of great and famous works as opposed to the emphasis on direct engagement with a much wider range of visual art forms experienced in the original, so highly prized in Wigan. This involves matters to do with scale, nuance of colour and form, and surface quality of paint, fabrics, etc. Robert Clement has written that, 'Even in reproduction it is difficult to observe any painting by Cézanne, van Gogh or Matisse without being aware of the way in which the artist uses both pigment and colour.'[10] This is, undoubtedly, frequently the case. Nevertheless, the reactions of many young people suggest that there might be an important distinction between the perceptions of the art teacher with knowledge of these artists' works seen in the original and those of young pupils who come to the flat-surfaced reproduction without any such prior knowledge: 'but when you get up to them you can see how thick he put the paint on, how rich they are'; 'but actually up close there were so many colours and there was actually so much detail in it'; 'because of its size it created an effect of harmony around you', etc.[11] The reproduction invariably only hints at these inherent qualities, and it is only in the study of works in the original that the full significance of process is revealed and understood. Interestingly, on a recent visit to New Zealand my attention was drawn to a debate there about the use of flat areas of colour in the work of many of their painters. It was argued that this had come about in response to the way objects appear under the sharp light of that country, but I met those who were adamant that it was because of the influence of European painters like Monet, van Gogh and Matisse, but known only through reproductions of their works, in the main.

In *Living Powers*, Robin Morris uses 'media' where Ralph Smith had referred to 'materials'. He identifies subject matter, form and media as comprising the 'special experience of the visual arts'. He advocates that 'due consideration must be given to each at all stages of development, in all sectors of education', suggesting that they also be seen as a structural link to other arts disciplines.

> In this way literature can be seen as possessing form and subject; music, form and media; and dance and drama as having all three. Thus, within the common framework set by the aesthetic field of making, presenting, responding and evaluating all the arts disciplines can be seen to share common constituents.[12]

Precisely so. But by substituting the more all-embracing 'process' for media, and with the addition of the fourth vital element of 'mood', it immediately becomes apparent that the three constituents of form, process and mood are common to *all* art forms. When it is considered that a whole body of music which has no obvious subject matter is certainly not devoid of content, the wider significance of this model across the arts and in relation to rich and varied arts links becomes clearly apparent; one sixth-form student, using it as an integral part of her art and design course, commented as to how it had also become an invaluable aid to her music course studies as well!

Many musicians are united in a view that, in the outstanding music examples devoid of subject matter, the form actually becomes the content. Here again, parallels exist between this notion and some of the notable examples of this century's non-figurative art. Diane Waldman, in a Rothko monograph, suggests that:

> Mark Rothko shares with composers of music an absence of explicit imagery and a correspondingly developed capacity to evoke content by association; an ability to engage ... the eye in a process that is akin to listening because it involves attention to consecutive passages; an interest in rhythmic passages ... and the use of color to achieve modulations that can be subtly chromatic or dramatically contrasted.... Rothko is a creator of melodic surfaces rendered vital and sonorous by means of a formal structure.... Finally, Rothko's orchestral properties are ... simultaneously ponderous and heroic, often lyrical in mood but never sentimental.[13]

Of the many parallels to which she draws attention, that of evoking content by association is particularly relevant to the notion of form in relation to content. This complex relationship has exercised minds for centuries, having been addressed long ago by no lesser a person than Aristotle, for example. It therefore warrants further attention here, and, in utilizing examples drawn from books about art and artists, a further important point is emphasized: art history books can seem dense and inaccessible to the young student, but content, form, process and mood provide invaluable criteria to provide clear access to the material contained within such books. I would like now to examine the categories in more detail. First, I will take form and content together and then process and mood separately.

PLATE 17.   Relationships between art and music being explored during the Colin Rose exhibition at Drumcroon; Rose's paintings derive from the moods and structures of music

Form and Content

> The greatest works in any medium ... are distinguished most remarkably by their sense of organisation, that organic sense of form on composition in which the parts truly resonate with and enhance one another. (H. Gardner)[14]

It is such formal qualities that Jacques Lassaigne homes in on in a description of a Matisse painting;

> In the 'Piano Lesson' the organisation of the picture surface by a combination of daring transpositions and more literal allusions, is an amazing tour de force. Demarcated by invisible lines, the big color planes are rigorously divided up by verticals and diagonals, onto which are grafted — like musical variations — graceful decorative arabesques.... The basic grey tone, stressed by the blue and orange bands of the window and curtain, accentuates the bright pink of the piano top, while the green wedge ... framed in the window and the converging lights playing on the small pianist's face amplify the sense of space.[15]

In marked contrast, Jean Clay writing in *Modern Art, 1890–1918*, provides the following much more content-laden description of the paintings of Ensor:

> Between the mask and the skeleton, the puppet and the cadaver, there is practically no place in James Ensor's art for the human figure. The social being, defined by cheap finery and grimaces, occupies the entire scene, and becomes all the more suitable for caricature because his agitation and

his mimicry of the 'conventional braggart' are doomed to final efface-
ment. The marks merely hide a skull. The society that Ensor judges is
not a theater. It is Grand Guignol, it is a sport of massacre. He constantly plays on the ambiguity of its decor: a theatrical scene with wings
and trompe-l'oeil openings or real space with windows and exits.[16]

This description also obviously conveys infinitely more than any bald list of
objects might do — hence the preference for 'content' rather than simply subject
matter.

The difference in emphasis between these two descriptions is too obvious
to need labouring even though, in the former, reference to 'converging lights'
carries hints of content while, in the latter, the idea of wings and trompe-l'oeil
openings likewise conveys overtones of formal qualities and design. There are
those who regard form as pre-eminent — 'sensory' types — and those who
incline towards content — the more 'temperamental' types — but the boundaries
between the two are often blurred, whereas the distinction between subject
matter and form is much more easily defined and therefore uncontroversial. The
significance of the content, form, process, mood model is that it is a means
whereby young people can approach art works with clarity, but fully and 'in the
round'. Debate and ponderings over the finer distinctions between content and
form are therefore preferable to thinking in terms of subject matter and there
being 'gaps' or a lack of real connection between it and form. It is therefore
worth attending briefly to the 'content versus form' issues first raised by
Aristotle.

A Professor Marigoni, writing in 1951, made the observation that: 'Now-
adays it is customary to say that the distinction between content and form is a
thing of the past ... since in every true work of art both are merged into one by
the artist's creative art. "Like content, like form".'[17] Though maybe alright in
theory, the synthesis is so rare in practice, he continues, that the contention is too
rigid and, besides, '... renders all criticism impossible, for criticism is essentially
based on an assessment of the relationship between form and content.' Nevertheless, a mere eight years later Clement Greenberg felt able to declare that: 'Content
is to be dissolved so completely into form that the work of art cannot be reduced
in whole or in part to anything not itself.'[18]

With the growing acceptance of the significance of the New York School
and Abstract Expressionism, the belief that from now on and for henceforth art
would be non-figurative seemed a real likelihood for a number of years. It led to
many art college students being trained to think in purely formal terms with
content completely disregarded. This bias, in turn, inevitably was reflected in
the school art and design studio and was to be further compounded through
the proliferation of design faculties throughout the 1970s. The irony of young
people in early adolescence nevertheless thinking in content terms and finding
motivation — at least initially — through these concerns is one of the underlying
factors in many of them producing a content-led 'home art', sometimes in direct
opposition to the almost exclusively formal-based school course on offer.

Even while Greenberg was heralding a content-free new age, though, the
Marxist-based thinking of Ernst Fischer was propounding a totally opposite
position: 'But let us be clear about it: the content, not the form, is always the first
to be renewed; it is the content that generates form, not vice versa; content comes

first, not only in order of importance but also in time....'[19] Wherever form assumes more importance than content, he maintains, 'it will be found that the content is out of date ... and at the time of the decaying bourgeoisie it is empty abstraction.' Forms, once sanctioned, have an extraordinary conservative character to which people cling, he suggests; he would doubtless identify with Fuller's concern at the student artist having to choose between 'infantalism and anaesthesia'. Even so, Fischer is conscious that form is far more than being,

> ... just a suitable vehicle for its content: it is an original 'elegant' solution of difficulties arising not only out of the content but also out of the artist's sheer pleasure in mastering them. Form is always a kind of triumph because it is the solution of a problem. Thus an aesthetic quality is transformed into a moral one.[20]

Sentiments, again, which closely accord with those expressed by Fuller, especially as his belief that it is the content that generates the form 'applies to nature, to society, and therefore to the arts.'

Dewey's notion that the art work is incomplete without the viewer ensures that this debate must run and run, for there will always surely be 'sensory' and 'temperamental' individuals amongst both artists and those who view their works. Returning to Rothko again, for example, he maintained that he was not an abstractionist and that, when viewing his paintings, if you are moved 'only by their colour relationships then you miss the point.' Through his art, his concern was in 'expressing basic human emotions — tragedy, ecstasy, doom and so on.' He added that people who wept before his pictures were having the same religious experience he had when he painted them. He directly invites such responses as those of Diane Waldman writing about his predilection for red 'as a carrier of emotion'. 'Perhaps Rothko was so drawn to red because of its powerful and basic associations; it is identified with the element and ritual — with fire and blood — and thus with life, death and spirit.'[21] Richard Wollheim's 'reading' of one of Rothko's Tate canvases reveals a further pondering over subtle relationships between form and content, for,

> ... the immediacy of Rothko's canvas derives from the way in which this expressive quality is provided within a formal counterpart: and that lies in the uncertainty that the painting is calculated to produce, whether we are to see the painting as containing an image within it or whether we are to see the painting as itself an image. Whether we are to see it as containing a ring of flame or shadow ... or whether we are to look upon it as somewhat the equivalent of a stained glass window.[22]

Did Rothko sometimes — or eventually — fail to reconcile these components? Robert Hughes asks whether there is anything other than emptiness left in the Rothko Chapel,[23] and to Fuller the final paintings leave only a 'black hole' where once an alternative world had been offered.

> These pictures are grey monochromes, in which colour and pictorial space, alike, have drained away. They are not elevating expressions of despair on the threshold of death — like, say, Poussin's great grey painting 'Winter' or 'The Deluge'. They themselves, are empty, dead. The

redeeming power of an aesthetic transformation has gone. This is what
I mean by anaesthesia. In gazing at these works we think of Lear's
utterance, beyond tragedy, beyond hope: 'Nothing, nothing, nothing,
nothing, nothing'. In these monochromes, Rothko's high sentiments
collapsed into the 'blinding square' and 'dead blank' of anti-art. Within a
few months, he himself lay dead in a pool of blood on his studio floor.[24]

The abstractions of Rothko potently highlight the importance of the complex
interactive relationships between form and content!

Returning to Dewey's notion of the viewer 'completing' the painting,
however, it might be appropriate to turn to one of Rothko's colleagues, Jackson
Pollock. C.H. Waddington, himself a scientist by training, argues that throughout this century there have been close parallels between painting and scientific
developments — even if revealed more clearly through the artist's writings than
through those of art critics! Artists, whether consciously or unconsciously, are
affected by the concerns and discoveries of their time with many links, for
example, between the shapes and forms which some utilize and microelectronic
diagrams. However, his 'interpretation' of the detailed surface of a Pollock action
painting is so romantically content-laden, in addition to reference to scientific
imagery, as to suggest that there is no end to the extent to which the human
imagination is capable of being triggered and stimulated by works of art and their
powers to transform.

> They can be 'taken' in many senses and in many scales; for instance,
> 'Autumn Rhythm' of 1950 is not only the winter twigs of a forest
> against the sky, it is not only the veins of a heap of dead leaves whose
> substance has vanished; it could be the electrons buzzing round the
> atomic nuclei of a complex molecule, or the stars slithering along their
> orbits in the galaxy. You can see in it a macrocosm or a microcosm: the
> landscape of withered grass stems you will see if you lay flat on a winter
> meadow and looked at through the eyes of an ant, the hair of the Virgin
> Mary falling over the crib of the infant Jesus, the whips of the Fate's
> scourging man through the universe, the smoke billowing from the
> bonfire of autumn leaves, the interconnection of everything with every-
> thing else, the flickering surface of evanescent thoughts just below the
> threshold of consciousness. You can explore it in a search for whatever
> you may bring with you to find.[25]

'Whatever you may bring with you to find.' Few who knew the Pollock canvas
in question could believe for one moment that Waddington is attempting to
provide a literal description of its subject matter, but in the fascinating interplay
between art object and viewer, he arrives at an extraordinary statement about
content, the criss-crossing veins and skeins of paint having triggered his imagination and subconscious feelings and images into active life.

This involvement, no longer passive, can stimulate a use of language which
is both expressive and precise, born of a need to match as effectively as possible
the world of verbal language to that relating to the visual and tactile. An important distinction between content and form is that one, with its concerns for what
the work is about, is likely to invite use of a highly descriptive range of vocabu-

PLATE 18. The formal values of a Howard Hodgkin print emphasized by its forms and colours being extended into a high school still-life arrangement

lary, while the other stimulates use of vocabulary to do with the structural. Clay's description of Ensor's art conjures up imagery in a vivid way, and Giorgio Vasari does the same in a fascinating way in relation to Uccello's 'Flood' — fascinating because in its now badly damaged state, what Vasari describes can only be imagined today. How wonderful it would be to be able to see, as originally depicted:

> ... the dead, the tempest, the fury of the winds, the flashes of lightning, the rooting up of trees, and the terror of men ... a dead body, foreshortened, the eyes of which are being pecked out by a crow, and a drowned child, whose body, being full of water, is arched up ... various human emotions, such as the disregard of the water by two fighting men on horseback, the extreme terror of death of a woman and a man who are riding astride a buffalo; but as his hind parts are sinking they are despairing of all hope of safety.[26]

All rendered with 'diminution of the figures, by means of perspective' in a manner which is 'certainly very beautiful'. In the final analysis, content in art is as varied and endless as the countless aspects and facets of life itself.

Form, by comparison, emphasizes the structural aspects of art. Lassaigne, writing about the Matisse, refers to demarcation by invisible lines, planes rigorously divided up by verticals and diagonals, organization of the picture surface, and so on, making use of words like 'bands', 'framed' and 'converging' in order to emphasize how the work is shaped and its structural qualities.

As these have aesthetic implications, being embodied within an art object, it is commonly accepted practice to 'borrow' words originating in other art forms for this purpose, with their use now metaphorical. He, therefore, writes about 'daring transpositions' and 'graceful decorative arabesques'. The parallels between Rothko's work and music have already been noted, and in the supporting quotation Diane Waldman incorporates the 'rhythmic passages', 'modulations', 'melodic' and 'orchestral' in describing his work. The examples are countless — Robert Hughes refers to the 'rhymes and chords of shape' used by Seurat, and the fusion of Mondrian's 'love of boogieing' with 'the syncopated rhythms' of New York[27] — but they point to important links with all other art forms, for they, likewise, make use of terms which are literal when applied within visual arts contexts — words such as 'colour', 'line', 'tone' and 'texture'.

Hughes is referring to a specific work with an interesting title, Mondrian's 'Broadway Boogie-Woogie', and many artists have consciously given their works titles associating them with music, emphasizing these close ties. Monet gave his Rouen Cathedral canvases subtitles such as 'Symphony in Grey and Rose', Whistler called his Thames paintings 'Nocturnes', while Kandinsky would simply designate his as, for example, 'Improvisation No. 35'. Should not pupils be educated in such a manner that they are better able to understand these cross-arts associations and to know where a word is used in its literal sense and where it is being used metaphorically with a meaning which is closely associated with one in another art form?

There are, then, quite distinctive features which distinguish content from form, but equally there are strong areas of overlap which can make it quite difficult completely to separate one from the other at times, and it is for this very reason that 'content' has been preferred to 'subject matter'; the overall aim is to enable the pupil to explore *fully* works of art, and the nagging gap between subject matter and form therefore has to be plugged.

Process

Each time I start a piece of work it's terrifying, because I have a blank sheet of paper and there's no relationship yet with that. I look for hours at a blank rectangle and then almost dive at it as though into cold water.[28]

Amanda Faulkner provides a graphic description of the initial phase in the making of a work of art with which many artists are readily able to identify. As one of the finest of the new generation of women artists who consciously address feminist issues, she is concerned with content to an important degree. She is equally aware of what she is about in process terms as an accomplished artist, of course. Once a start has been made, she has 'something to respond to and the relationship grows from there.' Each artist has their own personalized approaches.

I always work on one piece at a time, because to work on a number would be like having a love affair with six people at once and I can't spread myself that thin! I make a mark on a surface and it won't be quite as I intended. I have to assess what has happened and either remove it or adapt my original idea to accommodate it or take ideas from it. The drawings take a long time to complete even though the marks are made rapidly and with force. I have to spend hours walking backwards and forwards to assess what is happening. Looking and thinking.

PLATE 19. Christine Kowal-Post at Drumcroon providing pupils with unusual insight into process through her collection of carving tools given to her by an African sculptor friend

'Process', too, has been chosen because it embraces more than is indicated by 'media', 'materials', 'techniques' and the like. It opens up a third, very distinct, area of access. From close-up a Monet canvas, for example, is at not too great a remove from that of the Pollock described by Waddington; the focus on paint as paint is very different from what it might suggest or represent in terms of content.

> 'At close range ... the image seems to disappear entirely and the spect-
> ator sees only the thickly encrusted surface built up of a myriad of small
> brush strokes of the most delicately varied tints' ... what we witness
> here is 'an absorption in the process of the brush, a simultaneous
> identification of the structure and direction of the paint with the artist's
> consciousness, in the course of which subject-matter as such, as a set of
> objects existing apart from the painter and his paint, has almost ceased to
> exist.'[29]

Such close examination can begin to stimulate wider speculation. In response to looking at works by George Grosz and Anthony Green in the Tate Gallery, a 15-year-old pupil begins to conjecture: 'the way they draw it doesn't look like they've just gone out and copied something as it is.'[30] As she does in her own work, it would seem that these artists, too, might prefer to observe, remember what they have seen, and then put it down. From the evidence in the works, the pupil has been led to much wider speculation about the artists' whole approach to the study of the world around them in relation to their concerns, illustrating that process has much broader implications than when it is narrowly thought of just in terms of how marks have actually been made and the like.

To take an extreme but illuminating example, again involving Monet, it is quite possible for the young student to begin to envisage how the actual conception and construction of his Giverny waterlily garden could also be inseparably

bound up with his previous experience of painting nuances of nature and therefore also with indistinct images in his mind's eye of possible paintings to come.
These images would only be more fully clarified by the act of first constructing
and then tending and cultivating the pond over many years while also studying it
on a regular basis by virtue of 'living' with it; what a profound insight into
process in its broadest sense such an example begins to open up. Robert Hughes
evocatively conveys this notion in *Shock of the New*.

> For the pond was as artificial as painting itself. It was flat, as a painting
> is. What showed on its surface, the clouds and lilypads and cats' paws of
> wind, the dark patches of reflected foliage, the abysses of dark blue and
> the opaline shimmer of light from the sky, were all compressed together
> in a shallow space, a skin, like the space of painting. The willows
> touched it like brushes. No foreground, no background; instead, a web
> of connections. Monet's vision of energy manifesting itself in a continu-
> ous field of nuances.... The pond was a slice of infinity. To seize the
> indefinite; to fix what is unstable; to give form and location to sights so
> evanescent and complex that they could hardly be named....[31]

Black and white photographs still exist of the garden as it looked in Monet's lifetime, but today many a gallery goer finds it as natural to make the journey
to Giverny to see the garden as it is to go to the Orangerie to be surrounded by
the waterlily canvases which fill those rooms — another fascinating example of
heightening of awareness through artist's vision.

Existing film and photographs, as well as written records, similarly ensure
that Pollock's 'action painting' methods are well documented, but the motivations leading him to that process provide a further profound insight into process.
They are particularly interesting in the context of the derision which such
methods, epitomizing 'modern art', can arouse in many young adolescents whose
prejudices are then further affirmed, rather than dispelled, by the teacher encouraging them to make splash and splatter paintings as a related exercise in intuitive
application. By contrast, awareness of one key formative experience on Pollock
invariably arouses interest because of the unusual insight into process which it
reveals, as highlighted by Bryan Robertson.

> The liquidation of the image effected by Pollock between 1947 and 1953
> came also from a most loving understanding of an extraordinary kind
> of pictorial art made by the Navaho Indian in New Mexico in the
> American South West. Pollock was born in Wyoming, and travelled in
> the South West in his youth. He made spasmodic trips to that area after
> he came to live in New York as a young man and his consciousness
> was conditioned, always, by early memories of the West. As fertility
> symbols, as invocations to the natural sources of rain, wind and sun
> which they see as gods, and as two-dimensional flat totems on the earth,
> the Navaho Indian made pictograms flat on the ground by spilling sand
> and coloured earth through their hands on to the earth surface.... These
> sand paintings, as they are called, are ephemeral. They are made at sun-
> rise, and the magic they are intended to invoke cannot materialise unless
> all traces of them are dispersed by sunset....

European art is permanent: we conserve it and restore it, we guard it in museums, and we buy and sell it as a commodity. The idea of a temporary art made only to serve a ritual mythology and placed at the mercy of the elements is strange to us. The idea was not strange to Pollock....

'I prefer to tack the unstretched canvas to the hard wall or floor.... On the floor I am more at ease. I feel nearer, more a part of the painting, since this way I can walk around it, work from the four sides and literally be "in" the painting. This is akin to the method of the Indian sand painters of the West.'[32]

Though Pollock's paintings are now conserved, restored, guarded and bought and sold for huge sums as Western commodities, knowledge of that initial experience can go a long way towards opening young people's eyes — and minds — to the significance of the actual act of applying paint to canvas, by whatever means, as something significant in its own right. It also, of course, provides a fascinating insight into the values and lifestyle of the Navaho Indian, with the processes integral to their art equally embedded within their lives and beliefs. This is distinct from Western notions of art as little more than a consumer commodity with its worth judged solely by market value in many minds.

Process and content are consciously fused by Kevin Johnson, a young British black artist, who consciously addresses black issues in his work. He has arrived at an appropriate range of processes to communicate the anger he feels about the treatment he, his family and friends have received.

Once I've got that stimulus in mind I have the block of clay, and the first thing I have to hack out is the neck. I beat it with the rolling pin and I get big chunks of clay and rip them off.... Once that's been done, I start to whittle it down to the eyes, the nose.... I never work against the medium by abusing it — I work with it.... I like to make them very tactile. I like everyone to touch my pieces.[33]

To this end he textures them and, when he is in full flow, 'people think I'm a bit demented', for he will grab lace, people's trainers, clothing with good textures — anything appropriate to texture the surface of it. The process then becomes very technical; he adds clay and treats it.

I'll roll out very fine bits to put against that, and the textures really come up. This is where oxides work really strongly because they really do pick out such textures.... I use manganese dioxide to cover the whole thing, that's usually my base. Then I use wire wool, or brillo pad, and take off the top surface.... You actually highlight certain areas by taking the oxide, or the patina, off the surface. Then I put cobalt dioxide on to give like a blue, and then I'll use copper to give the green. I sometimes put venadium in — it doesn't always come out yellow but sometimes you get a yellowish base.

This passage illustrates how process is the area which is most likely to throw up vocabulary of a subject-specific and *technical* nature. This vocabulary describes nuances of process in a very precise manner; Kevin gives a jargon-free and very clear description, but it is in this area that jargon can lead to obscurity in the wrong hands. Under process, then, a range of technical words can come into play such as: scumbling, impasto, coiling, slabbing, moulding, casting, frottage, collage, assemblage, registering, masking, etc.

Process, then, is a third generously broad category and one which includes, but naturally subsumes, the more specific aspects to do with media, processes and techniques. Though it is obviously quite distinct from content and form, there are nevertheless blurred areas of overlap where it can become difficult to distinguish between, for example, content-laden concepts and the process means whereby these can be realized.

Mood

'Although many of the carved details in the old doors and boxes give off an ancient air, which might be associated with a different age, I certainly don't want them to look as though they are relics from the past so I will usually include some object which is very much to do with the present.'
... In total the works appear imbued with a rich narrative capable of looking different from feelings and responses. Sometimes faintly sinister, sometimes vaguely nostalgic they draw the viewer into dreamlike surroundings.[34]

This passage evocatively conjures up the potent moods conveyed by the forms and imagery embodied within the carved doors and chests which Anthony Lysycia then stains and colours as well as using them as unusual large-scale relief printing blocks.

Mood is the most immediately obvious subjective area of the four, engaging feelings and emotions directly. It is the mood or atmosphere encapsulated within the work which is so central to that capacity of visual arts objects to make their impact and 'capture' the viewer within an instant, as that student so vividly encapsulates when she says she will 'always refer to that Rothko as that emotion that it evoked the first time.' In much calmer vein, in relation to distinctive qualities embodied in Seurat's 'The Bather', a fifth-form boy described it as creating 'an effect of harmony around you ... an almost unreal atmosphere — a sort of escapist feeling', these two examples highlighting how various and diverse the moods conveyed by works of art can be.

These and many other young people's responses illustrate the degree to which they can be powerfully moved and affected, in the most desirable and significant ways, and in the instant, by works of art. The human eye and brain both have remarkable capacities to range over and take rapid account of complex visual phenomena, involving the engagement of both feelings and thoughts. Roger Fry noted how 'One chief aspect of order in a work of art is unity; unity of some kind is necessary for our restful contemplation of the work of art as a whole, since if it lacks unity we cannot contemplate it in its entirety, but we shall pass outside it to other things necessary to complete its unity.'[35] It is in comprehending that unity, expressive of the overall artistic intention, that the work of art can rapidly exert its presence, and profoundly move us in quite special ways.

Formal ordering and mood can inseparably fuse and coexist to this end. In a letter to his brother, Theo, van Gogh emphasizes this close relationship. 'The colour should impart, by its simplicity, a grander style of things. It should suggest sleep and rest. To look at this picture should rest one's brain and one's imagination.... The shadows are suppressed. It is coloured in flat, frank tones....'[36] The painting in question is the well known one of his bedroom at Arles, and he makes it clear that it is the overall mood he is seeking to capture and convey which determines choice of colour scheme, paint application and the use of tone. His sentiments are surprisingly close to those of an artist who might be considered to be of very different disposition and temperament — Henri Matisse.

He sought 'an art of balance, purity and serenity, devoid of troubling or obsessive subject matter' that would act as 'an appeasing influence, a mental sedative, rather like a good armchair.'[37] To his way of thinking, expression,

> ... does not consist of the passion mirrored upon a human face or betrayed by a violent gesture. The whole arrangement of my picture is expressive. The place occupied by the figures or objects, the empty spaces around them, the proportions — everything plays a part.... A work of art must carry in itself its complete significance and impose it upon the beholder even before he can identify the subject matter.[38]

There is the famous incident of Kandinsky standing spellbound in front of a Monet canvas, only realizing later that it was of a haystack. Matisse, of course, is giving a painter's eloquent expression to Fry's assertion about order and unity and, not surprisingly, be brings the same attitudes to bear in his reactions to the works of other artists with which he closely identifies.

> When I see the Giotto frescos at Padua I do not trouble to recognise which scene of the life of Christ I have before me, but I perceive instantly the sentiment which radiates from it and which is instinct in the composition in every line and colour. The title will only serve to confirm my impression.[39]

The note of calm refinement characteristic of the mature Matisse is in marked contrast to the turbulence and troubled psychological world of Edvard Munch. Messer's description of the artist's 1906 'Self Portrait with a Wine Bottle' penetrates deeply into this disturbing world.

> The seated artist, surrounded by the flaming lines, seems to contemplate his own doom. Three distant, almost featureless and half-averted creatures face empty tables that make one think of white-clad coffins. Converging in the distance, these furnishings enclose the victim within an oppressive interior. Munch himself is the painting's oversized and egocentric focus. Everything in the work presses upon him and aims for his red necktie — a plausible substitute for his exposed jugular. Unexplainable, except in psycho-symbolic terms, is the oppressive red background shape that frames Munch's head and seems to advance upon him in an ominously engulfing movement.[40]

If Bonnard was prey to any such depths of despair, he certainly never communicated even a hint of them in his essentially sunny and optimistic art. He conveys relaxed and joyous moods at a far remove from the dark and morbid northern climes which imbue Munch's art. Bonnard was fond of saying that 'a picture should be a little world of its own, self-sufficing',[41] and in his description of one of these little worlds, the c.1932 'Nude in a Bedroom', André Fermigier evokes a parallel word-picture which is structured around the work's content and colour.

> Light streaming in the window of the bathroom ... the slats of the shutters through which the sunlight falls break up the light and make it iridescent.... The tiled bathroom floor is blue to the left, orange at the right, separated by a passage (which, to cap the climax, is a white shadow!) corresponding to the white of the stool and the linen on which the dog is sitting ... the painting is a mosaic of colors assembled patiently and shrewdly and with evident enjoyment of the refined variations in blues, mauves, lilacs and orange-pinks.... One could imagine nothing more sumptuous and more dazzling ... this dressing room is an incredible jumble, a profusion of tumbled linens and more or less identifiable utensils in the middle of which the alarm clock appears, like an ironic and helpless recall to precision.[42]

Within this profuse environment the young woman is bending forward turning her head, her position 'altogether charming and original'. Amongst the various objects described, there is an implicit reference to process in the 'patiently and shrewdly assembled mosaic of colours', reminiscent of Max Kozloff's description of the same painter's 'shreds and patches of porous colour — blond pinks sieved by lavender blues, surrounding greens freckled by spots of orange.'[43]

Combinations of elements of content, form and process all, then, determine and contribute to the specific mood and atmosphere of a work. This has led to the suggestion that what is here being termed 'mood' is, in fact, no less than the aesthetic experience proper. Indeed, such statements as that by Fry and that of Bonnard in which he insists that 'a picture should be a little world of its own, self-sufficing' are certainly alluding to that greater wholeness to do with the particular aesthetic appearance of the work in itself.

Nevertheless, the argument that mood cannot therefore warrant attention in its own right cannot be sustained. Elements determining mood can be carefully and consciously selected by the artist in the certain knowledge that they will then produce their desired effect. Irrespective of their many other qualities, the paintings of Picasso's Rose Period arouse a different range of moods than are stimulated by those of his Blue Period; he is fully conscious that the simple decision to allow rosy-pinks to permeate induces different feelings than when the more melancholic and sad blues predominate, just as some restaurants make use of warm-tinted glass in their mirrors to induce feelings of well-being. Likewise, Seurat consciously applied the notion that the use of verticals, horizontals and diagonals respectively produced feelings of stability, calm and life, while the Expressionist painter similarly matched the quality and nature of brushstrokes and use of paint to the feelings and moods he or she wished to communicate.

PLATE 20.   Young people of all ages have been responsive to the powerful moods which Ian Murphy, a young Wigan artist, evokes in his paintings: a detail of 'Ivory Stone and Perpetual Light', a work in oil, wax and Polyfilla

Such knowledge and awareness can be made use of by anybody, once known. In themselves they cannot guarantee aesthetic satisfaction or wholeness, though: a particular range of blues can be used by anybody in the knowledge that they have the capacity to induce feelings of melancholia, yet the viewer can be equally saddened because the work is both unsatisfactory and unsatisfying as an aesthetic entity!

The control the artist exerts over content, form and process, then, has a direct bearing on the mood of the work, yet its aesthetic essence lies deeper. Mood must, therefore, comprise an essential fourth element requiring consideration in its own right, for there is no guarantee that in addressing the other three, mood will be dealt with satisfactorily — if at all. As the final element it not only helps ensure more 'in the round' study, but facilitates this while also more positively bringing one's own feelings into play.

By its nature, mood encourages use of an *evocative* type of language appropriate to conjuring up the atmospheric and relating to emotions and feelings. Stephen, a 17-year-old student, certainly conveys atmosphere in a most evocative passage in response to Turner's 'Norham Castle — Sunrise'.

A mood is conveyed which makes the landscape pictured seem like an idea that Turner dreamed up rather than the actual reality of it. At that particular moment in time it must have been quite awesome to see the mists and colour swirling to and fro. And slowly, very slowly, the thin vapours joining together, becoming bonded and knotted, as they congealed into solid shapes. Like a gas condensing and forming a solid, they must have seemed as if some wizard had conjured them, to literally transform into solid matter. And the sun, constantly present, shining meekly through this unearthly apparition. Steadily becoming bright and real as its furnaces are stoked and fed. Condensing, with heat, the fine vapour into Norham Castle.[44]

Some Educational Implications

The four categories, content, form, process and mood, are therefore essential elements of a model which has a wide range of educational implications, the most important being its potential for student empowerment. It provides a means to enable them to engage in depth with art works, and to make a wide range of types of connections between them and other works, which, on the surface, would otherwise be seen as being quite unrelated. It provides an invaluable analytical tool for pupils to engage with art works of which they have no prior knowledge, enabling them to study them at more objective levels and to bring direct feeling responses to bear; this active participation is distinct from, and to be preferred to, the purely passive reception of the opinions of others. It offers criteria which can enable pupils to interpret, and make use of, material contained within books about art and artists which might otherwise be perceived as too dense and inaccessible. It can help them to make important connections between those art works to which they are personally drawn and responsive and their own studio practice. As the student quoted earlier testifies, these connections can feed the imagination to aid practical work with regard to 'colour combinations, structures of pictures, techniques and subject matter', as well as 'design faults'. Content, form, process, mood can, then, be an invaluable means enabling pupils to take responsibility for their own learning, by helping them to identify a wide range of personal interests and concerns with a bearing across the whole art and design syllabus. As such, it is in keeping with, and an aid to fuller exploration of, the aesthetic field as defined through making, presenting, responding and evaluating.

It also raises important initial and in-service teacher training issues. Many teachers were themselves subjected to a training in which the emphasis was almost exclusively on studio-based practice, the art history component — often of just a couple of hours' duration — seeming quite unrelated. Others complain that their exposure to, and knowledge of, art history is minimal through lack of exposure, one PGCE student admitting to her resulting lack of confidence in this area. She admits to art critics' terms such as 'movement', 'structure' and 'rhythm' baffling her, leading to a belief that the 'one unchallengeable interpretation would be found in books or on television by art critics and must be learnt.' Horrified 'by this dreary prospect', she confesses to shutting her mind off and deciding 'to suffer in silence.'[45] She is certainly not alone in this regard. Amongst the issues raised at the various Content, Form, Process, Mood Workshops conducted at both initial and in-service levels, one significant one must be the extraordinary hidden capabilities which many students and teachers begin to reveal, with implications for classroom practice and the evaluation of their pupils' responses and related practice.

Notes

1   Ralph Smith (1980) *The Function and Assessment of Art in Education*, Leeds, Association of Art Advisors (pages unnumbered).
2   Edmund Feldman (1970) *Becoming Human through Art*, Chicago, Illinois, Prentice-Hall.
3   See, for example, *Art Works* (1987) Ministry of Education (Schools Division), Victoria, Australia.
4   Taylor, *op. cit.*, p. 60.
5   Murray McDonald (1990) *Patrick Hughes: A New Perspective*, London, Flowers East (pages unnumbered).
6   Rod and Dot Taylor, *op. cit.*, p. 95.
7   Student Personal Appraisal (October 1989).
8   Maxine Greene (1990) 'Art Worlds in Schools', in *The Symbolic Order*, Basingstoke, Falmer Press, p. 218.
9   Al Hurwitz (1983) *The Gifted and the Talented in Art: A Guide to Program Planning*, Worcester, Massachusetts, Davis Publications Inc., p. 29.
10 Robert Clement (1986) *The Art Teacher's Handbook*, London, Hutchinson, p. 168.
11 Taylor, *op. cit.* Clement is making a distinction between photograph and reproduction as the basis for image by pupils.
12 Robin Morris (1987) 'Towards a Shared Symbolic Order', in *Living Powers*, *op. cit.*, pp. 201, 202.
13 Diane Waldman (1978) in *Mark Rothko*, London, Thames and Hudson, Preface.
14 *Art Works*, *op. cit.*, p. 269.
15 Jacques Lassaigne (1959) *Matisse*, Geneva, Editions d'Art Albert Skira, p. 86.
16 Jean Clay (1978) *Modern Art, 1890–1918*, London, Octopus, p. 99.
17 Prof. Matteo Marangoni (1951) *The Art of Seeing Art*, London, Shelley Castle Ltd, p. 59.
18 *Starlit Waters* (1988) Tate, Liverpool brochure.
19 Ernst Fischer (1959) *The Necessity of Art*, London (Eng. trans. 1963), Peregrine Books, pp. 138, 139.
20 *Ibid.*, p. 193.
21 Waldman, *op. cit.*, p. 58.
22 Richard Wollheim (1974) *On Art and the Mind*, Harvard University Press, pp. 128–9.
23 Robert Hughes (1980) *Shock of the New*, London, BBC, see p. 323.
24 Peter Fuller (1986) *The Australian Scapegoat: Towards an Antipodean Aesthetic*, University of Western Australia Press, p. 12.
25 C.H. Waddington (1969) *Behind Appearance*, Cambridge, Mass., Edinburgh University Press, p. 145.
26 John Pope-Hennessy (1950) *The Complete Work of Paolo Uccello*, London, Phaidon Press Limited, pp. 15, 16.
27 Hughes, *op. cit.*, pp. 116, 207.
28 *Amanda Faulkner Catalogue* (1989) The Drumcroon Education Art Centre, Wigan.
29 *The Impressionist Brush* (undated), Plate 27. Text incorporates quote from George H. Hamilton (there is no acknowledgment of book's author or publisher).
30 Taylor, *op. cit.*, p. 14.
31 Hughes, *op. cit.*, p. 124.
32 Alberto Busignani (1971) *Pollock*, London, New York, Hamlyn Press, pp. 21, 22.
33 Rod Taylor (1991) *Artists in Wigan Schools*, London, Calouste Gulbenkian Foundation (unpublished at time of writing).
34 *Anthony Lysycia 'Lifelines' Catalogue* (1989), The Drumcroon Education Art Centre, Wigan.

35 Roger Fry (1920) *Vision and Design*, Harmondsworth, Penguin Books, p. 34.
36 Germain Bazin (1958) *Impressionist Paintings in the Louvre*, London, Thames and Hudson, p. 230.
37 Lassaigne, *op. cit.*, p. 93.
38 Susanne Langer (1953) *Feeling and Form*, Routledge and Kegan Paul, p. 83.
39 *Ibid.*, p. 83.
40 M. Messer (1967) *Munch*, New York, Abrams, p. 130.
41 Antoine Terrasse (1964) *Bonnard*, Geneva, Editions d'Art, Albert Skira, p. 89.
42 Andre Fermigier (undated) *Bonnard*, New York, Abrams, p. 136.
43 Arthur Hughes (1981) *The Pull of the Future*, City of Birmingham Polytechnic Faculty of Art and Design, p. 25.
44 Rod and Dot Taylor, *op. cit.*, p. 106.
45 Rod Taylor, *op. cit.*, p. 260.

Chapter 5

Working with Teachers: Gallery Workshops

Candidates will be expected to demonstrate the ability to make informed responses to contemporary and historical art and design through an awareness of artistic qualities, an analysis and evaluation of design, and the forming and expressing of judgements. (NEA GCSE Assessment Objective 9)

Critical Studies, Examinations and Testing

With the acceptance of critical studies as an essential component of the GCSE examinations in art and design, an important move was made to ensure that a majority of 14- to 16-year-old pupils choosing to further their studies in the subject would have increased opportunities to engage with the visual arts as practised by others, in addition to pursuing their own practice. It was a close call, however; the Northern Examinations Association, for example, only added the above assessment objective very late in the day and, though most boards have emphasized the importance of critical studies in practice, some do not have assessment objectives which so clearly state the need for critical studies to be taking place as an essential component.

Though some of the resulting practice has inevitably been of mixed quality in the first instance, many teachers testified from an early stage to the increased levels of pupil interest, motivation and participation which the critical studies dimension brought about. Not only that, teachers began to recount how, on the evidence before them and in spite of reservations about the imposition on them of new demands through GCSE without adequate consultation, they felt the need to introduce a critical studies element into their courses throughout the school from year one. Some also expressed the desire that the process begin in the primary school, and, indeed, numerous primary schools have also initiated important developments of their own. Some have even incorporated critical studies approaches into whole-school policies and, in spite of the pressure placed on them through the demands of the National Curriculum, are keeping their nerve and even turning these approaches to advantage; there are potent dividends elsewhere in the curriculum with, for example, pupils developing listening and talking skills through the need to conjecture and clarify, as well as in writing. The Art Working Party has acknowledged these critical studies developments in their Interim Report recommendations; it is to be hoped that all pupils of all ages will, in future, receive an education in the visual arts which acknowledges their right both to know about art and design and to engage in its practice — with the proviso, of course, that art has been made optional at Key Stage 4 level.

It seemed inconceivable that such developments could ever take place during the 1970s when the emphasis on free expression was such that the argument forcibly held sway that the wider world of the visual arts as practised by others was 'out there' and irrelevant — even harmful — to pupil needs, at least prior to A-level. The introduction of critical studies at the GCSE level has inevitably posed problems for numerous teachers whose own education at the higher education level had likewise been deficient in this respect. Many who had been teaching for a number of years had rejected the type of art history lectures they had received themselves as being irrelevant to the pupils' needs and, in turn, had carried on their classroom practice without feeling any need to devise or adopt alternative strategies and approaches to address critical studies needs. How, then, might the resulting problems be addressed and teachers who had been sold short in their own training at least be helped to gain the necessary confidence to dip a toe into the critical studies waters?

The Implications for Teacher Development

Critical studies thinking has not been exclusive to the United Kingdom. It has been a widespread phenomenon throughout the later 1970s and 1980s, with developments taking place, for example, in Holland, Canada, Australia, New Zealand and the United States. Al Hurwitz describes how, in the States, he and a number of artists visited schools where they dealt with groups of up to fifty pupils at a time, demonstrating to them as artists. Starting with blank canvas, they would gradually build up a painting, but offering any pupils who so wished the opportunity to withdraw at the end of each key stage, one, for example, being when the design of the painting had been successfully established by being drawn out.

At the point when maybe five to ten pupils were left, Hurwitz felt the moment had come to work with these pupils by getting down

> ... to some 'serious discussions', about art, about artists, about art making.... I do not know for certain whether they are gifted in the critical or studio areas, but I do know that these children are intensely curious about art and eager to talk about it. If we could repeat this performance in every school in every community and gather all of the fourth phase students, we could help them develop their critical sensibilities — and perhaps ease the way for future art critics, historians and curators.[1]

I am a great believer in artists-in-schools programmes — but not to by-pass or as an alternative to the classroom teacher; when working together in genuine partnership, it is possible for teacher and artist to offer the young people in their dual charge a quality and range of experiences which neither, working in isolation, can otherwise offer. Also, the majority of teachers in this country, particularly at a time when their minds are focused on meeting the entitlement needs of all pupils, would find the strategy adopted to identify a supposedly interested group unacceptable and elitist, as well as logistically impossible to realize on any widespread basis.

Besides the need better to fund and resource schools, including the setting up of wide-ranging residency programmes addressing whole community needs, there are two overriding fundamental routes which are, in the long term, the essential ones to follow: those of addressing these issues at the initial training level and through teacher development programmes. If worthwhile critical studies experiences were to become a fundamental and ongoing part of all young people's education, would not the required art critics, historians and curators — as well as better prepared and informed artists and designers — still emerge, but naturally? In addition, might not they all have the rather important bonus of having a more informed, artistically literate and articulate, critically alert public with whom to deal? For this to begin to happen, it is surely absolutely essential that the teachers are fully involved — it is only they who, in the final analysis, can systematically address the needs of all pupils on an ongoing basis.

Most PGCE centres are currently taking these issues very seriously, but the in-service needs are great at a time of dramatically diminishing funding for such purposes. The introduction of GCSE, at least temporarily, provided both invaluable in-service funding and opportunities for all teachers to become involved in the issues of the day. As an important part of the Wigan GCSE art and design training days, a range of questions was structured around the areas of content, form, process and mood for workshop purposes. The aim was to explore how teachers might respond to engaging with original art works in the Drumcroon Education Art Centre setting with a view to them, in turn, more fruitfully engaging their pupils in the study of art works, including those about which teacher and pupil had no foreknowledge.

Though the authority pursues a policy of providing supporting information sheets, school loan works can nevertheless hang in schools and, because of uncertainties about their content or the processes used, etc., then not be used for teaching purposes to the extent they might be. Likewise, temporary exhibitions in local galleries invariably contain unfamiliar works, and no teacher can be expected to be fully informed about every work on permanent display in a public collection to which an individual pupil might be drawn. What clues might these works themselves contain? Do these not provide a sufficient basis for reasoned conjecture and exploration? Is there not a special bonus in that the focus is then directly on the art object in question rather than on surrounding data and facts? Obviously a wealth of information exists in books on art, and any worthwhile education is going to take account of this, but the absence of information about specific works need not be a deterrent and, indeed, can be turned to account by encouraging the processes of looking, responding, analyzing and conjecturing.

In addition to Wigan training day sessions, numerous similar workshops have been conducted elsewhere in the UK and abroad, and time and again the reaction of teachers is that they have never previously scrutinized an art object with such intensity and for so long, and that their training had not adequately prepared them for such undertakings. A range of questions, initially set out in the Wigan GCSE critical studies training day booklet, provided the basis for all these workshops. The questions are in no way the only possible ones and, where appropriate, teachers were always encouraged to formulate additional or substitute ones of their own. They were grouped under four headings as follows:

1   CONTENT. What is the subject matter of the work, what is it about? Is the subject matter incidental or is it a vehicle for the social, religious, moral, or political, concerns of the artist or client? Was the subject matter observed directly, remembered or imagined? Has it been treated representationally or is there deliberate exaggeration, distortion or abstraction and, if so, why? Is the subject matter surface deep or are there hidden, or not immediately apparent, meanings alluded to through the use of, for example, symbol, analogy, metaphor? etc.

2   FORM. How has the work been arranged? Is this in keeping with the content? Does it contradict or affirm the work's '*message*'? What kind of colour scheme has been used? Is it, for example, a harmonious one or one built up of contrasts? Does one colour predominate or do two or more have equal significance? Is there one main overall shape or is it composed through interrelating sequences of shapes? Are there recurring shapes, lines, rhythms, forms, etc., which determine the design of the work? Does the work have a variety or unity of texture? Does the work hold together as an overall entity, or is it pleasing in parts and yet unsatisfactory as a whole? etc.

3   PROCESS. How was the work made and what was it made with? What materials, tools, processes and techniques did the artist use? How and where might the artist have commenced the work? Through what stages did the work proceed from commencement to completion? Might the artist have made supporting studies — sketches, photographs, maquettes, collages and stencils, for example? Was the work executed rapidly or did it evolve slowly over a long period? What skills must the artist have required to produce such a work? etc.

4   MOOD. Does the work affect you, the viewer, in any way? Does it capture a mood, feeling or emotion which you have already experienced? Does it convey feelings about life and nature? Can you imagine what the artist's feelings were while producing the work? Is the work quiet/noisy, soothing/disturbing, happy/sad, relaxing/jarring, etc., in the mood which it conveys and the feeling it arouses? Is your mood simply the one of the moment or has the work in question directly affected you? If the latter, what are the qualities in the work which so affect you? etc.[2]

At one workshop with PGCE students, conducted in a major municipal art gallery, one of the students has a university art history degree rather than the more customary polytechnic practical art and design qualification. She expressed particular appreciation of the workshop because at university she had been subjected to the constant criticism that all her written assignments were too woolly and vague. She had accepted the criticism as justified but felt helpless over what to do about it, and the criticism was never supported by any criteria designed to help her address the problem. She wished that the workshop had been conducted earlier in her career, for she felt that it did indeed provide her with the necessary criteria she had sorely needed throughout her course.

Unusual Responses

One of the more beneficial ways of working was that of the teachers working in pairs, with one posing questions and the other acting as scribe to record their discussed comments and observations. Many of these workshops have proved to be particularly rewarding from my personal point of view, for the teachers' reactions never cease to surprise, and, on occasions, can even be quite startling. One course, held at a county residential in-service centre, had the walls liberally sprinkled with original works from the Authority's own schools loan collection. In truth, though, any attention paid to these works during the three days and evenings prior to the commencement of the workshop was, at best, scant. For the workshop session, these were supplemented through the addition of works brought from an upstairs storage area. Because of the pressure on the teachers to complete the practical work which was the main focus of the week, the workshop using the loan items was to be only half a morning's duration, with a ten-minute appraisal scheduled for after the coffee break.

When the coffee was served, two women — cups in hand — hurried back to their work, eagerly resuming their discussions. One commented on how much they were enjoying the activity, observing that she would never have dreamed that she was capable of getting so much from the study of a single work of art. In the ensuing group discussion, which unfolded throughout the rest of the morning in the event, they explained in relation to their notes that they had deliberately chosen a work they did not like because, in the school context, that would be one they would be unlikely to make use of. How did they feel about it now enquired one teacher? 'I wish it were mine! I would love to take it home with me — I could live with it now!', came the response.

Another teacher immediately stated that her experience had been the exact opposite. Initially drawn to a Terry Wilson screenprint by preference, she now positively disliked it. But why? That initial appeal had been at the superficial level, she admitted, and was soon countered by the realization that the work had deeper and more disquieting dimensions. Black marks on the background surrounding the single male figure's features, seen in profile, had a sinister quality to them. Gestural marks around the hands emphasized movement and the fact that they were being vigorously washed in a manner reminiscent of Lady Macbeth trying to wash out that 'damned spot'. This dark pervasive mood to which she was now acutely sensitive was further intensified by the recognition that the title was incorporated into the print itself. The artist had stencilled 'Anonymous Portrait No. 5' in a letter form suggesting that used on police file photographs. Suddenly the teacher realized that she was covered from head to foot in goose pimples, brought about by sensations identical to those she had experienced in 'real life' once when she had woken up in a cold sweat, having committed a murder in a nightmare. Such reactions are generally uncommon in the normal routines of everyday life and in dramatic and marked contrast to the lack of reaction to these same works hung in bland anonymity in the same building earlier.

Equally striking responses were engendered during a Service Children's Schools Course in Northern Germany. It took place in the Mönchen Gladbach Art Gallery which houses a collection dominated by large-scale German and

PLATE 21.   Two teachers using Content, Form, Process, Mood as a basis to study Segal's 'Artist in His Studio' in the Monchen Gladbach Art Gallery

American works of the post-war era — many of them of a challenging nature. During the evaluation session the next morning the observation was made that where no obvious content was apparent, it seemed to allow scope for the imagination to soar freely. Many of the teachers had come considerable distances, but one lived nearby and was a frequent visitor to the gallery. He could nevertheless acknowledge that the workshop had led him to focus in-depth on works which had never previously registered.

Two sculptures generated particularly interesting responses. One was the 1968 'Artist in His Studio' by George Segal. It consisted of: 'Two reclining nude figures on mattresses, one male, one female and a separate figure of Artist and a wooden table with charcoal drawing of head and breast of reclining female.'[3] In keeping with most works produced by Segal, it was white in.

> Plain plaster colour counterbalanced by contradiction of brown table/ fawn drawing paper and black charcoal — 'mundane vs aesthetic' though felt contrast pulls together, or links, group — unity of texture of figures broken by use of natural wood of table — reclining female out of proportion but does not detract from overall image — lack of colour emphasises form — holds together powerfully.

They found the piece 'disturbingly real' in its impact, with a 'feeling of startling realism engendered'. The work produced a feeling of a 'quiet working atmosphere — found ourselves whispering so as not to disturb artist — to stand behind artist and see what he is doing creates "weird feeling" — wanted very much to question him — feelings of voyeurism enhanced by juxtaposed figure of "Man sitting at table" (although unrelated originally) — keep coming back to it.' 'Man sitting at table' was an adjacently sited sculpture, also by Segal, at a remove but just close enough to suggest psychologically a fourth related figure to the artist and model group.

They conjectured that the 'plaster/bandaged figures' must have armatures, with the bandages giving a 'lighter quality', the whole arousing tactile sensations of a pronounced nature.

Would have liked to touch to test thickness etc. Close attention to detail
— lips, hands, jowls, toes, knuckles — suggest the hands have been used
solely as tools.

Sensitive features with detail suggest some kind of facial form beneath
plaster — fine mesh possibly??

They also conjecture as to whether the work was done from sketches or possibly
even a painting; but the group undoubtedly involved a '*Slow* process — gradual
buiding up of layers/in spite of quick-drying quality of medium. Reflects detailed
thought and long time scale. All form is built up and none indented or chiselled
or hollowed away.' The overall effect of this was 'very POTENT', with the
simplicity in no way detracting from the image. They found themselves 'both
drawn to the piece very strongly' to the point where even when they had
'officially' finished the exercise they felt compelled to return to it at intervals
throughout the remainder of the afternoon, so powerfully did it exert its presence
upon them.

Another work of dominating presence was a Joseph Beuys' sculpture, made
up of a number of separate sections dramatically spread over a large expanse of
gallery floor and so sited as to command immediate attention upon entering the
gallery. This is how two teachers described this piece:

2 railway lines sectioned at junctions 30ft. long straddled either side by
angled bolted metal rods (10) ... other side — 4 large hollow metal
barrel shapes supporting 15ft. cylindrical heavy metal form with a head
protruding from the narrow orifice. 2ft. along the cylinder a mythical
mouth protrudes. The appearance of the cylinder is that of an 18th
century gun barrel.... The objects at first sight appear to be man-made,
found rather than sculpted and fashioned for the purpose. However,
on closer inspection, the gun barrel and 4 supporting cylinders exhibit a
series of marks synonymous with casting methods. The unity between
the objects is enhanced by the rusting, aged, decaying, crumbling surfaces. The overall surface quality is brown, orange, grey, dull red as with
oxidating corroding metals.

The form of the piece is that of an 'essentially horizontal low level "sculpture"
with a strong linear directional basis' and the 'spatial arrangement is subtle with
play on intervals and spaces....' Under 'Mood' the writing becomes less objective and descriptive and more evocative: 'echoes of civilisations past and present
... ancestral voices', true meanings that are hidden and appear to be ambiguous,
etc. Through intense scrutiny and not a little thought allied to feeling, these
teachers went a long way towards coming to terms with challenging contemporary sculptures. In the process they also produced writing — albeit in essentially
note form made on the spot and without subsequent redrafting and refinement —
of a high standard in terms of art criticism and analysis.

A Need for Increased Visual Awareness in Society

Anthony Caro would doubtless have approved of their efforts: 'If a sculpture is worth looking at it needs time to take it in; it is no use hurtling past it.... People need to get more used to modern sculpture.'

> ... the general level of appreciation in art needs to be raised so that people recognise the good from the bad. And that takes constantly look-ing, discriminating, sharpening one's eyes, having faith in one's judgment.[4]

Anna Somers Cocks goes further, for she would certainly applaud the process involved in the teachers setting down their observations and responses in written form. As an assistant keeper at the Victoria and Albert Museum, the first thing she was taught was how to describe an object minutely. She believes that though this might produce 'numbingly boring prose', it is a valuable 'training exercise, a discipline' in the naming of parts basic to looking. She applies the procedure to a recently erected fountain of three ducks which, to her unpleasant surprise, has appeared on Bond Street. It is 'feeble in design', and does not work properly, the base being too small for the height, 'so the water piddles all over the pavement' and 'come winter it will doubtless cause the odd fractured elbow.' Her descrip-tion explains how, 'From a tripartite, lobate, carved base of stone in the Art Nouveau manner, rises an erect bronze column of spiralling lily pads, encircled at the crown by three flying ducks and dominated by three bull rushes from which issues water.'[5] Cocks bemoans the unthinking way we in this country stick flowers 'on toasters; on saucepans; on tiles, in a haze of pink, beige or grey; we print them all over sheets in pastel colours, we spoil high quality bone-china plates ... by enamelling them with weedy, asymmetric pseudo-modern floral patterns.' 'We are a nation of visual illiterates who need to be drilled in the naming of parts so that we might at least *notice* what we are buying (that being the first step towards looking at it critically).'

The V & A, she believes, should 'take up the cause of explaining ornament and design rather more vigorously ... instead of just leaving the objects to speak for themselves.' Whether the linking of at least some aspects of design with tech-nology through the National Curriculum will eventually assist this process remains to be seen, but if one consequence is that of artificially divorcing art from design, harm will certainly be done. In the meantime, the critical studies activities which can flow as a result of these content, form, process, mood workshops have implications across the whole art, craft and design spectrum — important because, as Cocks says, 'Your average duke and your average bus driver tend to agree about Carl André's Bricks. And yet modern art is not dispensable, because it is inextricably linked with creative modern design, the vigour that goes into one indirectly giving life to the other.'

This concern about art and design being separated by officialdom has been expressed by many — Sir Hugh Casson and Patrick Heron being two particularly articulate examples — though, as yet, to no avail. The idea persists that, whereas design relates directly to the technological needs of society, fine art is a non-functional luxury and indulgence. A student with aspirations of working in tele-vision as a producer recently recounted an incident very much to the point. At her college, fine art has been conveniently hived off to another site with inferior space and facilities. A noticeable and undesirable immediate outcome, she observes, has been a marked reduction in the use of drawing as an essential means of recording, developing and thinking through ideas in departments like her own.

The summer degree ceremony had been formal and dignified with local industrialists as well as the college hierarchy in attendance. At the conclusion of the proceedings one student, still in gown and mortar board, unexpectedly stepped forward and made an unscheduled speech. Did not the college hierarchy and these smartly suited business gentlemen realize what they were doing? Ideas both essential and regenerative to the fields of fashion and design had invariably been born within the fine arts. Diminish and impair the one, and the other is likewise correspondingly impoverished. The students shouted, applauded and threw their hats in the air, but the various dignitaries withdrew in aloof silence. When Cocks asked a factory manager why they did not produce anything in a 'clear elegant modern shape', the retort immediately came back, 'We are not in the fashion business.'

These issues extend right back into the mainstream school system. Young people should be enabled through their education to articulate their thoughts, feelings and observations, and to make informed critical judgments about a whole range of art, craft and designed objects throughout every phase of their school life. Fine art works are obviously significant to this process simply because they are so 'complex, demanding and puzzling.'[6] Great works are deep, and the more one tries to penetrate them, the more one becomes conscious 'that their central essences are hidden far further down.'[7] Is it not therefore appropriate to adopt approaches which encourage questioning rather than providing all the answers?

Previously Untapped Teacher Capabilities

As has already been indicated, the first content, form, process, mood workshop was on a Wigan GCSE training day, using school loan objects and displayed works. The Drumcroon exhibition at the time was 'British Relief Woodcarving' and, though maybe not 'great' works, there were certainly significant ones well worthy of study; to quote one teacher, 'minor art seen close to seems a great deal better than great art seen through reproductions and slides or seen from a distance.' To conclude this section, two of the teachers involved provide abundant evidence of an eloquence in their responses allied to a questioning and conjectural approach.

The Drumcroon exhibition catalogue describes the works of Lee Grandjean as follows: 'Old gates are the support and background for the elmwood slabs, forming the basic structural composition. The image is carved within and across the lateral divisions. Colour creates its own structure overlaying both the illusion and the real edge.' The structures looked impressive and imposing covering one of the Main Gallery walls, and one teacher chose to work from his 'Praise, Wonder and Despair' during the workshop, writing the following about it:

This large, wooden, painted relief (167 × 111 × 16cm) depicts three figures against a dark forest. Large pieces or planks (found ready shaped) of wood have been attached to a thick, wooden framework in a broken,

PLATE 22.   'Praise, Wonder and Despair' by Lee Grandjean in the Drumcroon exhibition

fragmentary manner. Strong vertical sections mainly representing the tree trunks and more branching, fan-like arrangement in the upper part representing the branches. The pieces have been fairly crudely carved into to describe the three-dimensional quality of the branches and to reveal the three figures in the lower half of the scene. The chisel marks seem fairly uniform in size over the whole piece, unifying the surface.

The figures are fairly evenly spread across the lower half of the relief. They are very simplified, angular symbolic versions of a figure. The figure on the left seems alone, he does not touch any of the other figures. He raises his arms straight upwards towards the sky and hangs his head back as if giving thanks — I feel he represents the 'Praise' in the title. The centre figure stands upright with arms and hands at his side but his head turned upwards to the sky. He is the most dominant of the figures due to his position in the scene and also the finer modelling and painted highlighting on the face and body. He seems to represent wonder, the light perhaps being a spiritual light, something breaking into the dark forest. The right hand figure is linked to the centre one by an overlapping leg — he strides to the right almost off the relief, his head bent onto his chest. The pose suggests despair.

The colour is mainly blue and brown with some shading — tonal-work is painted onto the wood fairly thinly — you can still see the texture of the wood and it has a matt finish. It helps separate more clearly sky tones from figures. The mood is not a joyous one because of the coolness of the colour scheme. Colour does not confuse. The fragmentary nature of the construction and composition helps create a feeling of movement from one figure to another and the diagonals in the branches of the tree echo the poses of the figures.

When first viewing the piece the apparent crudeness of construction and lack of finish make one immediately aware of the process the artist used. The images carved are very clear at a glance. The presence of the piece, its size, its bold imagery, primitive modelling and colour were what drew me to the piece. Yet it had some surprises; there are some very sensitive parts, particularly the face of the central figure.

This description illustrates how, in moving from one area to another, there is evidence of modification in the nature of the responses. By providing distinct ways in and an approach from a different standpoint, each of the four areas encourages the work to give up another aspect of its significance and meanings.

Another of the artists represented, Anthony Lysycia, had studied for his A-levels in a Wigan sixth-form college. He had, in fact, exhibited in the Centre at an early stage in its history while he was still a student. He was therefore invited to take up residency throughout the duration of the exhibition, causing him to bring additional works and to fill the upstairs Conference Room, which also became his studio area. One of these has since featured in the 'Lifelines' one-person show which the artist has subsequently staged at Drumcroon. It was then titled 'Two Brothers' but the teacher who chose to study it during the earlier exhibition was unaware of this title. The considered use of fourteen questions interspersed through the passage indicates just how significant a part conjecture can play in the process of engaging with such a work.

I am amazed to see a door hanging on a wall and out of context. My conditioning says it has a domestic connotation and here I see it presented as a decorative, yet thought-provoking, artifact — making me think.

At a content level I note the two figures, apparently intertwined — are they brothers? Do they represent a previously taboo relationship, for one looks at the other somewhat affectionately? The main figure clutches a container — holding the tools of his trade? Maybe he's a carpenter, or does he represent the artist maker? Does his expression — looking out and wondering — suggest that he is more intellectual; the artist as creator? In front of the container of tools a bird holds a worm fast in its beak whilst balancing on a perch — it seems to link up with the second bird lower down, gripping the vine leaves, and its beak pointing towards the bottle of wine. Have we a symbol here? Is the person who has made this work a lover of wine and good living or do the symbols have a broader implication? The symbols combine and underline the broader context, as the scroll relates and the fallen head on the ground reminds me of an ancient culture. Greek — Roman? It could be either, for the scroll forming the shape of an Ionic capital reminds me of Greece — but the Renaissance tights of the main figure bring me back to Florence and a night of revelry in August when a band of young people marched through the city 'decked out' as in Leonardo's pageants. The symbols

PLATE 23.   The 'Two Brothers' carving by Anthony Lysycia is on the right in this view of Drumcroon during a workshop session

continue around the work; lips, ears, eyes, noses — are they the fragmentations of a self-portrait? Do they suggest that the two central figures are being spied upon or observed? The pedestal supports the tools of *our* trade and the artist a bird — a sinister or happy element — is art alive or threatened? As I struggle to unravel the work I am delayed by knots in the wood and they combine to further the content; a hole for a latch reminds me that this door has been used to keep out the cold — to protect, to enclose — the protecting gesture of the second figure is in keeping with this idea.

It will be noted that eleven of the questions have already occurred during this extensive opening section devoted to 'Content', inspired by the ambiguities suggested by the artist's emphasis on the use of symbols.

The form of the work is challenging — it is a door transposed into art. The design appears intuitive but made to fit an upright rectangular shape. The artist seems to be using a form not unlike the book illuminators, surrounding the central image with an unfolding decorative edge — perhaps the artist has studied Gothic illumination, or maybe just likes doors! As a door has been used there has been no attempt to camouflage the diagonal planks which cut across the image or to conceal the damage caused by use and time. The outer edges, or frame, are door colour but as we view the central panel the colour 'springs to life' and enriches the forms. I like the way the artist has 'slabbed' the colour on, keeping it apparently fairly representational and clear — it being only affected to neutrality as it 'sinks' into the fabric of the wood. The central design is interconnected, based on a set of rhythms which constantly move the eye back and forth. The forms balance out — look how a tree is placed at the top left to echo the wine bottle in the corner on the right.

In writing about 'Form,' the teacher has inevitably made some passing references to process — his use of 'slabbed' colour, for example, and how the paint has been allowed to sink into the fabric of the wood in places. An interesting feature of the artist's approach to 'Process' is that, having carved chest or door, he will then use the surfaces as large-scale relief blocks from which to edition sets of prints which he then hand illuminates. He afterwards stains and colours the doors and chests, and these are then exhibited in their own right, often in conjunction with the prints to which they have given rise. However, the teacher here focuses specifically on the door itself.

> The process demonstrated within the work is totally seductive. The artist seems to have worked into this 'old wooden door' with aggression, yet sensitivity. He has apparently moved beyond the handling we normally associate with the carver, i.e. the manifestation of chisel and hammer and attacked the surface with a heavy implement — for the gusto demonstrated seems at one level crudely enacted — has he used an axe? Maybe in an effort to convey primitive force, alongside the elements of sophistication, he has seized the first thing to hand. Was the person enthusiastic, excited, eager when he made the work? The work is made in low relief — a difficult concept and the artist had to think of removing away, yet leaving what is crucial of the material to transmit an idea. It flattens the forms and sometimes the technique evokes as it would with low relief, a temptation to touch. His paint appears like oils — for it glows and reflects and in parts is in impasto. We have a craftsperson here.

The shortest section is the last one on 'Mood,' the teacher writing pithily and summarily on this aspect.

> When all this is combined and I conjecture in front of the work — its form, its process but especially its content helps me to relate to this person who has formed the image. The work is convivial, its symbols keep on taking my mind from this exhibition setting to another country which I know has been a major inspiration to the artist. The Cypress tree in a landscape, the dark-eyed youth (a self-portrait?), the wine and the ancient symbols remind me of Italy. An intense Chorley artist of Polish origins has made the work having soaked in the art and culture but especially the sun of the Mediterranean.

In concluding, the teacher draws upon privileged information about the artist; with him having been educated in Wigan and with his Drumcroon exhibition focusing on biographical, as well as artistic, material, most Wigan art and design teachers are aware that Anthony had spent two years in Italy as a Prix-de-Rome scholar.

A further important feature of the workshop was that, having addressed each of the four areas in relation to the chosen work, the teachers then took each area in turn to identify other works of art, from across time, place and cultures, which related in some way; which other art works manifested similar content, were ordered and arranged in similar or related ways, used similar techniques, processes and working procedures, and evoked similar moods or atmospheres or aroused similar feelings? Unfortunately, pressures of time invariably mean that this aspect of the workshop is rarely addressed with the attention, or for as long, as it warrants, though there is no doubt that most sessions conclude with the teachers fully aware of the importance of this process and of its classroom implications.

The teacher writing about the Lysycia door did not have time to address mood at all and process was obviously only looked at in the most hurried way. However, what was written was sufficient to illustrate how, starting from the in-depth focus of the work studied in the original, it is possible to open up for the benefit of young people whole dimensions of the visual arts, so that they are able to see relationships and interconnections between the most seemingly diverse and different works.

Under the 'Content' heading, the teacher suggested the whole of Symbolism and that the teacher looks at Flemish fifteenth century painting, the architecture of ancient Greece and Rome, the many references to wine in such paintings as those of Rubens and Titian addressing such themes as Silenus and Bacchus and Ariadne, Gothic imagery, Medieval crafts and guild systems, Italian Renaissance art — with the figure in doublet relating naturally to, for example, Masaccio's 'Tribute Money' fresco, van Gogh's treatment of cypress trees and Primitive Art.

In formal terms, amongst others, the teacher suggests the Ghiberti Doors in Florence, Gauguin's Tahitian carvings and all the German Expressionist wood block relief prints, Northern European medieval carvings, local and, indeed, worldwide carved church doors and so on. Had the teacher had time, cross-cultural references to Maori or Pre-Columbian carving would likely have been made, while the British Relief Woodcarving exhibition itself included many artists whose work related to African carving, and Lysycia's doors and chests certainly related to these also.

Teachers had literally to think on their feet to make these associations, and would certainly add more in a systematic way if given the time to undertake this aspect of the exercise more reflectively. Nevertheless, the examples indicate what rich networks of associations can be made through this further application of the content, form, process, mood model, and it obviously has important implications in relation to how a school's book, slide, reproduction and video resources might be used both in preparation for taking pupils to art galleries and to substantiate the experience afterwards. In the process, whole dimensions of the visual arts can be opened up and made relevant to young people which might otherwise remain closed to them.

All the teachers' workshop examples used in this section make use of descriptive, evocative and expressive language, and in a clear, unpretentious manner. There is a considerable body of equivalent material which could also have been used and which is consistent in this respect. As well as the teachers frequently expressing surprise at their literary abilities, of which they were but dimly aware, their engagement with a work to such an in-depth level helps to demistify it in the most beneficial way. Not only that, it can throw a new light on the texts of art history books. One of the fears which art and design teachers expressed during the CSAE Project was that of the expressive work which many saw as the sole function of the subject being replaced by glib rhetoric used for effect. By default, the extraordinary potential of the art studio as a richly language-laden area of the school was not always realized.

Through such workshops, though, teachers have gained the necessary confidence subsequently to engage their pupils in similarly constructive debate. The English NCC Consultation Report (November, 1989) makes the observation that 'Every attainment target (AT) in science and mathematics and in the proposals for technology contains reference to language skills but not all to the same degree' (p. 117). Art and design has a particularly rich contribution to make in this respect through the nature of the stimulus it draws upon and the alliance of thoughts and feelings that characterize practice within the subject. Through language, vital subject-specific concepts can also be articulated and clarified; to recall those words of Bruner, 'the limits of my language are the limits of my world.' Rather than the art and design teachers' attempts to help young people develop a critical vocabulary appropriate to their age and stage of development inhibit their expressive work, the reverse is, in fact, the case. The systematic use and application of the content, form, process, mood model, with the clarity of focus it provides, have a great deal to contribute in this respect. There is a growing body of evidence that young people can apply this model in both gallery and school contexts, sometimes to unusual effect. It is precisely this which I hope to demonstrate through the use of two case studies in the next chapter.

Notes

1 Hurwitz, *op. cit.*, pp. 29, 30.
2 Wigan Schools, *Critical Studies and GCSE Art and Design, op. cit.*, p. 5.
3 Taken from the teacher's note exactly as made in front of the work in the gallery. (All the examples of teachers' writing throughout this chapter are likewise taken from their notes or writings as made in the gallery and without the benefit of subsequent reflection or refining.)
4 Anthony Caro (1989) 'A Lesson from the First King Charles', *The Weekend Guardian*, New Year 1989.
5 Anna Somers Cocks (1989) 'Out for a Duck', *The Weekend Guardian*, 27–28 May 1989.
6 Smith, *op. cit.*
7 Kenneth Clark (1960) *Looking at Pictures*, London, John Murray, p. 17.

Chapter 6

Two Case Studies:
Amanda and Victoria

First, the process of practising the arts is in itself partly one of observation, analysis and evaluation of one's own experiences in relation to other people's.... Mere expression without reflection and evaluation need not lead to an understanding of the nature of personal feelings nor of the social values and acquired attitudes which influence them.... Individuality requires self-knowledge.... Cultural education is inquisitive and so is the practical process of the arts. Participation — practising the arts — is important for that reason.

Second, many of the products of the arts — plays, paintings, literature, music, dancing — are integral features of the social culture. For this reason they are among those things which people need to experience and understand if they are to make sense of their culture.... To come to know a work of art is to grapple personally with the ideas and values which it represents and embodies. By giving form to their own perceptions, artists can help us to make sense of ours. (The Arts in Schools, Gulbenkian Report).[1]

For students to enter the aesthetic field in ways appropriate to their individual temperaments and interests, it is essential that the teacher taps into their ideas and aspirations. This puts an onus on the teacher to provide the students with the means to communicate by written and spoken, as well as practical, means. This does not imply that the role of the teacher is a passive one: the course on offer must have its own rigour and structure if adequate numbers of students are adequately to define specific interests of sufficient intensity and depth.

Amanda and Victoria — like the five students already encountered in Chapter 3 — studied at Winstanley Sixth Form College. Their course was structured around the three fundamental areas of studio-based activity, the critical domain and the use of the sketchbook. By these means, students begin to discern important connections between the objective study and project developments of the studio and their home-based and location investigations facilitated by sketchbook activity. Both aspects are likewise fed and stimulated by the use of college, gallery and museum stimulus which, in turn, takes on added meaning through the students' own practical endeavours. Through this interactive process, each student begins to identify a range of artists who are especially significant to them as individuals. Their own practice then begins to develop in original and unanticipated ways. Amanda and Victoria worked in the same art room at the same time, yet both developed their work along quite different lines stimulated by and involving quite different artists. Important parallels can be discerned though — in keeping with an overriding concern of our time, both find ecological implications in the artists to whom they are drawn.

Amanda and the Pre-Raphaelites

The Pre-Raphaelites are also important in the way that they established an English tradition, preserving our view of nature. The modern world is quickly destroying our wildlife, either by pollution or urban expansion. I think that we are fortunate that the Pre-Raphaelites accurately recorded an aspect of our world that may one day cease to exist.[2]

This short paragraph appears in the 'Introduction' to Amanda's A-level 'Personal Study', a written assignment in the region of 3500 words. A much earlier written 'Assessment Review' from the lower sixth phase of her course, however, reveals the direct extent to which her interest in her chosen topic emanated from her studio-based practical work.

The theme for all my recent work has been plants and flowers, and I intend to retain this theme throughout the course. Initially I just did a little experimental watercolour of a group of simple flowers. I liked the result and followed it up by a larger piece. I much preferred my first picture, probably due to its miniature size and colours.

Having chosen to develop her ideas through textiles, for which she felt a much greater affinity than painting, she began to incorporate her observations of plants and flowers into her work in an increasingly systematic manner. In thinking about her written topic, she was conscious that she wanted to relate her chosen study to these practically-based concerns.

This term we have also had to give in our intended written examination project. My title is 'Use of flora in painting and its symbolism'. I think that I am going to study the Pre-Raphaelites, especially Millais and Hunt. I wrote off to a number of galleries, and have received replies from most. This work also incorporates itself with my practical work.

Not process-wise, of course, but certainly in terms of content. At the same time she embarked upon another textiles piece.

Just before we broke up for the summer holidays I dyed a piece of cotton using purple, turquoise and green, producing a mottled effect. Working off some earlier drawings of natural forms, I executed two lino-cuts, one of a leaf, the other of a flower. Once my dyed material was dry, I printed upon it with the lino in red, blue and green.

She took home a sewing machine 'with the intention of working upon the fabric' during the holidays. 'Once I had padded it, I worked into the veins of the leaves and flowers using a variety of threads ... using both zigzag and straight stitch. The sewing produced the desired effect, i.e. to make the surface raised and textured. Afterwards I handsewed on beads of gold, silver and more subtle shades.' On returning to College, she incorporated the '3-D leaves I had made', which were similar in shape to a waterlily. 'These were green, and really set the piece of work off, being sewn in strategic places. I am extremely pleased by the completed piece of embroidery, and intend it to be non-functional, except as a wall-hanging.'

Meanwhile, she had also begun her preparations for her written study, again seeing the summer holidays as providing an excellent research period to enable her to find out more about this 'group of artists who aimed to portray the absolute reality of nature and its colours.' Besides her personal liking for their paintings, she also felt 'that they would be beneficial in my own artwork as a reference to which I can associate.' A week in London would provide an ideal opportunity to see a group of Pre-Raphaelite paintings in the original, and she undertook research in anticipation.

> Throughout the summer holidays I continually researched the topic at Drumcroon Education Art Centre and Wigan Library.... On 4th August I went to these libraries and did some preliminary study — gleaning information on who exactly the Pre-Raphaelites were, their aims, history, etc. and, more importantly, to discover just what paintings were available for me to see in this country. I noted all the relevant books in the libraries, including page numbers and references.

Three days later her studies were continuing, but now in front of the paintings themselves in the Tate Gallery in London.

> The 7th–13th August I spent in London, which provided me with an excellent opportunity to view the Pre-Raphaelite paintings which were in the Tate Gallery (where I spent three days) ... making extensive notes on the content, form, process and mood of the following paintings: —
>
> 1 'Ophelia' by John Everett Millais.
> 2 'April Love' — Arthur Hughes.
> 3 'Our English Coasts' — Holman Hunt.
> 4 'The Girlhood of the Mary Virgin' — Rossetti.

The 'Plan of Procedure' which has to be prepared as a part of the study provides us with more insight into her approaches to note-taking.

> I noted the content, form, process and mood. I made detailed notes on the colour values, recording the exact colour (e.g. pine green, carnation pink) and I noted the thickness/quality of the paint. I also recorded where the paintings were situated, their frames and any other information that a mere reproduction is unable to produce.

The notes are extraordinary in their thoroughness and evidence of intense scrutiny and observation. Her most beloved Pre-Raphaelite painting rapidly became Millais' 'Ophelia', and some extracts from the notes for that painting will have to suffice in conveying something of their flavour:

> Tuesday, 8th August, 1989 — Tate Gallery.
> 'OPHELIA' 1851–2 — John Everett Millais (1829–96).
> Oil on canvas 76.2 × 111.8cms./30 × 40ins.
> Presented by Sir Henry Tate, 1894.
> Situated at the centre of the longer wall between Arthur Hughes'
> 'April Love' to the left, and Walter Howell Deverell's 'A Pet' (right).
> Painting surrounded by an impressive gilt frame. Painting rectangular shaped, except the top corners are rounded.
> *Face:* — glassy eyed, (blue), rosy lipped — mouth agape, upper teeth showing. The skin possesses subtle tints of pink on the cheeks, palest tints of moss green around the mouth, chin and forehead.
> *Dress:* — looks antique. Violety grey, hints of mulberry and storm grey/ blue. Lace bodice, intricate and fragile-looking, flowery design lace also apparent on the skirt of the dress, though the design peters out as the sides of the dress become submerged in the water.
> *Hair:* — long, auburn, floating wispily in the water.
> *Water:* — deep, midnight blue at the extreme left. As it becomes shallower, i.e. around the figure, it becomes transparent, lighter. Some areas possess luminosity, others seem murky and forbidding. Aquamarine, midnight blue.

She also deals with the 'Long grasses/reeds' (9 lines), 'Upper bank' (6) and the 'Top left' (also 6 lines), but is particularly interesting in what she has to say about:

> *Lower bank:* — Startling luminosity of colour. Tiny strokes of green: — leaf, mint, pine, olive, cucumber, moss green, mingles with rusty reds, mustard, and hints of similar shades of blues and greens that are evident in the water. Each tiny brushstroke mingles in, though evidently attention is focussed on the shape of the foliage, right in the centre, in olive green. Continuing along the bank and it seems that the foliage is lying down flat. Reeds? Here the predominance of green diminishes, and the teak browns and mustard yellows emerge. (Close inspection reveals that the greens are still there, but are underneath.)

It is when she moves on to the final section of the notes that her background research prior to the visit clearly affects her looking, for she reveals an unhesitating knowledge as to what the many flowers in this section symbolize.

> *Upper right:* — No less detailed, yet a different kind of foliage (to that of the top left) — much more flowery and decorative. Immaculately done, with extreme precision — each tiny leaf carefully portrayed. Replica of nature and its colours. Lots of plants and flowers.
> Daisies (right hand) sunshine yellow centre, delicate ivory petals.
> Purple loosestrife. Difficult to see brushstrokes.

PLATE 24. Mysterious, sad, alluring yet beautiful, 'Ophelia' became Amanda's favourite painting

Pansies floating on dress — symbolises thought, love-in-vain, scarlet red.

Chain of violets around Ophelia's neck — symbolise faithfulness, chastity, and death of the young — navy/purple blooms and touches of sky-blue.

Roses near cheek and edge of dress — strawberry pink, mulberry dashes and a delicate pink, almost white.

Poppy next to daisies — death.

Faded meadowsweet — (uselessness) — palest of pink with the occasional touch of cornflower blue and lilac, yellow centre.

Forget-me-nots — lilac, sky-blue, more faded in the foreground.

Though she indicates that she studies the works noting the content, form, process and mood, she stresses that she bears these in mind but does not separate her observations under these headings — except for mood, which she usually considers in its own right at some point. With 'Ophelia' she concludes with a brief reference not only to mood, but also to process:

PROCESS. Texture: — smooth in places, though in others it is possible to detect thicker areas of paint — slightly raised surface. It undoubtedly has a photographic quality, so accurately is the scene depicted and nature's colours conveyed.

MOOD. The painting has a quality that draws you to it — mysterious, alluring, sad yet beautiful — the idyllic, perfect place to die.

Back in the north-west, she was soon in the Drumcroon Library again, this time substantiating her firsthand observations and studies. She made notes about the location, Elizabeth Siddal — the model for Ophelia, exactly when the painting was begun and completed, etc., noting down two specific quotes about the combination of a 'Shakespearean subject with a Ruskinian intensity of natural observation' and the fact, to be repeated many times, 'that the idea of painting the mad Ophelia drowning was highly original at the time.' Her Tate studies were also replicated in the Manchester City Art Gallery, 'where I studied 1) 'Hylas and the Nymphs' — Waterhouse. 2) 'The Hireling Shepherd' — Hunt.' She continues (on 16 October 1989): 'Last weekend I wrote up my chapter on 'Ophelia' and handed it in for marking today. The project is to be completed by 1st February, 1990, and I feel confident that I will meet this deadline.'

Her 'Assessment Review' then moves back to her practical work, but let us first move to the chapter on Ophelia while the evidence of the gallery-made notes is still fresh in the mind. Besides incorporating the factual information already noted, she recounts what had happened in the play 'Hamlet' to cause Ophelia to be in that situation and adds information about Elizabeth Siddal posing: 'The bath water was heated by lamps situated underneath the tub, and according to J.G. Millais, the lamps once went out, and consequently Elizabeth contracted a severe cold, and Millais was forced to pay the medical bills by her extremely irate father.' As she gets fully into her stride, though, the worth of her gallery notes is clearly evident from the fifth paragraph onwards.

The painting is composed of Ophelia floating in the river which is surrounded by various kinds of foliage. Millais has endeavoured to capture her glassy-eyed appearance, and the subtle tints of pink and pale moss green on the chin, forehead and around the mouth make me believe that at this moment of depiction, Ophelia was still actually alive, and the position of the hands also contribute to this personal view.

The lovely antique dress which Elizabeth Siddal is wearing was bought by Millais for the price of four pounds. An intricate, fragile-looking lace covers the dress, which is flowered all over by silver embroidery. The outfit is generally a violety-grey colour, yet in some areas a hint of mulberry and a storm grey-blue is apparent. Around the figure the water possesses a degree of luminosity, and the design of the lace peters out as the dress becomes submerged in the transparent shallower water. In other areas the deep midnight blue seems murky and somewhat forbidding. The dress initially helps Ophelia to keep afloat,

'Her clothes spread wide,
And mermaid-like, awhile they bore her up' (Act IV, Scene vii)

acting as a sort of parachute, but unfortunately it inevitably also aided in her death,

'Till that her garments, heavy with their drink,
    Pull'd the wretch from her melodious lay,
    To muddy death.' (Act IV, Scene vii).

Surrounding the figure are huge masses of greenery and flora, which make it an ideal choice for my topic. When the flowers are interpreted symbolically, the whole painting can be read in a similar fashion almost as a piece of writing.

The lower bank is a startling luminosity of colour, and is composed mainly of weeds, which undoubtedly attributed to Ophelia's death, probably becoming entangled with her dress and limbs and gradually pulling her down. Close inspection reveals that Millais painted this area in tiny strokes of paint, a most painstakingly slow job. The tiny strokes of mint, pine, olive, moss and cucumber greens mingle in with occasional strokes of rusty red and mustard. The rusty red is also used to colour the robin's breast....

She describes the reeds to the left and how they are used to connect the upper and lower banks, while their roots are just visible though submerged in the water. 'The upper left bank consists of dense, thick foliage, and I interpreted it to be a fallen tree, for the branches appear tangled and inpenetrable. The trunk is executed in deep rich earthy browns, and the texture is effectively conveyed using deep purple paint.' Amanda finds the 'marvellous detail of this painting' to be 'quite unbelievable' and 'so accurate of nature that it has a photographic quality.' She goes on to say that 'Ophelia' 'contains much symbolic meaning' with the dozens of flowers painted with 'the most painstaking botanical fidelity'. She continues,

In some areas the flora stands out as if embroidered on the bed of weeds and grassy water plants in which the woman floats. When the flora is interpreted the whole painting comes alive and each flower has its own significance.

The chain of violets around Ophelia's neck are purple blooms with tiny areas of navy and sky-blue. In Act IV, scene v, Ophelia speaks of violets that,

'withered all when my father died'.

Thus an image is formed which associates violets with faithfulness. Violets, however, can simultaneously symbolise chastity and the death of the young, all of which we can associate with Ophelia.

In the same scene, Ophelia also mentions the pansies amongst the flowers that she has gathered in the fields. Thus Millais has incorporated the pansy in his depiction of Ophelia's death, and has painted it a scarlet red. The pansy can symbolise both thought and love in vain.

The roses near her cheek and at the edge of her dress, and the fieldrose on the bank, may be referring to her brother, Laertes, calling her 'rose of May' in Act IV, scene v. The roses in the water are a delicious strawberry pink, possessing also the occasional splash of mulberry red and a most delicate pink, almost white. The rose is known as the most beautiful of blooms with an exquisite scent.

The purple loosestrife in the upper right corner was probably interpreted by Millais from the 'long purple' in the text, although in actual fact Shakespeare meant the early purple orchid.

The daisies near Ophelia's right hand are delicately portrayed, possessing a sunshine yellow centre and ivory coloured petals. They represent innocence (and the willow and the nettle also in this area symbolise forsaken love and pain).

Amanda observes that by 'interpreting Shakespeare's blooms we are able to construct an accurate picture of Ophelia's wretched thoughts and emotions.' Those left are Millais' rather than Shakespeare's. The poppy, attribute of the Greek God of sleep, 'is also interpreted as meaning death. The forget-me-nots symbolise what the name suggests.'

These have been painted in a lilac and sky-blue, which gradually becomes paler in the foreground. The faded meadowsweet to the left of the purple loosestrife symbolises uselessness and has been executed by Millais in pale pink with the occasional stroke of cornflower blue and lilac, with a subtle yellow centre.

According to Tennyson, she continues, daffodils symbolizing delusive hope had been painted out on the poet's advice, because they would not be in flower in company with the rest, being out of season. Amanda concludes:

'Ophelia' by John Everett Millais is one of my favourite paintings due to its delicacy and accurate portrayal of nature. It is simultaneously mysterious, sad, alluring, yet beautiful, and I view its location to be idyllic, a perfect place to choose to die. Ophelia's last moments alive would have been beautiful — the sight of the flowers, the smell of the scent, the sounds of the river and the robin.

The value of her gallery-made notes as well as her background research does not need labouring; it has sometimes been possible to include whole phrases unaltered.

While working on this chapter, she was also engaged in her next embroidery piece for which she 'received inspiration at an embroidery exhibition at the Turnpike Gallery, Leigh.' Amongst other works, she was 'particularly impressed' by Janet Ledsham's 'Sunshine and Shadows', which was an 'interpretation of her life; the good times and the bad, using colour symbolically.'

It was constructed on a grid system, each window taken up by a panel of felt into which various dried flowers were arranged. This piece of work corresponded nicely with my already half-formed idea of working with a trellis. Originally I intended to place panels of embroidery into strategic 'windows' but I have started to construct a variety of 3-D flower forms.

Taking the machine home again, she constructed a sufficient number of flowers like a hydrangea with four petals sewed together and threaded through with wire to arrange them into 'a half-spherical shape'. She expresses dismay, however, at the inordinate length of time it takes to construct them.

Two months later (18 December 1989) it was almost completed, however, and comprised five panels in different tones of green, 'ranging from an olive/ moss green to a light green', the trellis itself being made of varnished wood yet 'largely concealed by the 3-D flowers and pieces of material which I have wrapped around the frame'. There are basically three types of flower, of which the smallest 'ironically took by far the longest to construct and these pepper the frame in various areas.' 'I think that the trellis has been successful.... I'm also pleased by the fact that my practical work has a close connection with my written project.... As I am studying the Pre-Raphaelites, and thus obviously like and admire their work, my work will reflect this.' She also likes the decorative frames that surround their work, and so 'I did a small, experimental embroidery and also executed a decorative frame which was arched.' The trellis being in low-relief indicates the need for further progress in this field, and 'in the future I plan to make a structure. As yet I am unaware of the design, and plan to experiment before I commence anything major.' This eventually took the form of a three-dimensional metal structure through which Amanda entwined her flower forms.

A final word about the trellis structure appears in her 'Study' in the chapter devoted to Rossetti's 'The Girlhood of the Mary Virgin', in which use is also made of a trellis.

> Also in keeping with my topic, the vine must also be studied and interpreted. Executed in deep, rich greens, the many leaves which travel the trellis in the shape of a cross, refer to the coming of Christ. As well as being symbolically significant, the vine is quite decorative, especially when viewed against the background of the deep blue sky. In my personal artwork I have designed a trellis (perhaps subconsciously influenced by this painting), which I have decorated with embroidered panels and flowers. Around the framework I have wrapped different materials, and I discovered that the colour of these fabrics affected the overall piece. Similarly I believe that Rossetti made a conscious effort to place the trellis in his painting against such a background, thus achieving the richness of colour.

Here, surely, is evidence of Amanda's practical concerns leading her to insights about Rossetti's thoughts and working procedures which are at a much more significant level than would be achieved through teacher-devised exercises aimed at affirming what is being taught through appreciation sessions on the Pre-Raphaelites.

She has obviously researched the Pre-Raphaelites out of interest and love born of related concerns, and is well-read. Her responses to 'Ophelia' experienced in the original are of a personalized nature, revealing the detailed nature of her investigations into that work and its content, but also they are fully imbued with all the intensity of adolescence. The Pre-Raphaelites can have a special appeal to the young adolescent, but when I was a student, the Pre-Raphaelites were held in such contempt that study of them was discouraged, even though they were

PLATE 25. Amanda's trellis, perhaps subconsciously influenced by that in a Rossetti, also drew upon qualities discerned in contemporary embroideries viewed at the Leigh Turnpike Gallery

particularly well represented in the city art gallery. Amanda's own practical work had led her to them by a natural route, and in her 'Study' she reveals an affection for their works which reflects her having 'discovered' them through personal needs and concerns; it is a generous course which offers young people sufficient scope to identify those artists and works which are relevant to them, irrespective of teachers' preferences. The process frequently becomes two-way, as in Amanda's case, with qualities she discerns in the Pre-Raphaelites — and in contemporary works — in turn informing her own practice. Considerable teaching skills and forethought, as well as flexibility while thinking on one's feet, are required in the devising of courses which are rigorously structured and yet generous enough in scope to enable students to identify interests and locate themselves within the broad cultural tradition. What Amanda reveals is at a far remove from the predictability of response which will invariably result from the exercises recommended by Ralph Smith (see Chapter 7).

Amanda discerns within Pre-Raphaelite art qualities which she sees as being a precious record of disappearing nature. Victoria likewise picks up on ecological concerns in relation to two contemporary sculptors — Andy Goldsworthy and David Nash.

Victoria and 'The Art of Nature'

Nature is humankind's key link to survival, so if we abuse it, surely all we would be doing would be securing the fate of the future of humankind. That is why it is so important for us to recognise the beauty of nature. In realising this, sculptors, such as Goldsworthy, explore nature and reveal it to us in such a way that we are more aware of our environment....[3]

These words appear in Victoria's 'Personal Study', 'The Art of Nature', in which she studies the works of Andy Goldsworthy and David Nash, many of whose

PLATE 26. In her A-level assignment Amanda successfully combined a wide range of processes and media (handmade paper, porcelain, embroidery, etc.) with her interest in her subject matter

PLATE 27. A detail of Amanda's A-level assignment

works are naturally located within the landscape rather than in the art gallery. It was her personal interests and concerns, of a long-term nature, which inevitably drew her to these and related artists.

Since I was young I have always been interested in nature, and in such a way that it reflects through and into my own work. At first it was not so apparent, but gradually my practical work all seemed to be based in natural forms. In Art History, when studying artists, it was always those who took nature as the main theme in their work who appealed to me most. It seemed obvious that when I chose my sculptors, I would choose those for whom nature was a critical motivating factor in the production of their work.

Through this long-standing interest in nature, and as a committed young art maker herself, she feels a close affinity with her chosen artists in ways which extend far beyond mere interest in techniques and outward appearance.

> Not only do I enjoy their work, but I admire their philosophy of art which is based in a sensitivity for the natural forms around us and also their abilities and sensitivity when working with such elements....
>
> 1　'I find myself drawn into the joys and blows of nature, worn down and regenerated; broken off and reunited; a dormant faith revived in the new growth old wood.' (David Nash)
> 2　'When historians look back I hope they'll see the art of people like me as the result of the time when we reassessed our relationship with the land, and began to value it in a way that it hasn't been valued for a very long time.' (Andy Goldsworthy)

Victoria is fully aware that Goldsworthy's distinctive leaf sculptures are based upon, and correspond to, the basic forms and structures of nature.

> By folding, twisting, weaving and pinning the leaves together with thorns, his amazing creations from nature arise. The veins of the leaves provide the skeleton of the sculpture which, as it does in our bodies, gives stability and strength. In over-lapping and laying the leaves in a circular pattern, cones, spheres, holes and other incredible leaf formations are created.

Le Corbusier stated that he had 'a soft spot for shells'. The shell is pure harmony and its concept is singular, he said. 'Its development is either the sunburst or the spiral, inside and outside.' These and similar qualities are discernible in Goldsworthy's work, and Victoria discovers many of these in a sculptural form constructed from chestnut leaves.

> This particular sculpture conveys to me the idea of a pod or shell, which has split open. Goldsworthy has carefully arranged and pinned the leaves by using thorns and small pieces of broken twigs, to create a sphere-like object. The split along the side enables you to see clearly through to the inside, which has a totally different surface to that of the outside. Here the smooth, flat, shiny, green surfaces of the leaves, create a deep velvet-like covering for the interior, making it warm and inviting. You could imagine an animal climbing in for comfort. All the main veins on the leaves are showing on the outside of the magnificent leaf sculpture, running parallel to one another. They seem to create a cupping-like formation, as though protecting something precious inside.

One of his works leads Victoria to wider speculation about nature than its more obvious outward appearances.

> Numerous patterns and shapes can be produced from leaves, and with the pattern of nature being circular, following the seasons in a year,

many of Goldsworthy's two dimensional leaf forms are circular also, or of a spiralling nature.

In one year the position of the sun in the sky is followed by all the living plants. They depend on the sun for their life. As we look at the bark of some trees it is evident how it twists and spirals up as it has grown throughout the years. Such movements of nature's elements are expressed in Goldsworthy's works.

An example of a circular and spiralling formation is created from rhododendron leaves, which, being smaller than the large chestnut's leaves, allow greater precision which is needed to create such an image.

The overall form is a large circle created from the leaves, about two and a half metres in diameter, with a small hole in the centre; this is where Goldsworthy started his creation. By working the leaves outwards Goldsworthy has produced this strange and mysterious art work, which, although it is two dimensional, gives us the sensation of looking down a tunnel, with an entrance at its far end, into which daylight is entering. Such a feeling has been created by smaller-scale leaves being used first at the centre of the form and laid closely together. They become progressively larger and more spaced apart the further out from the centre they are positioned.

The gently spiralling action produces a peaceful image as the mass carpet of leaves look cool and creates a soft appearance. The many shades of green are used to full effect against each other and in presenting both sides of the leaves towards us, Goldsworthy stretches possibilities further as he shows us the varying textures of the surfaces. When I first saw the form it was a temptation to reach out and follow the direction of the leaves with my hand. The form almost seemed to be spinning, and as I looked it took my imagination and staring for too long made me feel as though I was falling to its centre, the structure's simple power being deceptively strong.

Victoria here provides information which goes a long way towards dispelling the ingrained notion that studying art, in contrast to making it, is passive. She provides potent evidence of the physicality which engaging with art works in the original can involve. A description of another of the artist's works leads back to heightened environmental awareness.

Goldsworthy's amazing leaf blankets full of stunning autumn colours, look spectacular hanging in the crisp morning sunlight from the branch of a tree. Again he is giving back life to the leaves which maybe only a moment ago had fallen, probably from the same tree that supports them again in their new form. United together their beauty comes over more cogently. As some areas of the leaf blanket are only one leaf thick the sunlight penetrates it easily, creating areas of translucent yellows which in turn contrast those areas where the leaves have been purposely

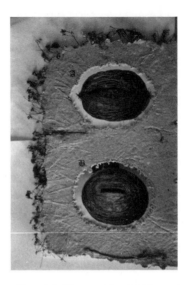

PLATE 28. A page from Victoria's 'Personal Study', illustrating how she used handmade paper embellished with seed heads to show off her photographs of Goldsworthy's work to effect

overlapped and layered to maybe three leaves' thickness. In those places deep reds and oranges are formed by the density of the colour. No glue or needle and thread holds this creation together; no man-made material has aided in the creation of such a powerful eye-catching form. All that holds the leaves in place are thorns which were maybe found from a nearby bush or perhaps sharp twigs which scatter the ground around the tree. Goldsworthy's leaf blankets hang from the tree by being pushed onto the ends of the branches where they pierce the leaves at the top of the form. This allows the sculpture to move freely in the breeze, for the bottom edge of the form is clear from the ground and can swing free from constraint, making its presence more obvious.

Goldsworthy's leaf blankets, as with almost all his other sculptures, do not last long, maybe a day or perhaps even a week depending on weather conditions.

'Once made and photographed, my sculptures are left to the mercy of the elements.'

Lasting only in photographs, taken by Goldsworthy as a record of his finished creations they do eventually 'die' and as ever return to nature to become loam or humus, to feed nature again.

It seems that wherever Goldsworthy goes a trail of ephemeral sculptures follow, maybe to the surprise of a casual passer-by who is suddenly confronted by a stunning mass of colour from a hanging leaf blanket, unaware that such beautiful colours have been surrounding him or her all the time. The momentary rejuvenation that Goldsworthy gives to the leaves causing this heightened awareness;

'I love to reveal the richness in ordinary things.'

Under the powerful impetus of Goldsworthy's art, Victoria, too, began to follow new and unusual directions. Goldsworthy expresses his aversion to his work leading to lots of 'little Goldsworthys' made by young people. However, Victoria picked up on some of the essential qualities inherent in his work without resorting to the imitation of its outward appearances. She had taken her own photographs of his and Nash's work, and to illustrate her 'Study', she mounted them on pages of handmade paper she had specially made herself. She embellished these by incorporating into them a variety of seed heads so that each sheet was individual and distinctive.

This, in turn, stimulated her to make large-scale and unusually thick sheets of paper at home, using the garage space for the purpose. Their thickness enabled her to carve out her design, in much the same way as if she were relief cutting a lino or wood block. Interestingly, her twin sister, Alison, was also studying A-level art at the same college, with relief printing using similar techniques as the main emphasis of her work. Once Victoria's design was cut out, though, she applied glue to the grooves and filled them with pot-pourri, adding — at least initially — scent to her distinctive creations. During her course she had seen slides of the beautiful marble floor tiles of Spoleto Cathedral, inspiring her to make studies of the mosaics in her local church; these provided the basis for her pot-pourri designs.

Next she translated her designs onto plywood sheets to produce an extremely large tryptych relief print, one block providing the central section and the other the two outer sections with each printed in reverse. Leonardo was insistent that all portraits were, in a sense, portraits of the artist as well as of the sitter, and the delicate, almost ethereal, pastel range colour schemes of these boldly abstract designs unmistakably embodied Victoria's gentle and sensitive nature and personality. Now at a far remove from Goldsworthy's art in any obvious sense, her use of handmade paper and 'recycled' plywood sheets was nevertheless born out of ecological concerns which had initially attracted her to the artist, and were deepened and affirmed through study of his works. She also made use of a range of techniques of which she was fully aware because they were being extensively practised by her twin sister who, in turn, began to print to effect on equally large handmade paper of her own. To satisfy their needs fully, each sister adapted means employed by the other in addition to drawing upon the works of mature artists. In these assimilation processes, each remained true to herself, giving expression to individual, clearly defined ideas.

Victoria provides further evidence of the special cyclical relationships between a particular view of nature, artist, the making of art, and its viewing which is characteristic of so much visual art as well as representing a means of charting the aesthetic field as represented by making, presenting, responding and evaluating. David Best warns against confusion of the aesthetic in nature with that in art, pointing out that '... if the same experience were given by our relation to these natural objects as by our relation to the arts, then we should not need the

PLATE 29.   Using large sheets of handmade paper, Victoria produced bold abstract designs utilizing pot-pourri

PLATE 30.   Victoria aided by her sister, Alison, holding one of the large plywood relief prints she produced based on the floor studies she made in her local church

arts to give the experience. 'Aesthetic education' could be achieved by taking children on nature walks, and encouraging them to be observant in various ways.'[4] It is an extremely important point, but the special relationship which exists between the aesthetic in nature and in the visual arts is so complex and interwoven that, in addressing the distinctions, the interconnections can also be better understood, reinforced, developed — and enjoyed. Art constantly replenishes itself by drawing upon and utilizing the experiences and sensations, along with the appearances, of the natural world. It simultaneously feeds on other art, both past and present; Cézanne set himself the task of 'doing Poussin again from nature.' In turn, it is hardly surprising that in responding to works of art, one can then become more sensitized to particular nuances and aspects of nature and the immediate world through the resulting heightened awareness.

Though certainly not exclusive to the visual arts, these interconnections are particularly acute and embodied within them to a more significant degree than appertains to other art forms. Artist and viewer alike are affected by a long history, extending back to the Lascaux Caves, in which there is a close association between artistic representations and their correspondence to the world of natural appearances; these associations are difficult to eradicate completely, even when one seeks to escape from them, whereas the musician *can* make conscious reference to sounds in nature but is not obliged to do so to any significant degree — though there are doubtless deep associations between the rhythms of life and of music, as there are between those in life and art.

In the ancient world sight was prized as the highest and noblest of the senses, a view affirmed in recent times, according to a recent TV scientific documentary, by scientific tests into the workings of the brain which indicate that 80 per cent or so of all we know and understand emanates directly from the sense of sight. Perhaps the main aim to be found in virtually all art and design syllabuses, that of developing pupils' visual awareness to its full potential, should be the most valued and carefully cultivated in the whole school programme!

Leonardo also emphasized the pre-eminent importance of the sense of sight, in the context of explaining that all our knowledge has its origins in the senses. 'The eye which is the window of the soul is the chief organ whereby the understanding can have the most complete and magnificent view of the infinite works of nature.'[5] He also maintained that '... the art of painting includes in its domain all visible things ... the painter's mind must of necessity enter into nature's mind in order to act as an interpreter between nature and art.' Many important issues can be seen to revolve around the relationships between art, nature and heightened environmental awareness. Victoria brings us right back to the concept of heightened environmental awareness, that important aspect of the illuminating experience which connects art to nature in special ways.

Notes

1   *The Arts in School, op. cit.*, p. 40.
2   All the extracts used in this part of the chapter are from the student's 'Personal Study' (1990) or from her 'Personal Appraisals' written during the year 1989–90.
3   All the extracts used in this part of the chapter are taken from the student's 'Personal Study' (1990).
4   David Best (1990) *Arts in Schools: A Critical Time*, The Birmingham Institute of Art and Design, an NSEAD Occasional Publication, p. 3.
5   Richter, *op. cit.*, p. 4.

Chapter 7

Art, Nature and Heightened Environmental Awareness

How it happens now that the work of Vincent Van Gogh immediately seized me, with a spontaneity and intensity that surprised even myself — so that I am hardly able to clear the after images of his works from my mind, so that I see his colors in objects everywhere around me, so that I am surprisingly able to see beauty where I never saw beauty before — that I do not understand. (Frederick van Eden, 1890).[1]

Special Responses to Nature through Art

1890 was the year of van Gogh's death and his work was still unknown to the wider public. In his first unexpected encounter with the artist's paintings, van Eden — never having previously even heard of him — provides a description of the moment which bears all the hallmarks of the 'Illuminating Experience'. As I outlined in Chapter 3, this is when, through a particular experience, previously held attitudes about or towards the art form are shattered or significantly modified. Though the experience is of an essentially emotional — sometimes even disturbing — nature, it is by no means devoid of cognitive elements. When it occurs in its most profound forms, the recipient will frequently comment on having lost sense of time and place: 'it was enjoyable, it just flew past ... it didn't seem like an hour and a half — more like 10 minutes'; 'your attention was drawn to it. That created an almost unreal atmosphere — a sort of escapist feeling.'[2]

While modifying previously held attitudes, it can also be highly motivating, causing an individual to want to know and to embark on a voyage of discovery. One student recounts, for example, how she now visits galleries wherever and whenever she can. But she remembers playing scrabble with her sister, bored out of her mind, in the National Gallery. A few months later, though, she describes herself as 'swimming in a world of colour' in the Monet waterlily rooms in the Orangerie in Paris.[3] The motivation generated through the Illuminating Experience is of the utmost educational significance.

Equally important, as a potential bridging link between the study of art and its practice, is the heightened environmental awareness which can also be generated; something of what has been experienced within the art gallery affects

PLATE 31. The artist helps us to see the familiar afresh; a detail of one of Ian Murphy's Wigan Parish Church series

PLATE 32. In his capacity as a Drumcroon-based artist, Ian also provides young people with opportunities to explore remote and dramatic aspects of nature: a pupil sketching during a residential week at Wigan's Lake Coniston centre

the way we subsequently see the everyday world around us once outside the gallery. Van Eden provides a vivid illustration of this phenomenon. After seeing van Gogh's paintings he suddenly sees his colours in objects everywhere around him, and he is surprised to discover that he is now able to see beauty where he was never aware of it before. In other words, the ordinary and the mundane have been transformed by becoming imbued with aspects of van Gogh's vision and artistic practice. As a consequence, the young student who has been dutifully working away in an honest but routine manner can, quite suddenly, find new impetus and higher levels of motivation born out of what has now become significant in life and nature. One student describes how, 'before, you'd just see something outside like the buildings, and you'd just draw that. You look at things differently now. Things that you wouldn't have found interesting before, now you do. It's changed the way that I look at things!'[4]

The way an artist looks at things, and assimilates these experiences, can lead to them being given expression through metaphor and analogy, playing on associations between art and life in unexpected but revealing ways. Giorgio Morandi rarely left Bologna and its immediate environs throughout the whole of his life, and is well known as a master of small-scale canvases of bottles. His intimate knowledge and love of his native city is nevertheless richly embodied within these paintings:

> Morandi said that even a still life is architecture, and his still lifes are like nothing so much as the architecture of Bologna. The tall thin bottles remind us that Bologna was known as the city of a hundred towers: two leaning towers (quietly upstaging Pisa) still dominate the city centre. The columns and arches of Bologna's arcades make rectangles and semi-circles as abstract as the geometry of Morandi's paintings. Bologna is like nowhere else. It has fine individual buildings but what makes the city so extraordinary is the place as a whole, and what gives it its unique and lovely cohesiveness is the arcades (the portici).[5]

The importance of heightened environmental awareness cannot be over-emphasized, bringing together, as it does, the two worlds of art and nature. Above all other art forms, the visual arts have enjoyed a particularly close relationship with nature, and feelings of an obligation to record, imitate and interpret it extend back to the extraordinary representations of animals and their movements achieved in the Lascaux Caves. Even the artist who consciously chooses the path of non-figuration does so in the certain knowledge that a majority of those viewing the resulting works will still seek to find associations with nature, discovering the horizon in the main horizontal — as the word suggests — for example. The artist, by virtue of being steeped in the study of nature's shapes, forms and colours, will likewise draw upon this stored reservoir of memories and sensations — however subconsciously.

It is possible to go even further by suggesting that it is the artist who has played the major role in determining how we actually see and look at the world. Clemenceau firmly believed, writing in the artist's lifetime, that Monet

> ... took a great step for us, towards the representation of the world and its elements, by light distributions that correspond to vibratory waves

such as science is revealing to us.... The genius of Monet has led us to a no less comparable progression in our sensations of the world, which we shall always have to account for, no matter what the future of our assimilations may be....[6]

Monet, of course, is but one noteworthy example in a line of artists extending through time and across places and cultures.

Nature as Stimulus for the Imagination

In addition, the visual arts — dealing as they do with all the major life issues which every art form addresses — are to do with inner and imaginative worlds, to do with profound thoughts, feelings and emotions. One of the strange, often unwritten, assumptions of art and design education, highlighted by Simpson in relation to the 'Visual Studies' movement, is that of treating objective study as being distinct from, and unrelated to, the use of the imagination. One sometimes still comes across school courses in which 'doing imaginative work' is a clear component — even accompanied by provision of lists of 'imaginative' topics — and divorced from the observational study which takes place elsewhere in the curriculum in prescribed slots. In reality, the continuous and rigorous study of the visual world can and should be one of the most fundamental means whereby the imagination is stimulated and nurtured. Leonardo maintained that:

> ... you must know that you cannot be a good painter unless you are universal master to represent by your art every kind of form produced by nature. And this you will not know how to do unless you see them and retain them in your mind. Therefore as you walk through the fields turn your attention to the various objects and look now at this thing and now at that, collecting a store of diverse facts selected and chosen from those of less value.[7]

Not only that, but he proffers further advice designed to ensure further retention in the mind's eye of what has been observed.

> I have found in my own experience that it is of no small benefit when you lie in bed in the dark to go over again in the imagination the outlines of the forms you have been studying or of other noteworthy things conceived by subtle speculation; and this is certainly a praiseworthy exercise and useful in impressing things on the memory.

That he is not just talking about remembering these things in a narrow and purely literal sense but as a means of stimulating the imagination is left in no doubt whatsoever through his additional advice, advocating that we:

> Look at walls splashed with a number of stains, or stones of various mixed colours. If you have to invent some scene, you can see these resemblances to a number of landscapes, adorned with mountains, rivers, rocks, trees, great plains, valleys and hills in various ways. Also

you can see various battles, and lively postures of strange figures, expressions on faces, costumes and an infinite number of things ... do not despise my opinion, when I remind you that it should not be hard for you to stop sometimes and look into the stains of walls, or ashes of a fire, or clouds, or mud or like places, in which, if you consider them well, you may find really marvellous ideas.[8]

By these means, he insists, the mind of the painter can be '... stimulated to new discoveries, the composition of battles of animals and men, various compositions of landscapes and monstrous things, such as devils and similar things, which may bring you honour, because by indistinct things the mind is stimulated to new inventions.'

In similar vein, Max Ernst made extensive use of a 'frottage' or rubbing, technique, one which is still extensively used in schools, but which all too often remains just at the level of texture exercises. Max Ernst made use of it in such a way that:

... before his eyes these produced 'human heads, animals, battles that finish with a kiss'. 'I insist on the fact,' he affirms, 'that the drawings obtained in this way lose more and more, through a series of suggestions and transmutations ... the character of the original material and acquire the aspect of images of an unbelievable precision....'[9]

Likewise, the sketchbook is often seen as being at variance with imaginative approaches and, indeed, when the approach is that of producing homeworks of a cup and saucer, a matchbox or crumpled can, a teapot and so on, the sketchbook can become the epitomy of 'a spade being a spade' kind of objectivity. In the hands of a Henry Moore, though, it becomes something more, with him maintaining that:

One doesn't know really how any ideas come. But you can induce them by starting in the far little studio with looking at a box of pebbles. Sometimes I may scribble some doodles, as I said, in a notebook; within my mind they may be a reclining figure, or perhaps a particular subject. Then with those pebbles, or the sketches in the notebook, I sit down and something begins....[10]

He always professed that it was the human figure that interested him the most, 'but I have found principles of form and rhythm from the study of natural objects such as pebbles, rocks, bones, trees, plants etc.' Through such areas of study, the artist's imagination is constantly being nurtured and stimulated.

The reciprocal nature of the process of an artist feeding off these basic forms and structures of nature leading to that 'no less comparable progression in our sensations of the world' taking place is vividly illustrated in one young student's reponse to a piece of sculpture in her A-level 'Personal Study' on the theme 'Man, Woman and Their Sculptures'. She focuses on the works of Henry Moore and Barbara Hepworth, who came from the same region and shared similar outlooks and preoccupations. In describing the bronze 'Single Form' of 1961–63 by Hepworth, Clare highlights another important feature of the Illuminating Experience

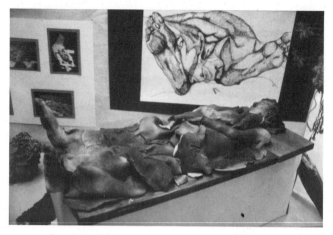

PLATE 33.   Clare's interest in Hepworth and Moore led to her making sculptures of her own; this piece is based on studies of herself

— students who might struggle to communicate ideas prior to such experiences frequently manage to write beautifully and evocatively subsequently simply because they now have something genuine and personal to say. She poetically highlights the powerful allusions to forms in nature encapsulated in the work also as a direct consequence of the artist's equally avid study of them, in keeping with Moore's attitudes to the laws and principles of form and rhythm to be found in natural objects.

> The sculpture has a basic form that makes you remember the years of your youth, when whilst walking along a beach you occasionally picked up the timeless Mussel Shells gradually being ground down by the sea and sand into soft shapes. The colour of the sculpture also makes you reminisce of the blue and green colour of the shell, giving 'Single Form' another subtle connection to nature.[11]

Sculpture, of course, invites inspection in the round — sometimes causing surprise.

> As I looked at the sculpture I thought at first that it was very dense. However, when I walked close to it I discovered that it was flat on one side.... As I looked back at my photographs (taken of it) an afterthought I had about the sculpture was that it looked like a smooth 'Skimmer' pebble that can also be found on a beach. The surface of both sculpture and pebble look like they have been worn down by the sea's constant battering of one form against another.

'Single Form', for all its associations with natural forms has, however, been made by an artist with intent, and Hepworth does not let us forget this.

> The hole in the sculpture is cut by a machine, a 'Woman' made hole, which cuts perfectly through the form. I think Barbara Hepworth pro-

duced the hole so mechanically for the purpose of making an abstract statement, to show that even though the sculpture may look like a natural form, the hole shows that a person has actually been here and made it, thus humanity works with nature.

Whenever someone looks at the sculpture they usually relate it to something they have seen in nature as I myself did. There is a realistic parallel between her naturalistic ideas of sculpture and where Hepworth has implanted her notions of abstraction onto a form which we could see every day. In doing this she changes nature into Art.

Like the painter and sculptor, the architect, too, can, should and does draw inspiration and knowledge from this intensive study of nature and natural objects. Le Corbusier was of the opinion that 'There is nothing more beautiful than a shell — it is pure harmony; it is the law of harmony. The concept is simple, singular. Its development is either the sunburst or the spiral, inside and outside; it is quite amazing.'[12] Working, as he did all the time as an architect, 'with planes, sections and cross-sections', he discovered equally important properties in bones, maintaining that:

... a bone is a wonderful thing, made to resist jumps, punches, kicks — anything you like — and to support dynamic exertions. Each particle of bone is delicate — extremely delicate — and a cross-section shows you all that. And if you look at your piece of bone and you think about it, you realize that there is a lot more you can learn from it. When you are building with concrete, a sawn-off bone is an eye-opener.

There is no need for artist and designer to go out of their way in search of the unusual and extraordinary — on the contrary.

These objects are the things you find everywhere — the most important thing is to notice them, to observe them, to recognise them and see that they are wonderful. Because for the most part they express and contain the laws of nature, and it is a fine education. It's the real education that I've always sought. The only education that I've had is looking at nature, studying it — and accepting what it teaches.

Ways in Which Art Grows out of Art

The 'only education', he says, but, as with all artists — however consciously or through subtle assimilation — this keen scrutiny of nature and its principles was counterbalanced and informed by his equally avid studies of art and architecture. A major influence on 'his formal idiom was his involvement in modern painting', which, perhaps unusually amongst recent architects, he also practised to a significant level of proficiency. Equally, though,

His formal language was based on a passionate enjoyment of two systems of form which seemed diametric opposites but were, in his view, similar: classic Doric architecture, in all its lucidity, and the clear analytic shapes of machinery....

Corbusier strove to celebrate what he called the 'White World' — the domain of clarity and precision, of exact proportion and precise materials ... 'the informed, correct and magnificent play of forms under light.' That one phrase condenses his passion for the Pentelic marble, the whitewashed Aegean walls and crystalline sea-light, amid whose Doric antiquity so much of Corbusier's imagination was shaped when he was young. [13]

During that formative stage in his life, '... he wandered around the Mediterranean, stopping off at Athens and visiting the Middle East, looking particularly at the white houses which are indigenous to the whole Mediterranean culture. His study of these houses was to be an important influence on his later work.' [14]

Moore's studies of natural forms were likewise complemented by an immersion in the world of sculpture, inevitably involving European examples but also extraordinarily wide in the cultural sources and traditions embraced, with him increasingly aware that:

... a common world-language of form is apparent in them all; through the working of instinctive sculptural sensibility, the same shapes and form relationships are used to express similar ideas at widely different places and periods in history, so that the same form-vision may be seen in a Negro and a Viking carving, a Cycladic stone figure and a Nukuoro wooden statuette. [15]

Amongst the 'greatest sculpture of the world' he includes Sumerian, early Greek, Etruscan, Ancient Mexican, Fourth and Twelfth Dynasty Egyptian, Romanesque and early Gothic, from all of which he drew inspiration at various times. Nevertheless, according to David Sylvester,

... Moore reveals a profound instinctive allegiance to the classical and Renaissance tradition. The clearest demonstration of this is his strong preference for the reclining figure as a theme.... And the reclining figure is virtually a prerogative of the European tradition.... Moore's art, then, has always been more or less involved in reconciling certain modernist assumptions with the European tradition against which modernism has rebelled; throughout most of his career he has tended to give his sculpture the sort of complexity of articulation which that tradition has nourished....

Alongside their studies of nature's basic forms and structures, therefore, both these artists — architect and sculptor — reveal evidence of complex layers of influence which the study of the art of the past and present has upon them. Some have found this idea of being influenced and affected by the work of others problematic in educational terms, such has been the degree to which they have prized the notion of individual children's natural creativity and originality. The truth of the matter is, of course, that all children are subjected to all manner of influences

PLATE 34.   A ceramic display in a high school art and design suite helps pupils develop their discriminatory powers while making them more aware of possibilities for their own work

through advertising, the media and so forth, from long before they even begin school. The real issue would seem to be how we best harness this process to educational advantage. Natural assimilation is a crucial part of the process, as an important sculptor contemporary of Moore — Jacob Epstein — seeks to clarify.

> Of course I have been influenced. No artist evolves altogether spontaneously out of nothing, and there is no such thing as an entirely clean slate. The word 'influence' however needs very careful explanation, as it is very loosely used by critics to mean anything, from merely mechanical copying.... The word 'influence', as I understand it, means a full comprehension of both mind and technique that go to the composition of a work, and a translation of that, according to the personality of the artist. A complete re-creation in fact through a new mind.[16]

In this way, he suggests, the influence of Rembrandt on van Gogh and of Ingres on Degas are very real, 'but in neither case is there a trace of copying.' Every artist 'without exception is influenced in this manner, often quite unconsciously. The word though is now dangerous through constant misusage.' Constable's assertion that, 'A self-taught artist is one taught by a very ignorant person', has already been noted. He added, 'nor did there ever exist a great artist who was so.'[17] Matisse, at the forefront of the avant-garde in his day, could nevertheless likewise declare, 'I owe my Art to all painters.'

The implications for art and design teaching in the schools sector are clear: in schools devoid of appropriate resources and without any systematic policy of organized visits to galleries, sculpture parks, artists' studios, etc., their pupils are being denied the necessary opportunities for this essential assimilation, sometimes conscious, sometimes not, to take place.

Likewise, the study of the natural world is vital, and can stimulate the imagination as well as developing powers of observation and skills in recording. Many art rooms are stimulating places, being unusually rich in resources to develop work of this kind. Regular use of the sketchbook is also vital, as this provides opportunities for pupils to explore environments which are entirely of their own choosing in response to personal needs and concerns. Through this combination of the study of art and of nature, young people can be put in touch with their inner selves in extraordinary ways; one young student describes spending a considerable time on one study, but being motivated to complete it by obsession!

The Aesthetic, Artistic and Designed

These interconnections are worth keeping in mind when considering the distinctions between aesthetic experiences to do with nature on the one hand, and through responses to works of art produced by people 'with intention' on the other. Roger Fry makes the clear distinction between qualities of 'order and variety' possessed 'in a high degree' by certain things in nature and works of art made with an 'intention of purpose'. Through this intention, the work of art can reveal something to us about ourselves which, once revealed, we recognize as having been within us, but latent, all the time. This recognition is another important characteristic of the Illuminating Experience: 'It was like a seed that was there — but it has to be triggered off', is one student's graphic encapsulation in words of this notion. In the light of many other similar testimonies by young people on the power of these experiences, it is clear that the argument can no longer be sustained that adult artists' work is 'out there', both irrelevant and potentially damaging to children's interests. Indeed, it now seems strange that it carried the weight it did for as long as it did.

In a long and fruitful life, Louis Arnaud Reid — like Fry — delved deep into these matters; he, too, similarly distinguishes between the aesthetic in nature and in art, also emphasizing that art is made with

> ... aesthetic intention (whether fully conscious intention or not) something that can be contemplated and enjoyed for its own sake, and also something which expresses and embodies in a perceived material medium values, ideas, meanings, which could not possibly be expressed and embodied — and so known — in any other way.[18]

In addition to what might be termed clearly designated 'art' works, Reid identifies a range of things capable of inducing aesthetic experiences, pondering over some which maybe fall into a grey area between art and nature. There is perhaps something of an archetypal nature about the enjoyment of natural beauty which is stimulating to all the senses. There are the broad sweeps of nature: 'The sense of the ambience of the natural world — sky, light, clouds, sea, distant horizons, the air breathed deeply, the support and smells of the earth and growing things.'[19] These, he suggests, can be a constant and unending source of joy. Homing in on the 'physically smaller aspects of nature', he draws attention to '... forms, textures, colours of trees, flowers, fruits, animals large or small ... "found" objects of every kind.' All of these are worthy of study in their own right, 'simply for what they are.'

Turning to the 'built environment' and the areas of design and craft, we are back to things made by humankind which can possess 'important aesthetic aspects', but without them necessarily being designated 'works of art'.

It is debatable whether some churches, public buildings, country mansions, gardens, whole areas like Hampstead Garden Suburb, can unambiguously be called 'works of art'. The same applies to the shapes of motor cars, fridges, kitchen and tableware, furniture.[20]

'Art and the Built Environment' focused upon even more unprepossessing aspects of the urban and built environments and vernacular architecture, often finding distinctive and aesthetic dimensions there. Will technology, as a 'new' National Curriculum area, faciliate the extension of critical studies approaches and strategies across this whole spectrum of the built, manufactured and designed worlds to which Reid draws attention? Will it enable pupils better to make all manner of connections between their own practice and this vast and extensive world of made objects which might then, in turn, be better understood and made more relevant through heightening of awareness?

Reid's own description of an admittedly somewhat special spoon reveals details and inherent qualities which all too frequently pass unnoticed and are taken for granted in the hurly-burly of life. This is especially so when the object in question is functional and not 'officially' art with the added care in presentation to which it then becomes entitled. 'Perhaps a utensil has never been so affectionately described', suggests Ralph Smith.

The lines are smooth, easy, liquid, flowing; the handle is deliciously curved, like the tail of a leopard. And strangely, without contradiction, the leopard's tail is finished with little raised nodules like small grapes. It is a queer mixture of a leaf and a leopard. The texture is grey and dull like river mist, and is lit with soft lights shining out of it like the moon out of a misty sky. The sheen is white-grey satin, the bowl is delicately shaped with overturning fastidiously pointed fronds; it is restrained and shallow, yet large enough to be generous. The lines are fine and sharp, with clear edges.[21]

He is fully aware that such a fulsome description may sound absurd and incongruous, 'But if you hold the spoon in your hand, you feel it is a kind of poem, which in a strange way unites all these, and many other, values into a single whole. You feel as you see it that you are living in a gracious world, full of loveliness and delight.' Clearly this is a special spoon worthy of particular note. But is there not a whole range of readily available manufactured objects of varying quality which could be brought into schools on a regular basis with a view to inviting considered study? Could not the inevitably varying qualities be turned to account by leading to the forming of judgments, discrimination, and a realization as to why one thing might be preferred to another? Could this process not lead to a greater consciousness and awareness of the things that help make up our everyday world?

This discriminating process could also focus on the various aspects of 'modern architecture' which also make up the environment which young people inhabit. Though so-called 'modern architecture' has had such a bad press of late that prospective clients are deterred from approaching certain architects, there are modern buildings which undoubtedly warrant serious consideration, and which deserve a better fate than to be stereotypically lumped together with the most

PLATE 35   Increasing awareness of the designed world; Ian Horne in residence at Golborne
High School, with his Sock Shop designs, fascinating to pupils, on display

misconceived concrete blocks of the 1960s, inhuman in scale and designed without consideration of local communities and the environment. Across the art,
design and technology spectrum there should be scope for young people to
address this area; but this will only begin to happen to any adequate degree if the
expertise in critical studies which art and design teachers are now beginning to
manifest is allowed scope to involve technology, an area where such expertise has
traditionally been sadly lacking. In other words, as the National Curriculum dust
begins to settle, it is essential that art and design teachers are allowed the necessary time and space both to meet their subject-specific foundation obligations *and*
to make a positive contribution to technology with additional time allowed; no
teacher, however brilliant, should be expected to shoulder the burden of constantly having to meet two sets of distinct and different — if sometimes related —
obligations.

With regard to modern architectural achievements, Stephen Gardiner highlights a satisfying fusion of architecture with nature achieved in, of all places —
one might think — an office park! The 'combination of trees and buildings fastens
the attention on detail', but gradually 'the detail and its interest, brings the eye
back to the drop-scene for the landscape' because they have been conceived 'to
have an affinity with nature'. A neutrality has been sought, but with the
contributions of others helping to bring vitality to the whole.

At Stockley, there is an astonishing example of the point: a white, steel
and glass three-storey structure backing on to the Grand Union Canal,
and it's by Norman Foster.

There is nothing neutral about this. The suddenness of its impact is
thrown up purely by an extraordinary version of glass and a powerful
expression of its enormous structure in the form of a high canopy that
has a subliminal echo of Le Corbusier's Zurich Centre, also set in a
park....

> The sheer glass wall overlooking a lake is an invention — the very strange effect, designed to reduce glare, suggests a mist rising from water. In responding to water, and the glare it creates, the image of the misting over is an evocation of its atmosphere.

> Here is a stunning example of the imagination that is unique to modern architecture. It provides, moreover, a screen of privacy for the interior is effective as a net-curtain wall; from the outside, there is no hint of the enormous space within, the vast entrance, for instance, which opens up this building to the landscape.[22]

The link is made with Corbusier, and the blending of architecture with water and landscape is a concept and ambition which has been sought by architects in many places through time. Architecture is uniquely placed finally to fuse art with nature in the most literal sense.

While princes and critics are having a field day at the expense of modern architecture, with it lumped into one amorphous whole, painters like Brendan Neiland are sensitizing us to nuances of the modern cityscape exemplified through the use of new materials and technologies. Gardiner refers to the 'silver glass wall' at Stockley, and Neiland exploits the surfaces provided by glass facades to focus upon the unexpected flux of nature to be discovered right in the heart of the built environment. To do this, he has to look upwards: 'There's a whole world going on up there', he muses. In turn, Tracey, an A-level student studying his paintings, finds her angles of vision being determined by the artist: 'Neiland often looks upwards.... Therefore when we look at his work we are thus encouraged to look up once we get outside.' Once having looked upwards, unexpected connections are to be made: 'Neiland, like Monet, sometimes achieves the feeling of motion in his paintings, particularly in the prints which feature clouds. The clouds appear to be moving past the top of the buildings.'[23] Studying the acrylic canvas 'Silhouette', she notes how

> ... the painting is made up of undulating forms as if rain is falling on the windows and distorting the reflections. This wavy effect is broken up by part of the structure of the building, which appears in the form of three lines which seem to run parallel to the top and bottom of the painting, but are, in fact, slightly diagonal. These lines play an important role as they appear to hold the rippling forms together and prevent them bleeding out and becoming 'too wild'. Such a quality Neiland would never have allowed, hence the rigid grid structure.

Such structures are both those of the modern cityscape and of a whole tradition of pictorial composition, leading Tracey to draw a further parallel with Vermeer who, like Monet, is another of Neiland's acknowledged loves.

> An obvious link between Neiland and Vermeer is the use of a grid system. In both artists' work there is a strong emphasis on straight lines, horizontal, vertical and diagonal, and this adds a sense of order. It is obvious that the forethought that has gone into such a work also compares to Neiland's method of preparation.

The dominant quality in Neiland's work which enables Tracey to place him firmly within a cultural context and tradition also enables her to relate to a dominant feature of the modern cityscape. 'All these lines are part of the basic skeleton structure of the building. Within this linear structure are more slightly angled lines, these represent the frames holding the glass in the building.'

Some Implications

Like Fry and Reid, David Best also differentiates between the aesthetic in art and nature.[24] He suggests that for clarity, and to avoid confusion, 'aesthetic' be used specifically in relation to qualities inherent in nature, and that 'artistic' be used in relation to such qualities with regard to art works. This avoids looseness in usage, but does, nevertheless, pose the problem that young people would still encounter the word 'aesthetic' in almost every art book already published. Ralph Smith, addressing the same issue, also suggests use of 'artistic', but only insofar as it would provide a useful means to 'gather up whatever the aesthetic leaves out.'[25]

Interestingly, he then moves on to what he regards as a by-product of such artistic experiences and comes very close to describing heightened environmental awareness!

> Furthermore, since the undivided attention that must be paid to artworks presupposes uncommon perceptual acumen, it seems reasonable to suppose that aesthetic experience can lead to an improved ability to notice things generally, especially their more subtle aspects. If this happens, then more of nature's qualities and more aspects of human relationships could become accessible to persons as a result of their having studied art.

This he welcomes as an undoubtedly desirable, even if not central, bonus of art study. However, he relegates in significance the pupils' own practical activities without acknowledging how these can blossom and develop in unusual and sometimes extraordinary ways under the impulse of heightened environmental awareness. 'The proper object of study in art education is the study of the art work', he asserts, and practical activities only have a function as 'learning exercises' to this end. In so relegating them, he diminishes access to the full aesthetic field of making, presenting, responding and evaluating, just as the system did when it placed undue emphasis on making at the expense of the remainder.

In the process, he also reduces the power of practical activity to function fully even at a 'learning exercises' level. Only rarely within exercise contexts will feeling and reason genuinely come together to provide the kinds of rich, involving and rigorous arts experiences for which Best so cogently argues. Yet once practical activity assumes its rightful place within a framework which includes appropriate critical studies approaches, young people demonstrate sometimes quite extraordinary capacities to make crucial connections between their own practice and that of others, to the enrichment and enhancement of both. These are of a different order than when, for example, pupils do a cubist exercise to further learning about Cubism. This purely intellectual activity fails to involve the whole person and his or her concerns.

This chapter has touched upon the significance of the rigorous study of both nature and the works of artists and designers to the built environment and functional objects. A relatively unexpected bonus of the National Curriculum would increasingly appear to be that of the visual arts imbuing technology as a foundation subject with the aesthetic. One of the proposed general aims of the new GCSE technology examinations,[26] for example, is about stimulating 'curiosity, imagination, creativity, and the ability to operate effectively in the made and natural world.' Another is to do with promoting the 'ability to communicate information and ideas through a variety of media.' Specific aims of the design and technology component emphasize 'aesthetic awareness in the context of fitness for purpose' and the development of critical faculties and the making of 'informed judgments about the appropriateness of the outcomes.' The contribution of the visual arts to these processes is not simply desirable, it is essential.

The benefits of a rigorous study of nature and of art are finally illustrated by Rosemary, a student coming to the A-level course late and after only six weeks' experience.

Looking at dried flowers through a magnifying glass was a new approach to studying natural form. I found this illuminating in that the intensity of detail which could be seen on the petals was breathtaking. The intricate patterns which the tiny rectangular petals of the chrysanthemum made gave me a determination to capture this mass on paper.... I started to use watercolours, this seemed to be the perfect medium in which to depict such delicate flowers.

At home I have been continuing to study flowers and leaves, incorporating coloured pencils and watercolours into my drawings in an attempt to give the flowers a three dimensional effect and to help the drawing to gain some of the reality of life the original possessed.... I began to understand just how difficult it is to give life to a drawing but, after initial disappointment, I realised that my drawing had a decorative quality.... I am also touched by the delicate, wistfulness of nature which was captured so beautifully in a painting of Turner's I have seen. This decorative approach is being developed as a preparation for the February examinations....

I enjoy the rich colours that I have found the watercolours producing and have received inspiration from the 'Altarpiece' by Jan Van Eyck which we have studied in Art History. The jewels he crushed and mixed into his oil paints produced such vivid, literally, ruby reds which virtually convinced me it was a photograph not a painting I was looking at. The decorative jewellery in this painting relates to my work and I hope batik or embroidery techniques will help to produce such a wealth of detail in my own style. I have used deep purples and maroons to complement fragile, nearly transparent violets in my classwork and rusty browns, brassy yellows and blood reds in studies out of college....

I love drawing natural form; it relaxes me and gives me a great feeling of fulfilment on the completion of a flower.

... I also hope to visit some art galleries to fully appreciate original works.[27]

Any worthwhile course of study in this area of the curriculum inevitably leads the pupil to original works in the art gallery.

Notes

1 Susan Alyson Stein (Ed.) (1986) *Van Gogh: A Retrospective*, New York, Hugh Lauter Levin Associates, Inc., pp. 242, 243.
2 Rod Taylor, *op. cit.*, pp. 65 and 63.
3 *Ibid.*, p. 220.
4 *Ibid.*, p. 226.
5 Richard Boston (1990) 'Gotta Whole Lotta Bottles', *The Weekend Guardian*, 24–25 November 1990.
6 *Claude Monet at the Time of Giverney* (1983) Centre Culturel du Morais, p. 188 (published on the occasion of exhibition on above theme, 6 April–31 July 1983).
7 Richter, *op. cit.*, p. 218.
8 *Ibid.*, p. 182.
9 *Max Ernst, Histoire Naturelle* (1982) Arts Council of Great Britain Catalogue (pages unnumbered).
10 *Henry Moore at the Serpentine* (1978) Arts Council of Great Britain Catalogue (pages unnumbered).
11 Student A-level 'Personal Study', 1990.
12 'Illuminations' (1987) Channel 4 TV programme on the artist, October 1987.
13 Hughes, *op. cit.*, p. 190.
14 *Discovering Art, Twentieth Century: Part 1* (1966) Paulton, Nr. Bristol, Purnell and Sons Ltd, p. 148.
15 David Sylvester, 'Introduction' to *Henry Moore at the Serpentine* (1978), *op. cit.*
16 Jacob Epstein (1931) *The Sculptor Speaks: Jacob Epstein to Arnold L. Haskell* (a series of conversations on art), London, Heineman, pp. 95, 96.
17 Ernst Gombrich (1982) *The Image and the Eye*, London, Phaidon Press Ltd., p. 230.
18 Louis Arnaud Reid (1981) 'Assessment and Aesthetic Education', in *The Aesthetic Imperative* (Ed. M. Ross), Oxford, Pergamon Press, p. 9.
19 Reid, *op. cit.*, p. 10.
20 *Ibid.*, p. 11.
21 Smith, *op. cit.,* (pages unnumbered).
22 Stephen Gardiner (1990) 'Enter Excess at Exit 4: On Stockley Park, an Office Extravaganza', *The Observer*, 11 February 1990.
23 Student A-level 'Personal Study', 1990.
24 See David Best (1985) *Feeling and Reason in the Arts*, London, George Allen and Unwin. Having distinguished between the aesthetic and artistic, Best develops the argument that, 'at least in many cases, a work of art can be considered from both the aesthetic and the artistic points of view', p. 157 (a revised version of this book will appear in the Library on Aesthetic Education).
25 Smith, *op. cit.*
26 SEAC Draft GCSE Criteria for Technology, Consultative Draft, applicable for examinations in and from 1995.
27 Student 'Personal Appraisal Statement', February 1991.

Chapter 8

The Drumcroon Education Art Centre: Policy and Issues in the Gallery Context

If you are going to take children a long way to the art gallery, if you are going to disrupt timetables, I think it has got to be an experience that they'll remember — something that is valuable to them, something which they can recall with some pleasure and feel that they really have made some breakthrough in their perception of art works. It's taking children to an art gallery for the first time that really is of great import-ance.... (Head of a Secondary Art Department)[1]

I'd always felt that galleries were wonderful resources and I'd been enjoying them for years and years. I was very conscious that most people didn't go into them ... and I felt that the sort of gallery that this should be very popular and people should feel that it was easy to come into and work on that sort of level. (Gallery Exhibition Officer)[2]

... even though the class may all be studying the same theme in the same gallery, it allows each child a personal response to a particular exhibit. This response will be partly aesthetic and partly the result of curiosity, and it will involve associations that differ from individual to individ-ual.... The enclosing classroom is becoming obsolete; the scope of the school has widened beyond its walls. Children develop in a broader environment; the surrounding world serves their schooling. (*Pterodactyls and Old Lace: Museums in Education*)[3]

Gallery and Community

The Drumcroon Education Art Centre is not just an art gallery; it is far more besides. It provides a whole range of visual arts resources within its walls, but which also progress outwards into the schools it serves. In fact, Drumcroon is probably the most original innovation of an ambitious education authority which has positively addressed the entitlement needs of all those in full-time education. Its uniqueness sometimes masks the fact that each of the strategies it employs is transferable, for all have been devised in support of the conviction that all pupils are entitled to a visual arts education designed to help them know about art as well as to make it; they are therefore relevant wherever that basic belief is shared, as Peter Abbs emphasizes.

> I associate the Drumcroon Centre with activity, with artistic making and artistic discourse. I associate it with people: with children, adolescents, teachers, artists-in-residence, educationists, visitors and people coming in from the community. I see it as a great initiative to make art central to human existence. I think its worth has now been demonstrated and the Centre should be regarded as a model to be adapted and developed by other educational authorities. In brief, a success story which in our period of cultural laisser-faire needs to be told again and again.[4]

Named after a successful turn-of-the-century racehorse, the turreted 1903 building, close to the town centre of Wigan in the urban north-west of England, was a doctor's house and surgery prior to 1980. It is open to the general public, but was conceived primarily as a much-needed resource for the 160+ schools and colleges of Metropolitan Wigan, an area with a population in the region of 320,000. The high unemployment levels of the 1980s reflect the socio-economic problems of a community which was originally founded upon the coal-mining industry, but Drumcroon was born out of a conviction that cultural deprivation was an equally serious disadvantage which had to be addressed. There is now considerable evidence to support the belief that the confidence gained by pupils through recognition that they have special talents revealed through artistic achievement washes over everything else that they do. This is reflected in external examination success terms across the curriculum, but Wigan's Director of Education believes that the real significance is in terms of how they develop as human beings. 'The arts give pupils power by enabling them to communicate.'[5] Drumcroon provides the spearhead of an authority arts policy designed to empower young people in this way.

The initial reaction of most first-time visitors to the Centre is to the richness and attractiveness of its environment. Simon Richey both conveys this response and indicates wider significances.

> When I first visited Drumcroon I was struck by the colour and abundance of it all: the proliferation of pictures on the wall, the hanging tapestries, the wood carvings and sculpture. Open any one of Drumcroon's publications today and it is these qualities that you notice first. I was aware of the Centre's role as a kind of interchange of creative influences, for many such influences are brought to bear at Drumcroon and they flow in many different directions.... All of these influences may feed back into the regular cycle of Drumcroon exhibits and sometimes you can spot them, like a family resemblance.[6]

Underpinning it all, Richey emphasizes, 'is the belief that children are entitled to the highest quality of artistic experience, both as makers and observers, and that pictures and artefacts should be a natural part of their everyday lives, there to be handled, to be liked or disliked, to be argued over, there to illuminate....'

Exhibitions are of contemporary works, but these are contextualized in such a way as to make the art of the past accessible to even the youngest of visitors.

PLATE 36.   The Artists in Wigan Schools exhibitions always provide rich and stimulating environments, fully contextualized, which are fascinating to young people of all ages

The use of current art also provides children with the opportunity to meet the artists concerned and to work with them or with others who share similar concerns. The children's own work, often related to Drumcroon stimulus, is regularly displayed within the Centre, sometimes alongside the mature art to which it was, in large measure, a response. Some of this work is produced in workshops which are part of a Drumcroon visit, much of it is produced in school subsequent to a visit, but now embedded within the curriculum. It is through this constant ebb and flow between Centre and schools that the 'interchange of creative influences', to which Richey refers, is generated.

This integration between schools' needs and gallery philosophy gives Drumcroon its special ambience, as another gallery director testifies:

> Drumcroon rather defies description; although it is called an 'education art centre' its emphasis is on educating everyone in the broadest sense through their experience of art.... Their philosophy is to consider education as an intrinsic part of their exhibition planning rather than as the kind of cultural cosmetic job, an extraneous activity hitched onto an exhibition that it so often is. Here we have the essential difference of Drumcroon from a normal art gallery, the heart of the unique atmosphere that children and adults alike who visit the centre try to articulate.[7]

Gallery windows, which afford views of a life-size shire horse made by primary pupils or the unusually shaped and vividly coloured off-loom weavings of Tadek Beutlich, help attract passers-by who want to examine or scrutinize more closely what they have glimpsed from the street. Drumcroon's influence is not simply at a local level, though; in a typical year gallery staff, school teachers and art educators visit from all parts of the country and from abroad. These include considerable numbers of PGCE art and design students attracted, according to one lecturer, not just by the attractive environment but because the Drumcroon approach seems to 'synthesise what had previously come across as disparate or even intractable ideas and issues in art and design education.' As an essential part of the course, his students employ 'strategies developed at Drumcroon, for example the Content-Form-Process-Mood model for engaging learners with art, craft or design objects.'[8]

Another lecturer, also a frequent visitor, emphasizes the degree to which Drumcroon has become a resource on a very broad basis.

> There has never been anything quite like Drumcroon in British art education. It is simply unique.

> ... it has opened up the world of contemporary art and craft to the region. More than this, it has taken on the status of a national centre, representing all that is good in educational practice in the visual arts. Day in and day out, children, teachers, parents, artists and students visit Drumcroon to see work in progress by artists and craftspeople, view important exhibitions, study or practise art or simply drink coffee in this delightful building. Drumcroon and its work in the region have set the standard against which other arts centres are measured and ... it is known by artists and educators throughout the country.[9]

What is now termed 'outreach work' is another important criterion by which art galleries are judged today. Drumcroon's outreach work is so extensive and fundamental to its workings that the very word 'Drumcroon' has assumed two meanings — one to do with the actual building and its programme, the other with everything that epitomizes Drumcroon philosophy wherever it manifests itself throughout the authority — most specifically in the form of an abundance of rich and vital children's art. This outreach work has led to close working partnerships with schools and a number of ambitious projects, such as that leading to four large murals made by primary children being permanently sited in the new Wigan Children's Library. These reveal a spontaneity and boldness of execution, yet also abundant evidence of assimilated responses and references to the work of such artists as Bonnard, Klimt, Picasso, Renoir, Millet, Cassatt and Bruegel. Having seen them in situ, a teacher from overseas discerned an unusual level of achievement made possible through the partnership principles which underpin all these initiatives.

> One of the most impressive examples I saw of child art displayed for the benefit and pleasure of the community was the 'Four Seasons' murals in the Children's Library. The history of this work and the teaching involved reads like a masterplan for successful art teaching.[10]

Two major resources essential to the realization of such ambitious projects which constitute the cornerstone of Wigan's outreach work are the Artists in Wigan Schools Scheme — Anne-Marie Quinn, the artist involved in the 'Four Seasons' project, was a founder member, starting in 1984 — and the Wigan Schools Loan Collection, begun in 1974 and now containing 1500 original works in all manner of media. These works are available to all schools and colleges, who request specific examples in relation to projects and topics as well as simply receiving works delivered on a rotation basis. Loan works therefore inform teaching situations as well as making school environments rich and stimulating. The Schools Loan Collection is a vital resource in that it provides the means whereby children can have access to original works on a daily basis throughout their school lives.

Most schools have also now had the benefit of in-depth residencies of several months' duration, necessary for the artists to have time to address whole-school populations. A number of artists in the scheme were themselves educated in Wigan, giving them a natural ability to communicate in many ways and at many levels. They recognize themselves as they used to be in the pupils with whom they now work, who likewise readily identify with artists who have travelled the same road as they are now doing. Many of Drumcroon's visitors have a desire to see these residencies in action. One, a New Zealand college lecturer, having witnessed a number of residencies, saw important implications for practice in his own country.

> Sure this has occurred in isolated spots in New Zealand, but not in the concentrated way as in Wigan. Here you have an entire community involved in the Arts, i.e. Children through Artists — Artists through Children, Parents through Children to Artists, Artists to Parents through Children, etc. The most excitement for me was gained through the observation of the children's art that came from their workshop experiences with the artists. Their work revealed an enrichment which goes beyond just acknowledging adult art through observation. At Wigan they experienced a total immersion into the wonder of Art.[11]

Exhibition Planning and Usage

The bedrock upon which all these activities are founded is, of course, the Drumcroon exhibition programme. Exhibitions have traditionally occupied half-term periods, averaging six a year of at least six weeks' duration each. As a consequence of poll tax 'capping' in 1990 the number had to be reduced to five; the criteria for designing a balanced exhibition programme are inevitably complex, and therefore are realized on a broader basis than through what is displayed in any one year. The main criteria are to be discerned within the Drumcroon Policy Statement, which is a summary of well-tried practice over many years as well as being a statement of intent. Drumcroon policy aims:

> To give all Wigan's young people — irrespective of age — their teachers and the local community access to the range, breadth and variety of the Visual Arts through the focus of contemporary makers, taking into account such issues as those of race, gender and special needs. To give further insight and understanding, the Centre provides its visitors with opportunities to engage in related practical activities, and it also attempts to place each exhibition into a contextual framework by demonstrating process through resident artists and craftspeople and through the use of secondary source material which has the potential to range across time, place and cultures.

'Range, breadth and variety' demand a balance in the work of male and female practitioners and of processes and media ranging across the whole art, craft and design spectrum. Exhibitions featuring the development, or a specific aspect, of a single artist's work are contrasted with those which focus on a theme or process — Landscape into Art, Urban Images, Intimate Settings; Wood, Clayworks, the Pure Art of the Potter. The special nature of Drumcroon inspires many artists to aid in the contextualization of exhibitions in unusual ways through the loan of stimulus material which they have collected, sketchbooks or preliminary studies and, always of particular interest, student and childhood works which have survived. The outstanding example of this is the donation to the Centre by Michael Rothenstein of his 1912–25 childhood drawings, which gave rise to the Past and Present exhibition, covering seventy-eight years of the artist's life and illustrating the significant links relating what he was doing at 4, 5 and 6 to his work at the age of 80.

The Policy Statement was formulated in early 1987 while the GCSE training booklet, which gave rise to the content, form, process, mood questions set out in Chapter 5, was also at a draft stage. Policy has subsequently been realized through the systematic application of that model. The British Relief Wood-carving exhibition was on display at the time of the GCSE workshop, and was also the first exhibition to be directly affected by use of the model, with the catalogue and teachers' notes both being reproduced in the GCSE booklet as examples. In terms of presentation, usage and content it therefore illustrates a number of important Drumcroon approaches.

Of the eighteen craftspeople featured, three had already previously exhibited at Drumcroon, with one a former sixth-form student in Wigan who had become a woodcarver via the relief printing processes begun while a sixth-former. One of the exhibitors, Emmanuel Taiwo Jegede, was African, while a number of others had strong African connections and had experience of working there. There was a range of approaches evident, some polishing the surface, others leaving evidence of the toolmarks, but the overriding impact was that of the physicality and effort required by the process. 'A sense of mystery, magic and hidden meaning pervades the exhibition. The viewer is constantly reminded of the fact that carving is an ancient tradition for many cultures and that it is capable of generating extremes of expression and emotion.'[12] There were strong narrative and story-telling elements, with echoes of ancient myths in the recurrent use of such symbols as serpents, monsters, fish, trees and fruits.

Many woodcarvers 'testify to their feelings of kinship for other practitioners, past and present, and acknowledge influences that are steeped in tradition and history. Celtic, Mediaeval, Egyptian, Classical, African, Oceanic and German Expressionist influences can all be discerned by the perceptive viewer', the catalogue recorded. Needless to say, these links were all made explicit through the presentation of book material drawn from the Drumcroon Library, which was displayed with care for maximum clarity. One immediate important bonus of the content, form, process, mood model was that a perfect sequencing and matching of catalogue statement and teachers' notes could be achieved, as the teachers' notes made clear:

The introduction to the catalogue 'sets the scene' and attempts to place the exhibition in context. The comments on the exhibition are ordered so that they relate to the four basic standpoints from which an art object can be approached, namely PROCESS, FORM, CONTENT and MOOD, in the belief that this might establish criteria for profitable engagement with original works. Information relating to those artists who are represented in the Schools Loan Collection could be used in conjunction with original works in the classroom and may also prepare pupils in advance of any meeting with either Anthony Lysycia or Ted Roocroft in the Centre.[13]

Ted Roocroft worked in the Centre for one day a week, transforming a branch of wood into a pig sculpture to the delight of numerous young visitors who had fond memories of his thirty or so pig sculptures which had graced his earlier Drumcroon exhibition. In the event, Christine Kowal Post also spent two days in residence, introducing pupils to the work of an African sculptor friend, demonstrating the tools he used in his work as well as discussing her own.

Anthony Lysycia was in residence throughout, with the upstairs Conference Room his studio. He filled this with carved doors as well as additional carved chests to those in the 'official' exhibition. Each carved surface had also been used as a relief printing block, so large prints became an additional feature of the exhibition. Relief printing therefore became a basis for numerous workshops, and young children enjoying donning safety gear and experiencing what it felt like to carve into wood; 'I caught sight of one small boy wearing goggles and using a hammer and chisel ... for a moment he WAS a sculptor, and you could see it on his face.'[14] Three sixth-form students also spent a week 'off timetable' working alongside Anthony, experiencing the rigours of sustained effort demanded in practising art full-time. One of the chests contained all the artist's sketchbooks, extending back to his A-level days in Wigan. These became another special feature of the exhibition, revealing many of the sources of the artist's inspiration, with one of the earliest sixth-form sketches providing the factory motif which appeared in the most recent of the carved doors.

The teachers' notes also made open-ended — as opposed to prescriptive — suggestions about related activities which might be used in the classroom in preparation for the visit, each of the four areas of content, form, process and mood providing specific focus for the suggestions. Under process, 'the mark making and "drawing" potential of implements and tools' can be explored 'with obvious consideration for safety and the age of pupils involved.' Similarly, it is possible to 'experiment with stains, polishes, colour, sanding, varnishes' and to decorate natural wood surfaces by painting over them, as some of the exhibitors do. Some of the suggestions are simple, but nevertheless invaluable as preparation, such as familiarizing pupils with the work of artists who have influenced the exhibitors through use of books, reproduction and postcards. Once in the exhibition, the model can provide a constructive basis for fruitful discussion by and with the pupils. It can also help teacher and guide to recognize when the discussion has shifted from one area to another, enabling either to 'accommodate and make a positive response to that important recognition' on the part of a child, as opposed — as is often the case — to seeing the child as having gone off at a tangent by making a diverting interruption.

Whatever the content of the exhibition, its contextualization through book material can introduce a multicultural aspect, with the four areas of the model each having the potential to extend to any time, place or culture. This can be fully exploited in some exhibition contexts, and remain at a more nominal level in others. It is therefore necessary to ensure that the intrinsic content of certain exhibitions directly addresses multicultural and anti-racist issues. Three instances provide widely varying examples of this process in action.

Taking Account of Cultural Diversity

Anthony Daley's exhibition increased awareness of the whole genre of still-life painting both through its content and contextualization. Yet, strangely, he was born in Jamaica, being a black artist who chooses to work within the European tradition, for an important formative experience was seeing Rembrandt in reproduction form as a child. He is interested in how a chair becomes an icon in van Gogh's hands, and a guitar one in those of Picasso. The contextualization of the exhibition opened up the whole history of still-life painting, providing some fascinating insights. On seeing a large reproduction of a Chardin, many pupils were unable to discern whether they were looking at a photograph of a still-life arrangement, an actual painting, or a reproduction of a painting; as part of critical understanding, modern printing and reprographic processes need to be understood, providing an important area of discussion in their own right.

Daley works in series which can assume an overall pervasive mood when hung together, and the artist sets considerable store by these moods.

> The mood of the picture is of central importance really and what happens is that pictures painted in close proximity tend to have similar moods. Sometimes I will try to create different moods in a sequence of works, but they are not to do with any particular place or time of day or night — they're dreamtimes.[15]

This linking by mood of series determined the hanging of the exhibition. The most recent works provided the fulcrum of the show and filled the Main Gallery. Though at first glance abstract, all were actually based on a blue swan jug and flowers, and the mood was so pervasive that one 8-year-old exclaimed, 'I would just like to lie down on the carpet in here on my own and feel peaceful and restful looking at them.'

The large-scale canvases surrounded the viewer, and the supporting material included a lavishly illustrated Monet waterlily book, opened at a fold-out page where the connection between Daley's work and the harmonious mood of Monet's all-enveloping Orangerie canvases was clear. A GCSE pupil was introduced to Monet by the exhibition and found the Main Gallery paintings graceful and the room 'calm, peaceful and relaxing'. She was in Drumcroon for three weeks on work experience. Having never experienced seeing art of this scale or type before, she was initially bemused but became immersed in Daley's work, though discerningly critical of some aspects of it. She worked from related stimulus herself, using charcoal for the first time since primary days, working with fluency on a larger scale than at school, where there was a copying regime.

PLATE 37. Young people discussing an exhibited Anthony Daley still-life painting with the artist during his Drumcroon exhibition

> Most stimulating of all was being able to actively use an art vocabulary. At school there is only my teacher and my friends, and my friends are not interested in art. If I used certain words to describe a picture to them they'd look at me as if I was strange. But when I came here and everyone was using these words, it was fun! It's fun describing a painting, I like it. It's a bit like English when you're writing a story, using your metaphors and your similes; it's like that talking about paintings.[16]

The pupil provides a sad insight into peer pressures in a school context where critical studies approaches are not yet in place, leading, in turn, to the supposition that pupils cannot talk about art and should therefore devote all their time to making it. The National Curriculum, with an attainment target proposed for understanding and evaluating, will hopefully begin to erode the resulting low expectations.

It was interesting that an exhibition by a black artist should open up such issues and increase understanding of the very Western European genre of still-life painting. It also demonstrated, though, that the Afro-Carribean artist is quite capable of competing on the same terms as the European artist if he or she so chooses. Norma Tait, a ceramicist member of the Artists in Wigan Schools Scheme, illustrates a reverse process. During Connections, her work was displayed alongside that of the special needs sector pupils with whom she chooses to work. The catalogue states:

'I have empathy with other cultures who revere the earth and think that it is precious and my pots have always been earth coloured....' Norma Tait derives inspiration from a variety of sources including Pre-Columbian, Oriental, African and Aboriginal artefacts which often have symbolic or ceremonial significance.... She likes a lot of African pots and carvings because 'although they are highly decorative and quite ornate they still have that feeling of powerful simplicity' and is always striving to make her own work more complex without losing 'that simplicity of appearance'.[17]

All these interests were made explicit through the displayed support material of Schools Loan kelims and batiks and through a wide range of books and reproductions. Here was an example of contextualization literally ranging 'across time, place and cultures'.

Kevin Johnson is a member of the Black Artists Alliance and he addresses black issues head-on. Two of his striking ceramic sculptures were featured in the Wigan Schools Loan exhibition and are also well known to many Wigan pupils through their use in schools. They are designed to be displayed at eye-level to maximize their confrontational impact, and they frequently provoke heated debate, revealing deep-rooted attitudes. While he was a member of the Artists in Wigan Schools Scheme, Kevin also demonstrated his abilities to communicate verbally in both formal and informal contexts, as two student responses reveal.

It is really sad that minority groups can't feel proud to be who they are, that we should make them want to be white like us. What Kevin said was shocking, as obviously his experiences during his childhood had been, and you could sense his anger and resentment in the way he expressed himself through his art. He said that art was the way he let out the feelings he had bottled up inside him....

The talk by Kevin Johnson made me realise how much prejudice there is against blacks in Britain. His talk about his sister's experiences was very moving. I thought that in his sculpture of heads he captured the pain that blacks suffer very well. One particular sculpture of his mother when I first saw it seemed very insulting towards her but after his explanation I think it captured everything she must have endured in her life. Before his talk I would have never known black artists suffered any more prejudice than white artists.[18]

Sarah gets to the essence of 'Pride', one of his ceramic busts, but focusing mainly on the neck and its significance; one of the features which brings student writing about living artists to life is that of being able to glean information directly from the artist!

The long straight neck is also a common feature in Kevin's work. He sees the neck as an important form of communication, the way a person carries his or her neck as a way of judging their own self-worth. The neck, and therefore the angle of the head in Pride, immediately conveys everything the title suggests. The importance that he places on the neck stems from his interest in dance. '... African dance in particular. It shows much strength, dignity and tremendous power and it seemed natural to combine dance with the strong message that I want to convey.... This strength is magnified even more in the muscular tone of each neck, antagonistic muscles bound like the black body in which they are contained.'

The neck holding the head upright shows Kevin proud of what he is — black. To a white person it may seem a strange concept to be proud of your colour, but he feels that he has to be proud to make it through everyday life, to be resilient to racism. As a black person, in a predominantly white society, he had more to deal with than most people, and therefore has to be consciously stronger. He believes that everybody should learn to accept themselves and to be proud of what they are. He relayed a saying to me that he and many blacks live by, 'You can't know where you're going, if you don't know where you're coming from'. Basically meaning that you have to accept you are black if you want to progress in this society as a black person with values of your own.

Despite the proud neck, the anguish which is the central theme of the work is clearly visible. The brow is furrowed and the mouth is downcast, the eyes appear sorrowful and questioning. Naturally Kevin knew about racism at this time but the bitterness ate him up inside and he talked about his feelings very little. In the work Kevin wanted to show the pain inside.[19]

She describes Kevin's 'need to be "physical" with his medium, to attack the clay', of his expressive texturing of surfaces and how first 'his emotions began to manifest themselves in his work, and then in turn, in his speech.'

He began to talk quite openly about racism, the graphic articulateness feeding his verbal articulateness. He has had to work hard for this acceptance of himself, it has not come overnight but he can now see how important it is to accept oneself, as the insecure are the most likely to lash back.

One student made reference to the 'white ghetto' of Wigan; there is still a widespread belief that issues of race and multiculturalism are not the concerns of predominantly white communities. Those being educated today will lead their adult lives in a multicultural society, and perhaps racist attitudes are equally, or more, prevalent in essentially white communities, born of ignorance. Kevin Johnson did a great deal to modify such ignorance in Wigan. One of the seven Wigan principles, underpinning its entitlement curriculum policy stipulates, 'Education must take place within an International context as opposed to the National context within which it has operated to date.'[20] Each of the above three artists contributes to this process in dramatically different ways. The white artist acknowledging her debt to cultures who revere the earth, the black artist successful in working within the European tradition by choice, and the black artist forcefully revealing black issues and what it is like to be black in Britain today are all part of the same important continuum, and each increases awareness of facets of the same related set of issues.

These approaches provide a generous framework which, in turn, can encourage teachers to broaden the scope of courses to allow for cultural diversity and young people to address concerns relating to their cultural contexts, which frequently embrace two distinct sets of cultural values. Renu, for example, was born in India but has spent virtually all her life in this country. For her A-level Art and Design mock examination, she chose to address a question 'about the life of a relative or a friend and the ways in which it interested me.' In doing so, she found a personally relevant way into the aesthetic field which could never have come about through a teacher-led approach in a context devoid of negotiation. Renu records,

> I decided to do my mother. I chose this shape since it is a traditional Indian shape found on sarees and Indian jewellery. I have made the embroidered panel into a small purse ...

> The symbol of the ring represents an Indian saint. My mother is very religious — so I decided to include a peacock feather which is worn by one of the Indian Gods on his crown. The simplified shape of a peacock is an earring which fits the whole ear ...

> I'll use silk and chiffon for the panel. It could be made into a small bag or cushion. Most of my mum's sarees are brightly coloured — her favourite colours being cerise and mustard yellow.

The resulting beautiful small bag was eventually displayed in Drumcroon with others of Renu's work in the context of a textiles exhibition. At the preview, Renu's mother modelled a whole range of her sarees and jewellery to Indian music of her own choosing. One visitor described the session as 'entrancing.'

Gender Issues and Women Artists

When interviewed prior to her Drumcroon exhibition, Amanda Faulkner focused almost exclusively on the content of her work and its evolution in relation to her attitudes as a feminist. Yet when pressed about the other three areas, she could supply the relevant information rapidly and concisely. The mood in her recent works is calmer. 'The marks are quieter, there's more reflection, looking, changing, building up and in some sense I'm more at ease now.'[22] Yet the mood is determined by strong feelings about life and society caused by 'despair in the patterns of human behaviour and interaction — the need for and abuse of power, violence, war, greed, the destruction and neglect of the environment, but somehow I am not intrinsically pessimistic myself ... there's a lot of irony and absurdity in my work. It needs that. I need that. I laugh a lot when I'm working.' She confirms something universal in her work 'because I really do think that art links people to people and that is a positive (and political) thing to do.'

Her observations about mood inevitably lead back to content. Each exhibition is preceded by a teachers' meeting, and Faulkner's views in relation to her work's content threatened some teachers while invigorating others; but there were young people who identified so strongly with her work that they are still pursuing these interests two years later in personal study investigations. The artist acknowledges that:

> Before I discovered feminism, I just thought that my work and way of seeing myself grew out of my inner world and had little to do with any wider social pattern. But then I felt a growing awareness of how much people lack a sense of ease with themselves through to obvious social injustice. I recognised that we are all living under this oppressive and patriarchal structure and how that structure pervades all aspects of our lives and determines how we see ourselves. This has relevance, not just for women, but for everybody. I began to understand that my use of the female as protagonist in my work was making visible female experience, anger and dignity. Recognition of damage and the possibilities for change and growth have sustained my work for a long time.[23]

Such concerns, made tangible through dominating, large-scale works, full of symbols, and a recurring searing red which is all her own, made the impact of her Drumcroon exhibition both disturbing and unforgettable. She provides eloquent testimony to the need for content to have a rightful place in any National Curriculum structure (see proposals and suggested modifications in Chapter 2). Her imposing images drew forth powerful responses in pupils through their subject matter.

> ... because it seemed to trigger off some response in terms of feminist issues and attitudes that they believed in — and I'm not just saying girls, but boys as well. I remember very, very clearly one lad who came in with a *Daily Star* under his arm, and once we had talked about some of those issues in relation to an Allen Jones reproduction of a glamourised figure in a Page 3 sense of glamour, dropped that paper. There was nothing in the discussion — it was the recognition on his part.[24]

The then Gallery Education Officer trained in the 1960s, and, like so many of his generation, received tuition in which all the emphasis was on formal concerns. Having made systematic use of content, form, process and mood, he now recognized 'the narrowness of my training'. It would have, perhaps, helped his painting develop, for 'a lot of the abstract work I did was firmly fixed in real experiences of the world that were very difficult to acknowledge' in the art college climate of that time. Rose Garrard was studying in the same institution at the same time. It was only with hindsight that she realized she had *only* been taught by male lecturers throughout her years of art college study. She, too, recalls the formal bias and the relief she felt having plucked up the courage one day to acknowledge that column structures were actually based on the human form, and to shape them accordingly. Drumcroon's policy has led to equal representation of female and male exhibitors, and female artists frequently testify to traumatic art college experiences and of being marginalized by refusing to conform to the norms of the imposed styles and values of their lecturers. Students still complain of similar treatment today. The more sensitive are often affected by the macho bullying they receive; it is particularly at the foundation or general art and design level that they are susceptible to these approaches, having not yet developed the maturity or confidence to resist.

Art history has also been unkind to women artists. There is no one definitive art history: there are many art histories each of which tells a particular story. *The Story of Art* by Gombrich is but one version, albeit the most widely read. In a recent letter to *The Guardian*, a mother complained that her son was studying A-level art history, but that:

> The main textbook is still Gombrich's *The Story of Art* which mentions no women artists at all. Therefore my son is learning the names of Michelangelo, Fra Lippo Lippi, Monet and Chagall; he is not learning of Artemisia Gentileschi, Elizabeth Vigee Lebrun, Mary Cassatt or Berthe Morisot.
>
> Worse, he now believes that the male artists are the truly great ones because they appear in his textbook, and when he learns of the women later, they will be additions, late-comers.[25]

My 1960 edition of Gombrich has 370 plates, not one of a work by a female artist. There are over 400 plates in the more recent editions, but still no female examples.[26] The mother lays the blame at the door of the examination board, while I would blame the school for attempting to make one textbook suffice where no one book can.

The Drumcroon exhibition of Rose Garrard's wallworks covered forty years of her life. Called 'Portrait of the Artist as a Woman', it throws special light on the vertical and horizontal axes of creativity. 'Threshold' is a self-portrait of the artist aged 17 years, painted in 1964. She looks defiantly out of the canvas — she will go to art college, despite her mother's opposition. It is the first painting encountered on entering the Main Gallery, acting as a link between the mature works displayed there and the childhood works in the Small Gallery. She had lived a solitary childhood life on the top floor of her Victorian home, and her numerous self-portrait studies are an intense example of home art pursued over many years. They eventually show evidence of her discoveries of cubism and expressionism — her 'modern art' discoveries made in the local library, for she was allowed to go there on Saturday mornings.

Her parents had military backgrounds, and the earliest displayed drawing had been sent to her father, serving in Egypt, when she was 3. Her mother's army belt made a sinister exhibit, for Rose was regularly hit with it by her mother, though it is only recently that she has recognized that she was actually an abused child. She frequently drew to provide offerings to appease her warring parents, for both shared a love of art. Art has been of singular importance to her ever since.

> I really think that the way art has functioned for me is as a vital and healthy resource which has kept me sane and balanced throughout a very peculiar life. For most artists that's how it functions on a personal level. It's a route through life which is extremely spiritual and helpful and healthy — a way of examining things that gets beyond words.[27]

PLATE 38.   5.00 p.m. on a Friday evening; GCSE pupils working in Drumcroon in their own time on a school-based project during the Rose Garrard exhibition

She recalls visiting an exhibition one day at Nottingham Castle Museum. It was of 500 years of women's art, and its impact was considerable. 'Suddenly I had this total realisation that I had never experienced this situation before — of being totally surrounded by brushmarks by women that went right back through history.'[28] The male artist quite unconsciously makes constant links with any number of other artists, but she believes that women artists can feel as if they are in a black void, divorced from tradition, when working in the studio. This dilemma was resolved that day in Nottingham. One of the artists represented, Judith Leyster, had affected Judy Chicago when she first encountered her self-portrait. She '... describes her meeting with this painting at the National Gallery of Art in Washington, D.C.: "I was deeply moved. I felt I was seeing an echo of my identity as an artist across the centuries".'[29]

A self-portrait by Artemisia Gentileschi, a seventeenth century Italian artist, likewise affected Garrard. She found she wanted to *know* the paintings, so went to her studio 'without any sense of what I wanted to do other than instinctively to reproduce this painting; what I call "replicate".' Elizabeth Vigee Lebrun, Judith Leyster and Artemisia Gentileschi, in particular, provided her with the links with tradition she required; in one canvas she places her self-portrait in sequence with replications of theirs, emphasizing the importance of this lineage to the living woman artist.

She still makes use of the gilt frames inherited from her mother's antique business. A favoured device is that of breaking the frame, allowing the image to escape out of it, symbolizing 'the release of woman's art from the domination of art history scholarship'. In recent years many rediscoveries have been made; a number of Frans Hals key works are now known to be by Judith Leyster. Cleaning has revealed her signature beneath his, forged over the top for purposes of commercial gain — but many others are lost forever through neglect.

PLATE 39.   Anne-Marie Quinn's 'Mother and Daughter (Me and Mine)' pastel painting generated subtle student responses to do with mood

Through Drumcroon's approaches to contextualization, contemporary women artists are increasing knowledge of women artists of the past and their social circumstances. Because of the power of the original, though, it is through direct engagement with images by contemporary women that evidence of empathetic identification and insight is most clearly revealed. Sarah describes Anne-Marie Quinn as 'a local contemporary artist, whose recent work explores not only the experience of motherhood but also that of pregnancy.'[30] Anne-Marie Quinn is well represented in the Wigan Schools Loan Collection, the examples extending back to sixth-form college days. She was a founder member of the Artists in Wigan Schools Scheme in 1984, with subsequent experiences of working in every type of school. Her work has contributed to numerous Drumcroon exhibitions, and her residency at the Turnpike Gallery, seven miles away, culminated in an exhibition there also. The most recent display of her work at Drumcroon was in 1990 in 'Intimate Settings', where Sarah was able to study 'Mother and Daughter (Me and Mine).' Sarah records that:

The work seems so intimate, that to look at it is almost like intruding. Her work is not like a diary, recording day to day events but more like a treasure box where things are kept to remind the owner of a particular, special time.

She descibes the piece as focusing 'on the bonding between a mother and daughter', with the central image that of 'Anne-Marie lying down with her baby who she is breast feeding.'

There is a border which cuts off the image just above the knees and continues half way up each side of the work. This partial border is filled with various images, collage and pieces of writing. Anne-Marie almost encircles the baby showing the intimacy of the relationship. Her leg is bent slightly upwards and her left arm is coming round Bella whom she is looking down at.

The work is in pastel, and Sarah analyzes in detail the use of colour, of the mostly warm, skin tones. 'These range from a pale salmon and cerise, where the light hits the skin to a much richer indian red in the darker areas' to smaller areas of burnt sienna where little light reaches with deep red/browns, mossy greens, slate grey and cool turquoise in shadowed areas. The shadowy colours are carried into the sheets, and all the colours are repeated in the border so that border and central image create 'a pictorial relationship between them so that they are not viewed as two separate images.'

Although it was not planned, the images in the border became a natural progression showing the growing relationship between Anne-Marie and Bella. From the pregnant figure in the left of the border the eye is led up the arm of the central image of Anne-Marie, then across her and her baby and down the hand to her holding Bella as an older child. The idea of the present being held in by the past and the future gives a sense of security to the progression of the relationship.

Through her skilful use of borders in relation to main image, Anne-Marie has therefore achieved an unusual form of simultaneous narrative, such as was practised by, for example, numerous Quattrocentro Italian artists. In this respect, Sarah also picks up on the important presence of Anne-Marie's mother 'mostly obscured by collage and now very vague' in the border, for 'in the same week that Anne-Marie discovered that she was pregnant her mother was diagnosed with cancer. From the bitter irony of that time, the union of the three is no doubt strengthened now, with Anne-Marie illustrating the love within the relationship.'

Sarah describes the work as not looking conventionally finished, 'for it does not have a defined edge nor does the border come to a crisp end', suggesting that the artist could continue work on the piece 'recording the next stages in the growing relationship between mother and daughter'; it is, overall, a painting which has a soothing mood.

The work has a peaceful, tranquil effect. The serenity of the image and the fact that the baby is encircled gives a sense of complete love for Bella. The colour throughout the work is unified and the harmonious atmosphere is equal in the main image and the two images in the border.

This bonding is created by the carefully modulated formal relationships so that nothing appears out of place, or shocks the viewer. An air of security is evident, enforced by the fact that the two are held in by the border, as if it were a support or protection.

Sarah's beautiful evocation of the mood of the work is in response to the artist's complete understanding of her subject. 'Who else could have such a real understanding of the relationship between herself and her daughter?' In the hands of the woman artist, therefore, the time-honoured theme of mother and child takes on new connotations, enabling young people to recognize latent qualities within themselves, reconciling art with life and adolescence in important ways.

The tranquil mood to which Sarah has been so responsive is at a far remove from that of 'Mona' by Amanda Faulkner, as Nina makes clear.

When I first saw this picture I was physically repulsed by the vulgar images set down on the paper. There was a poignant air about this work which made me feel slightly inhibited. The brash and violent images made me imagine the artist at work attacking the paper, motivated by her strong emotions. This is shown by slashing marks at intervals throughout the picture. However, in places there is a calmness in the pastel work where the colours just flow into each other and become elusive; these areas of pastel seem to reflect the artist's more placid mood.[31]

Nina conjectures that the title might be consciously derived from Leonardo's 'Mona Lisa', an icon of female beauty, with Amanda deliberately choosing to make her woman ugly and repulsive 'to get away from the traditional art stereotype women who are idealistically beautiful.' The artist does this with devastating force:

... the smaller figure on the right, maybe a child, is wearing a dress with a scarlet band of shadow down the left of the bodice.... From the dress hangs the right breast, it appears sharp and penetratingly frightening, the nipple is portrayed as piercing and pointed. Over the top of the breast is a block of colour in deep red. The ferocity of the drawing of the breast gives us clues to Amanda's views concerning women.... 'Breasts are not either pretty things for men or food sources for babies, they're nasty droopy things. Breasts are erotic and maternal and they're quirky and individual things whatever state they're in.' The left breast also hangs out of the top of the bodice, but is rounded and appears stretched. Amanda emphasises the stretching by making slashing directional lines in blood red towards the nipple, possibly portraying an aspect of motherhood....

The arm is drawn in a childlike way as if to indicate the uninhibited quality of children's art, while the face is flat and mask-like, as if hiding the true identity of the child.

Maybe the mask-like face is representative of Amanda when she was a child.... This childlike figure may be indicative of aspects in her life and

PLATE 40.   Amanda Faulkner's 'Mona', situated above the fireplace (left) in the artist's Drumcroon exhibition, physically repulsed Nina when she first saw it

> her problems as a child going through puberty.... Amanda shows the child in a dress and also out of it, like a discarded skin. The breast emerges, symbolising the new woman. The breasts are depicted as ugly, possibly signifying Amanda's reaction to her own development and therefore she sees these sexual organs as ugly and intimidating.

Perhaps the flowing, washed-out pink ribbon on the dress relates to the artist's childhood and was used to tie up her pigtails, Nina conjectures. 'As the figure holds onto the ribbon, this may signify Amanda's reluctance to let go of her childhood, and the faded colour could signify her childhood draining away as she goes through the physical metamorphosis into adulthood.'

Both works are clearly content-laden, and it is easy to see why adolescent female students can identify with them so intensely. Yet Rose Garrard recalls her art college tutors cornering her on one occasion, demanding that she talk about her work. She was relieved to discover they were only interested in her formal concerns, as she did not choose to discuss intimate content without there being mutual trust. Nina feels that the mask in Amanda Faulkner's painting reflects her need of privacy, and relates this to the artist's student days at Ravensbourne, and her approaches to content then. 'They became camouflaged, partly for my own protection because so much was coming to the surface.' Faulkner and Quinn both use pastel extensively, yet as a student Quinn was 'persuaded' to work in the more acceptable medium of oil paints for her degree show — losing the intimate relationship between content and process, so fundamental to her work, through having to conform.

The potent descriptions of Sarah and Nina, with their insight into essential content, make interesting reading alongside Judy Chicago's observations about the students she teaches in the United States.

> As students become successively connected with themselves as women, they usually go through a stage of making very overt art. This art is often awkward because it is an attempt to articulate feelings for which there is, as yet, no developed form language. As the women develop as artists, they build skills that are relevant to their content. Their work improves and they become sophisticated, but that sophistication is built on a solid, personal foundation and is not the result of imitating prevailing art modes.[32]

In the process, women artists often find themselves occupying previously unoccupied territory, broadening the scope and range of artistic endeavour to the ultimate benefit of *all* artists, for there are many male artists as well who fit uncomfortably into 'prevailing art modes' — whether of school art, or art college, or determined by gallery and dealer through their control of the marketplace.

The teaching implications are profound. The content, form, process, mood model is used consistently by many young people in Wigan. It informs their practice and their thinking as manifested through personal appraisal statements. Viv took hers with her to the interviews for the General Art and Design (GAD) course at a local college as a prerequisite to her BA Honours studies. The interviewing tutor recorded the following: 'Draws big trees. No sense of positive or negative.' In contrast, Viv's wide-ranging concerns are apparent through this personal appraisal passage.

> At first I chose to draw a dead tree near to where I live. This tree interested me partly due to the relative positions of, and shapes formed by, its branches. I chose a dead tree as the hard edges and sharp angles of the branches would not be softened or interrupted by masses of leaves. My photography influenced me in that I began to represent the smaller branches as fairly flat forms, rendered black by the bright white of the sky. I chose a fairly low eye-level from which to draw the trees throughout the project, in the hope that the immense size of the trees would be obvious from my drawings. The bushes around the tree contrasted quite effectively with the tree itself. The random, curved, rapid movements of the leaves counteract the sharp hard angles and shapes formed by the branches. The huge tree evokes a feeling of security and permanence — despite the fact that it seems to be dead and lifeless, it remains standing and refuses to be defeated by the elements. This contrast also evokes the idea of life versus death.[33]

As the tree dies, it gives way to the bushes below, a higher form of life being replaced by a more primitive one. 'Is this picture optimistic or pessimistic?', she asks. That Viv makes use of strong, positive and negative shapes is not the real point — what is important is that she is capable of providing insight into the full range of her concerns, and there is an onus on any tutor to take consideration of these when addressing her work. That student and teacher work in harmony in this respect at one phase of education, then the student finds her concerns disregarded as her work is subjected to the criticisms of the assumed expert at the next, is all too common but nevertheless unacceptable.

Gallery-generated Classroom Practice

'Earthworks' was an authority-wide venture focusing on the environment and ecological concerns, with the Changes exhibition at Drumcroon and the sculpture and handmade paper works of Christine Merton and Elizabeth Stuart Smith at the Turnpike as the spearhead. One high school transformed an art room into the Rain Forest and struck up a working relationship with Greenpeace; a primary school constructed a sculpture trail along the school corridor and round the school grounds, utilizing the work of artists but also that of pupils, as the sculpture trail leaflet makes clear:

> Look at the work on the walls here. It was done by Y4. It is about the environment, our world, living nature. Now our world is getting more polluted. We should take great care of our world. We did them because we are concerned about our world and how we treat it. Soon it may be hard to find sticks and stones.[34]

At Lowton High School fourth-year pupils began their exploration of possible usages of natural materials 'blind', the staff choosing to involve the pupils in their collection and use in advance of them visiting Andy Goldsworthy's exhibition at Drumcroon. Sarah found this disconcerting at first because it contradicted her usual routines of working and notions as to what art was.

> The project began by walking to Pennington Flash, a local nature spot. There we collected large quantities of natural materials — there was lots of choice in this area of parkland. *But* never having worked with natural materials before I found it difficult to choose the correct material for me to work with.[35]

She selected willow twigs and bullrushes, but was unsure where to start. Her brief was to work with nature, creating a 'shape' outside rather than within the familiar security of the art room. Sarah felt this was 'a waste of time — I liked to work with more traditional materials like paint, pencil or clay'.

The visit to Drumcroon and seeing Goldsworthy's work completely changed her perceptions. It made her realize:

> ... it was possible to produce a really good piece of work from natural materials ... his work gave me the incentive to produce something better ... at the weekend I picked some long grass from the field in front of my house. I tried weaving it together in many different ways ... finally I came up with a circle design which went on to form my final piece. In the end I saw the idea through ... my piece was finally mounted on a piece of handmade paper which used natural materials in its construction.

PLATE 41.   A pupil working with natural materials in the environment in relation to the stimulus of Andy Goldsworthy's work

This project illustrates the pivotal position of the Drumcroon visit in school-based work which takes place both in preparation and as follow-up to the actual gallery visit. Through its close working relationships with schools, Drumcroon stimulates a great deal of practice of this type. Its dramatic impact on work which then takes place outside it is further demonstrated through the three-week work experience placement of Jane, from the same year in the same school. Pupils recount many horrendous negative experiences of these place-ments, most of which have little or no relevance back in school afterwards, while the insight into the workplace can be of a cautionary nature.

Jane's teacher saw her Drumcroon placement as having transformed her from 'a talented and interested student, conscientious by nature, keen to learn yet lacking the confidence and impetus exhibited by a few other students in her art group' to one 'shining all over' on her return to school.

> She was full of it and related many instances of things that had hap-pened — things she had done — things she had drawn — people she had met and most importantly artists she had spoken to, listened to and had seen working.[36]

She helped in the setting up of 'Intimate Settings', in which Anne-Marie Quinn was one of four women contributors. Jane found the experience a positive one from the outset.

> In the past I enjoyed Art but had no particular aim — I flitted between different aspects of the subject. As soon as I stepped into Drumcroon I

saw things more clearly. I had the opportunity to work with different people, artists, children from various schools — every experience taught me something new.... I learnt to work with new materials and a new subject — figure/portraiture/interiors. I was nervous at first but soon discovered that I felt really comfortable working in this way.

Realizing the importance of showing 'your own feelings and emotions ... gave my work a positive direction — a sort of theme', with Anne-Marie Quinn's work probably the biggest influence on her, for,

> ... the moment you walk into Anne-Marie's room at Drumcroon you can sense an air of closeness and intimacy — you feel as if you are invading someone's privacy. The theme of her work was mainly to do with family relationships — memories — old photos — letters — recipes — poems. She often uses these in collaged areas or frames for the work. Many of her pieces are very large and dominant — it is easy to feel a bit embarrassed when you look at them especially when there are other people about.

She discerns the many layers of meanings in these works, 'and these were revealed to us as we sat in Anne-Marie's room and listened to her talking about her work.'

Jane describes returning back to school 'armed with loads of new work and a head bursting with new ideas.' Her teacher testifies to a 'spectacular leap in Jane's output of work. Not only has she produced a lot of work in the form of large drawings but she has learned to use her sketchbook more profitably.'

> Her drawings are now bold and immediate in their execution and it seems appropriate to give Jane a corner of the art studio to display her work (whilst she is feeling so confident and 'good' about what she has produced).

Jane's peers responded enthusiastically to her work. This added to her sense of confidence as a person and as an artist! 'The most pleasing response has been that of a fellow 4th year student who found inspiration in Jane's work and has since begun to produce a volume of work herself more specifically focused on cropped imagery of interior settings/scenes.' To foster and further these new developments, the teacher contextualized what was now being done by displaying, in reproduction form, all appropriate examples of the paintings of Bonnard, Vuillard, Sickert and Degas — all of which had been influential, at various times, on Anne-Marie Quinn. The impact on Jane of seeing beautifully presented works in the Drumcroon gallery setting was capitalized upon in the school by the special presenting of Jane's work and built on further by the considered use of reproductions to support wider developments stimulated by Jane. In the process, Drumcroon had a profound effect on school practice.

Drumcroon is attractive in its own right, but the real evidence of the Centre's significance is highlighted in the practice of many schools, as is its influence on their methods of presenting children's work and the art of others.

The Visual Arts in the School Environment

Only a decade ago it was relatively uncommon to see other than the pupils' art work displayed in schools. It is significant, therefore, to discover a third-year junior pupil, David, writing, 'Wigan is an artistic place. We have been down to Wigan to visit with our school. There is a link between our school and Drumcroon — it is that they have got pictures on the wall.'[37] The environment of his school, Tyldesley County Primary — known locally at TCP — is unusually rich, and it always contains examples of mature art as well as those of the children. It also contains an art gallery of its own — a mini-Drumcroon. It is called the 'Murphy Room', and is named after Ian Murphy, a young member of the Artists in Wigan Schools Scheme who was in residence there, 1986–87. His studio is the area which is now a gallery, and it is a kind of oasis within the school, pupil after pupil being responsive to its unique atmosphere: 'It is a quiet place for concentrating and for looking and feeling at pieces of work'; 'I feel like I am part of the room because when I come in I keep quiet and all the room is quiet'; 'We are lucky to have a room to go into for quiet and enjoying the pictures.'

It is fascinating to discover evidence of young children, working within this conducive environment, assimilating structural concepts like content, form, process and mood and making them their own in their engagements with art works, as when Vicki writes:

I feel I know a lot of information from the pictures even if I have only been there ten minutes. I look at these pictures by carefully looking at what the picture contains, the mood that the artist felt and what I feel, and the process, how the picture is made, and what materials were used.

Stimulus provided by Murphy Room exhibits gives rise to a constant flow of pupil responses, some of which find expression in the form of beautiful creative writing. Louise, aged 11, for example, has the following to say about 'Eruption' by Ian Murphy,

Rushing and racing.
Rocks and water.
Full of excitement.
Ripped up paper thick with paint.
Marvin, making it look like water colliding with the sharp jagged rocks.
Fragments of blue and black.
Vertical, horizontal, rugged and sharp.
Rapid and swift.
Rocks leading to others,
Making you carry on the picture,
Even when you've ended the picture on the frame.
Your imagination carries on thinking,
What will come next?
From massive giant rocks, to tiny segments of slate.

Such responses are commonplace in a school where the arts are essential to a whole-school policy 'consolidated by active partnership between teachers, chil-

PLATE 42.   A corridor display of pupils' work generated by their visits to a Michael Brennand-Wood exhibition illustrates the richness of the TCP environment

dren, parents, governors and between the school and its outside community.' The work and philosophy of this school will be fully explored in *The Arts in the Primary School*, also in the Falmer Library on Aesthetic Education.

The divide between primary and secondary practice has been referred to in Chapter 2, as has the deep-rooted imperative to engage children in making to the subordination of all other visual arts education requirements. The appointment of an arts coordinator at Hawkley Hall High School led to critical studies approaches being adopted throughout the school, directly benefiting incoming first-year pupils. Their secondary education began in a manner which grew out of the best of primary practice, constructively building upon it.

The existing first-year syllabus commenced with a 'Me, Myself, I' project, and he addressed this by combining self-portraiture with the study of Expressionism. 'It was a magical moment for me ... the children *wanted* to talk about art, and they *wanted* to talk about other artists' work, and they *wanted* to explore what was going on in those pictures.'[38]

A forthcoming Drumcroon exhibition, Past and Present, was designed to celebrate seventy-six years of Michael Rothenstein's art by juxtaposing his 1912–25 childhood works, presented to Drumcroon by the artist, with the works he was now producing at the age of 80, demonstrating the developments and constant elements in his work. The line drawings in ink of his teenage years photocopied beautifully and, with accompanying teachers' notes, were made available to schools six months in advance of the exhibition.

They related ideally to the project, for they had humour and elements of caricature, were a record of the life and antics of the artist and of his immediate family and friends, and they captured the life of a bygone era in a way which fascinated the pupils. Each of the recurring characters was instantly recognizable,

PLATE 43.   Part of the Hawkley High School displays arising out of the 'Me, Myself, I' first-year project during which the pupils explored Expressionism

however small in scale in any particular drawing. These naturally led to the study of works by George Grosz and Ralph Steadman and, in turn, to portraits by Tom Phillips, Peter Blake, David Hockney and artists 'you wouldn't associate directly with portraiture'.

From this base, the pupils' own practical work evolved. How might they show aspects of a person's life not necessarily made apparent through physical attributes? They came up with the idea of showing and communicating emotions, initially simply writing down words and discussing. 'I think that is something we tend to run away from in art — we throw that conceptual stage out because we feel this desperation to get them drawing something or painting something.' The time spent in discussion and in 'getting hold of ideas' enabled the project to start more unusually than, for example, by the pupils simply recording the person sitting opposite. The ground laid also ensured that there was a genuine variety of approaches adopted and responses; they began by drawing themselves in their sketchbooks at home.

> When they brought these back, I started exposing them to the German Expressionists, showing them the work of Otto Dix, Max Beckmann, Kirchner — that whole range of artists — and I asked them what was happening in these pictures. The beauty of it by then was that they had got hold of the whole idea that a portrait didn't have to be a likeness in a photographic sense, so they were relaxed with that whole concept.

The classroom developments therefore reflected their 'sensual explorations of the image and their ideas' in the use of colour, rather than it being treated literally, theoretically or through demonstration. Likewise, line, tone and texture were treated as essential component elements, rather than in isolation as is often the case at this stage. The criteria and strategies used in looking at artists' work were also applied to the pupils' practice, with a common vocabulary used with regard to each. The pupils' work was characterized by an unusual freshness, and the teacher likened the project to taking one's foot off the brake 'and being prepared to let it go' by allowing trust in the pupils — something 'we're too often frightened of.' He felt there was 'an exact parallel with painting itself'.

> Francis Bacon talks about this all the time — taking chances and taking risks, taking the moment or the happy accident and using that, and that is when you progress. I thought, 'Well, actually that is what is happening here with the children'. I'm allowing them that but at the same time I'm keeping the parameters there. I'm not imposing them but they need a structure.

There certainly was a framework, but a generous enough one to allow each pupil scope for individual manoeuvre facilitating personal, as opposed to conformist or generalized, statements.

Though some might see the practical phase as unstructured, the teacher knew that this was not the case. The thorough preparation ensured that the pupils, by being informed, were enabled to operate in a relatively independent manner, with striking technical implications.

> The actual use of a brush and the textural rendition of paint ... you obviously want to make them familiar with concepts like texture, but not as an isolated concept — and that is something that can be found in all sorts of art forms and in all sorts of ways in the world around.... The children were quite happily putting all that together: the mark-making, the textural, the gestural, the hot/cold continuum, and mood — all put together in one image with them having total control over what they were doing.

Basic art approaches are often used at the commencement of secondary schooling on the assumptions that nothing of worth has been previously experienced and that a basic vocabulary, incrementally acquired, is necessary for future endeavours of a more holistic and expressive nature — the pupils' needs at their current stage of development being sacrificed in the process. These pupils demonstrated that, through a critical studies approach, they were perfectly capable of effectively combining the elements of colour, line, tone and texture within one coherent and expressive statement.

Their work was then displayed in a relatively unusual but effective manner which brought every dimension of the project together. They fitted two deep on the display panels, but intervals were left in which the stimulus reproductions which had been used were also displayed. Captioning also emphasized the dual portraiture and Expressionism dimensions of the project. Further use of reproductions and books on the worktop below helped contextualize the displays, as did the use of Schools Loan original examples. A striking feature of the room as a whole was the obvious quality in depth of the children's work and its variety. Increased understanding had opened up a wider range of possibilities with *all* the paintings valued in their own right, as opposed to a handful being deemed worthy of display as most fully epitomizing the teacher's instructions or representing the more 'talented' pupils. The teacher was gratified by 'the sheer preponderance of work' which the project generated.

At the back of your mind you sometimes think, 'Have I failed two or three children in this group? Have they not grasped what is going on?' I did not feel that with that project. I felt every single child felt valued for what they had produced and that it was valuable in terms of what they had learned about art and artists — and that, sadly, does not always occur in secondary teaching.

A High School Gallery

He now feels that it is 'a nonsense to talk of critical studies on the one hand and art education on the other. I cannot separate them any more, my mind won't do it.' Instead of starting from process, he now increasingly asks himself, 'What environment do I want to create? And by environment I mean both a visual environment to draw from literally, and a visual environment from which to respond in terms of conceptual thinking — to be within it.' Schools Loan works became fundamental to this process, but there were inevitable problems getting '15 or 18 children round a picture, they were clambering over tables.'

> The adjoining room had been a home economics textiles room and it really became a dumping area for storage ... it had to become a usable teaching space, and what better teaching space than for the fundamentals of what I was teaching — and that was critical studies. I approached the Head, who was *very* supportive, and it was built in an evening, it was there. It was painted in the holidays, and from there we've never looked back.

And so was born the Hawkley Gallery. 'Every teaching situation either comes from Drumcroon, the Turnpike Gallery, or the school gallery. It's as simple as that basically!'

A friend, Ken Cottam, had been in residence at Drumcroon earlier and now willingly provided the inaugural exhibition. His treescape paintings and drawings were not conventional landscapes, the trees suggesting animal and human forms with the element of metamorphosis ever-present. This aspect was reflected in the contextualization.

> In terms of use of reproductions and resource material, areas of the gallery could reflect a certain nuance, if you like. So, on one side, we would have lots of postcards of the nude, the figure in landscape through the ages. On another, we would have a whole range of reproductions on the madonna and child theme, because both these elements were features of Ken Cottam — not in that traditional sense, but they were there and gave a wider context to how this artist was part of a greater continuum.... Knowing Ken, I was aware of his processes and the way he worked and knew what his interests were.

Sutherland was a favourite of Cottam's, and artists like Max Ernst were obviously included, but some of those represented were quite surprising.

I knew that some of the last work was influenced by the Three Graces by Rubens and, interestingly, Jim Dine — of all people — was on one side influencing him and Rubens on the other. Now, knowing that and knowing Ken's interest in Stravinsky and the Rites of Spring, and jazz, and the whole ideas of the rhythmic aspects of nature and the cycles of nature of growth and decay, and so forth — you can then put the emphasis on those different aspects in the way you lay out the books, use the reproductions and the way you label the works.

Each exhibition is treated in an organic way, appropriate to the school context and its function within it.

It's a growing environment. It's not something that's just set, like any other art gallery exhibition and then that's the end of it. It grows. The exhibition evolves as we use the gallery. People say, 'Oh, I must bring in my book on so and so!' The Arcimboldi book was a case in point. That came in two weeks after the exhibition had started through talking about it.

Such related stimuli as tangled roots, branches and plants were set up in the central gallery space, meaning that the pupils' practical work based on these provided a further vital organic element. The gallery space being clearly visible from the art room meant that small numbers at a time could make use of the stimuli, yet all engage with them during the course of the exhibition.

The gallery 'did feel claustrophobic with Ken's work in there', so the second exhibition was chosen to contrast with it. Norma Tait's ceramics and the delicate embroideries set in plaster by Sue Peterson provided its content. The staff set it up during a half-term holiday, and pupil reactions were fascinating.

When they came in the room on the Monday morning it was this new clean environment — and it did have an impact. The first thing they said was, 'Wow, doesn't it look different!' There were literal gasps. I used that in the first part of the teaching. They influenced me where we started — we started with Mood simply because they said, 'Wow!' I said, 'Why is it so different?' 'Oh well....' They suddenly realised that you had to look very hard. It was the macro and the micro; there were little treasures to be revealed in Sue's work, whereas with Ken's work — it was there.

Each exhibition is planned to 'complement and best be utilised in response to what is going on at Drumcroon and the Turnpike', and this was no exception.

I knew that the 4th year had all seen the Still Life touring Arts Council exhibition at the Turnpike Gallery. I knew I wanted to get an exhibition in school, and I couldn't get a better example than Sue Peterson because she responds to still life — but it was totally different. They didn't expect anything like the plaster works.

On occasions he has managed to get every pupil to a Drumcroon exhibition, but the whole school has access to every one in the Hawkley Gallery. Not that this is

PLATE 44.   Ken Cottam's 'Treescapes' provided the inaugural Hawkley Gallery exhibition

PLATE 45.   The pupils' immediate responses to the contrasting calmness of mood helped determine teaching approaches to the second exhibition

easy; the school is split-site, with the upper school over a mile away, meaning that care has to be taken to ensure that no third-year group upwards misses out. The school will eventually come together on the upper school site, meaning that a mobile classroom will be used as an interim gallery, but a purpose-built gallery will be provided in the next building phase.

Pupils will use it who already have a knowledge of numerous artists and an understanding of their relevance to their own practice. This is, in turn, helping to determine the nature of practical lessons, as when second years worked from a

Manet-like pose of a girl at a café table set against a heavily patterned background in the manner of Vuillard.

> Now I wouldn't have done that had I not known that in the first year those same children had been exposed to Amanda Faulkner and issues to do with the iconography of women, to Gustav Klimt, to a whole range of pattern. So building on that knowledge it is very gratifying when they start talking about artists naturally, saying, 'Oh, his work reminds me of Gustav Klimt', when they come across Vuillard.

Drumcroon enjoys a close working partnership with many schools. TCP and Hawkley Hall illustrate how schools are building upon the kind of stimulus provided and developing it in unusual ways within the school context in order to meet the entitlement needs of *all* their pupils. Numerous mini-Drumcroons have now been established within schools, though, obviously, a variety of constraints restricts many others. Nevertheless, many schools have successfully identified more modest areas where the work of both pupils and mature artists can be effectively presented and utilized. As a consequence, the majority of Wigan pupils now have ongoing access to original works of art throughout their school lives. The Winstanley College students, whose testimonies and examples of practice are interspersed throughout these pages, provide eloquent evidence of the virtues of an education founded upon the principle that all young people have the right to have access to the art of others as well as to making their own; many of the Winstanley students of today first visited Drumcroon while at infant school.

Conclusion

Advocates of child art, though alert and sensitive to aspects of the vertical axis of creativity, have often denied their pupils access to its horizontal counterpart, to the ultimate detriment of each and children's overall education. Likewise, a whole tradition of art history and appreciation has artificially divorced the study of art from its practice — many of the teachers of tomorrow are still being subjected to such approaches in the higher education sector. Both sets of attitudes are responsible for denying many young people proper access to the aesthetic field as active participants. However, recent developments in the visual arts have ensured that there are young people who are receiving a much more balanced and rounded education than seemed feasible even a decade ago.

The National Curriculum, from its inception, has failed to acknowledge the rightful place of the arts in the curriculum, both in terms of their intrinsic worth and as aids to learning in the wider curriculum sense. Nevertheless, in spite of some inevitable setbacks, the visual arts flourish and remain popular with large numbers of pupils. It is also possible to envisage modifications to the Art Interim Report which could lead to a set of programmes of study and attainment targets, each forming the essential component parts of one organic and interactive whole. If this can be achieved, the National Curriculum will — ironically — have provided the necessary vehicle for the visual arts in education to, at last, become a cohesive whole. This will only have been achieved when the majority of pupils, irrespective of age, background and assumed ability, can enter and constantly revisit the aesthetic field through a balanced and interactive participation in the activities of making, presenting, responding and evaluating. The holistic view, sought by the Art Working Group, would then have been achieved and the visual arts' potential to inform, enrich and illuminate young people's lives and to put them in touch with their inner selves in essential ways realized: the visual arts have a vital role to play in education in our materialistic times.

Notes

1   *Educating for Art, op. cit.*, pp. 134–5.
2   *Ibid.*, p. 149.
3   *Pterodactyls and Old Lace: Museums in Education* (1972), London, Schools Council, Evans/Methuen Educational, p. 10.
4   *Drumcroon: The First Ten Years Catalogue*, Drumcroon Education Art Centre, 1990.
5   Rod Taylor (1991) *The Artists in Wigan Schools*, London, The Calouste Gulbenkian Foundation.
6   *Drumcroon: The First Ten Years Catalogue, op. cit.*
7   Jill Morgan (1982) 'A New Way of Looking at Art', *The Artful Reporter*, North West Arts, May 1982.
8   James Hall (1990) Letter to author on occasion of the Drumcroom: The First Ten Years exhibition.
9   Arthur Hughes, in *Drumcroon: The First Ten Years Catalogue, op. cit.*
10 *The Artists in Wigan Schools, op. cit.*
11 *Ibid.*
12 *British Relief Woodcarvings Catalogue*, Drumcroon Education Art Centre, 1988.
13 *British Relief Woodcarvings Teachers' Notes*, Drumcroon Education Art Centre, 1988.
14 Anna Comino-James, in *Drumcroon: The First Ten Years Catalogue, op. cit.* Anna Comino-James observed this incident during Anthony Lysycia's Lifelines exhibition, 1989, when he was again in residence as he had been during British Relief Woodcarvings.
15 *Anthony Daley Catalogue*, Drumcroon Education Art Centre, 1990.
16 From recorded interview between author and the pupil on the last day of her work experience placement, Drumcroon, 1990.
17 *Connections Catalogue*, Drumcroon Education Art Centre, 1988.
18 Written student responses to Kevin Johnson's presentation to over 100 students and staff at Winstanley Sixth Form College, March 1989.
19 Extract from student's A-level 'Personal Study', 1991.
20 *Red Book 3: The Wigan Chapter* (1984), Wigan LEA.
21 From statement written in support of student's mock examination practical work, 1989.
22 *Breaking Water: Amanda Faulkner Catalogue*, Drumcroon Education Art Centre, 1989.
23 *Amanda Faulkner Catalogue, op. cit.*
24 From recorded interview by author with Keith Walker, then Drumcroon Gallery Education Officer, March 1990.
25 *Guardian* letters, 1990.
26 Ernst Gombrich (1960 ed.), *The Story of Art*, London, The Phaidon Press Ltd.
27 *Rose Garrard: Portrait of the Artist as a Woman Catalogue*, Drumcroon Education Art Centre, 1991.
28 *Ibid.*

29 Karen Peterson and J.J. Wilson (1976) *Women Artists: Recognition and Reappraisal from the Early Middle Ages to the Twentieth Century*, London, The Womens Press, p. 38.
30 Extract from student's A-level 'Personal Study', 1991.
31 Extract from student's A-level 'Personal Study', 1990.
32 Peterson and Wilson, *op. cit.*, p. 138.
33 *Approaching Art and Design, op. cit.*, p. 71.
34 Tyldesley County Primary School (TCP) Sculpture Trail Leaflet, Spring Term, 1990.
35 From 'Mini-Drumcroons', occasional publication material, 1991. Pending publication.
36 *Ibid.*
37 Documentation of TCP passage provided by Glennis Andrews, deputy head-teacher at the school. (Glennis Andrews and Rod Taylor will co-author *The Arts in the Primary School*, a forthcoming publication in this series.)
38 From recorded interview with Nigel Leighton, Head of Arts, Hawkley Hall High School. All Hawkley Hall quotations from this interview were conducted in March 1990.

Index

(Page numbers in *italics* refer to illustrations)